J.82- 1341 868 (D. Hreeson)

The Master Musicians Series

DEBUSSY

SERIES EDITED BY

SIR JACK WESTRUP
M.A., Hon.D. Mus. (Oxon.), F.R.C.O.

THE MASTER MUSICIANS SERIES

DEBUSSY

by

EDWARD LOCKSPEISER

*With eight pages of plates
and music examples in the text*

LONDON
J. M. DENT & SONS LTD

FARRAR, STRAUS AND CUDAHY INC.
NEW YORK

© Revisions, J. M. Dent & Sons Ltd, 1963
Made in Great Britain
at the
Aldine Press · Letchworth · Herts
for
J. M. DENT & SONS LTD
Aldine House · Bedford Street · London
First published 1936
Revised edition 1963

PREFACE TO FOURTH EDITION

AT THE time of Debussy's death at the end of the First World War, and even during his lifetime, it was generally admitted that he was a figure who had radically changed the course of music, that he had struck deep at our whole conception of music, and in a way from which there was no going back. We still feel this, but perhaps it is only about now that we may begin to see what it was that Debussy changed and to measure the extent of his influence. When the first edition of this book appeared, twenty-seven years ago, I was aware, despite its acclaim in both literary and musical circles, that I had only touched on the fringe of a vast subject which would take many years to explore. One aspect of this subject was the inter-relation of the arts peculiar to the movements of Symbolist literature and Impressionist painting, themselves rooted in a musical ideal which found expression in Debussy's many-sided art.

Over the years I pursued my researches into the hinterland of Debussy's world, bringing out a second, slightly revised edition of the book towards the conclusion of the last war, and in 1951 a completely revised edition. New facts which had come to light were incorporated in the biographical section of this third edition, while the critical section was completely re-cast. I was impelled to undertake this large-scale revision partly because of the availability of new letters and other documents, but also because it became evident to me that no study of Debussy's work could ignore the many literary and pictorial associations by which it is inspired. It is this version, in which certain inaccuracies have been corrected and in which the

v

bibliography has been brought up to date, that is now presented as the fourth edition.

Many delicate problems confront the biographer of Debussy, some of a moral nature requiring considerable tact, others of an aesthetic nature difficult to gauge. This is because biographers who attempt a psychological interpretation of a composer's music in regard to his inner life must deal with a form of creation which is nebulous and unyielding by comparison with the revelatory prose or poetry at the core of biographers of literary figures. It is nevertheless essential, in my view, to correlate Debussy's aesthetic with his personal character. In simple terms we want to know what the composer was like and how it came about that this music was written by this man. This is obviously the main purpose of musical biography, but although there has been a number of lives of Debussy his personality has largely eluded us. Discretion and the fact that some of the composer's relatives and friends were still living at the time of the last revised edition naturally forbade the publication of many essential documents. Yet the portrait I was able to present within the limited framework of the Master Musicians series did attempt to bring into relief certain psychological and moral problems which were intimately connected with Debussy's character. As I stated at the time, I touched upon these problems in the hope that a larger study would eventually investigate them on a deeper level.

It has been generally agreed that the present study of Debussy's life offers a fair assessment of the man as he was, and that it goes some way to defining both the nature of his sensibility and the unconscious forces at the root of his inspiration. I have nothing to retract from this study. But there is indeed much to add. I have been fortunate in having eventually been able to undertake a work of more considerable proportions, and the large-scale study, of which I have dreamt ever since the first edition of this book appeared in 1936, is now in course of publication.

Readers, therefore, who, as I hope, have been encouraged to acquire a closer understanding of Debussy's life and work in the course of the present volume may be recommended to my work, *Debussy: His Life and Mind*, Volume I (Cassell, London; Macmillan, New York, 1962), and also to two specialized publications of mine in French, *Debussy: Lettres inédites à André Caplet* and *Debussy et Edgar Poe* (Éditions du Rocher, 1957 and 1962). The first, besides presenting much new material, is a study of the mind and work of Debussy based on a broad approach. The French studies deal with particular aspects of Debussy's work, the latter investigating the far-reaching influence on Debussy, as on other French artists of his period, of the dreamlike tales of Edgar Allan Poe. The size and scope of the present volume naturally preclude the incorporation of material from these later studies, yet I have no hesitation in presenting once again this concise study of Debussy's life and work, the result of many years' communion with his art and with the worlds of literature and painting with which he was so intimately associated.

E. L.

London, 1962.

PREFACE TO THIRD EDITION

In presenting this edition of a book first published fourteen years ago and revised now as completely as the original structure has allowed, it is my first duty to inform the reader that these intervening years have brought a surprising number of both biographical and critical studies of Debussy, several of them of remarkable perspicacity and shrewd judgment, and an inspiration to me in the task of recasting my earlier book which, after many hesitations, I felt bound to undertake. The new work by Léon Vallas, the principal French authority on Debussy, the American study by Oscar Thompson and the compact *Life* by Rollo H. Myers are those I am especially anxious to acknowledge. A selection of many other available studies is listed in the form of a short bibliography in Appendix D. New letters, too, have been published, notably those to Robert Godet, André Messager, Pierre Louÿs and Gabriele d'Annunzio, and such biographical information as they yield has been utilized. Several other important series of letters, however, still remain unpublished. I will not say that the recently published letters, displaying many lively aspects of the composer's epistolary gifts, go very far to illumine the more intimate episodes of Debussy's life. Discretion and the fact that some of the composer's relatives and friends are still living have quite naturally forbidden the publication of documents which future generations may interpret and re-interpret, for I cannot imagine that the complex and sensitive character of Debussy will ever receive a final psychological assessment.

In the meantime I have been impelled not merely to add such biographical data as have been made available (and also to correct certain inaccuracies), but, through the longer experience of years, drastically to revise my earlier portrait of Debussy as the hedonist of composers, the creator of a sensuous art magnificent in its isolation, but unable to bear the tension of his life and eventually distintegrating behind a screen of bristling irony. Time brings a sense of wholeness, and while I may still hope to celebrate the aesthetic of pleasure and gratification which Debussy so gloriously revived in French music, the remote other-worldliness of his later works, far from marking a decline, proclaims them, in my opinion, as the creations of a hedonist who had become a stoic. I do not know what the letters of the latter part of Debussy's life may yet reveal; but I am convinced that the determination and tenacity of this great explorer, afflicted throughout this period of his life with a dread and incurable disease, can only be interpreted as an amazing triumph of the mind. In recognizing this ultimate conquest I have attempted to eliminate disparities of judgment as between one aspect of the Debussyan art and another, and also between the material existence of the musician and his creation. From first to last the man and his music are one, dedicated to the discovery of new provinces of the musical unconscious.

The later chapters of the biographical section are therefore those that have been more noticeably amended, while the chapters in the critical section have been either completely rewritten or recast. Once the emphasis or focus is altered in a survey of this kind—the modest equivalent, let us say, of a Debussyan gallery—there is nothing to do but to abandon the whole lay-out and start afresh. My hope is that these chapters may here and there offer a stimulating line of thought to the listener or provoke an associative idea in the mind of the inter-preter. Mere words cannot be expected to do justice to the miracle of music, and if my efforts can contribute something to the inspiration of others I shall be content enough: the critic can only learn vicariously.

Finally, I have eliminated the chapter in the earlier editions on Debussy's influence. There may have been in the 1930s a need to trace the immediate influence of one of the most arresting and original figures in music on the work of subsequent com-posers. To-day Debussy is no longer considered a revolu-tionary or an iconoclast. Nor, with the passage of time, can he be considered as merely a French composer. Indeed, in Eng-land as in other countries, the present generation revere him as Mozart revered Philipp Emanuel Bach: 'He is the father of us all.' And the impact of Debussy's wonderful offerings, uniting the nineteenth and twentieth centuries, as Beethoven bridged the classical and romantic eras a century earlier, extends far beyond a definable influence, illuminating not only the future of music but its past.

E. L.

London, 1951.

PREFACE TO SECOND EDITION

WHEN this short account of the life and work of Debussy appeared eight years ago it contained, as I was well aware at the time, many fogs and gaps. They were perhaps to be expected in the life of an artist who was himself so elusive and so laconic and who, in any case, was only just receding into history. On several periods only the scantiest of information was available, and often the few traces I managed to discover of his activities led only to further mysteries. Yet I liked to think that these quests, disappointing as many of them were, seemed to have some symbolical affinity with Debussy's very nature. It is said that a biography of a composer must make some attempt to relate the man to his music. It might go further and humbly attempt to imitate his art. At any rate, looking back now on the character I tried to reveal, I cannot help feeling that something unexplored must necessarily remain in any study of Debussy.

No further explorations have been made in the present edition, not because of any satisfaction with biographical half-tones, but because of the practical impossibility of communicating with France during the war. Hence, apart from one or two minor corrections, and certain additions to the bibliography, to the list of published letters and to the list of unpublished works, the book remains unaltered. I shall certainly be envious of the future biographers of Debussy who will, no doubt, be able to draw upon the long series of letters to his intimate friend, Robert Godet, of which only a small selection has been published, the letters to his two wives, Rosalie Texier and Emma Bardac, and those to Ernest Le Grand and to Charles Koechlin. When, after the war, these documents are made available, we may expect, if not a more brightly illuminated portrait, at any rate a more precise one that will elucidate many puzzling episodes in the life of a great artist.

How it was that such music came to be written by such a man is the central problem for the biographer, and what is particularly interesting in both the character and the art of Debussy is the amazing combination of an intimacy almost embarrassing in its truthful detail with a vague, phantom-like quality that belongs to a world never to be seen. I suppose it is here that we must reckon with the world of dreams, not the dreams of a sentimentalist, but the courageous visions of an artist who has dared, as Nietzsche put it, 'to become himself.' The main demand we make of an artist is: 'Does he create a world?' Debussy's world was a new province of the unconscious mind, so new and, at the same time, so real that Saint-Saëns and Rimsky-Korsakov saw it as a dangerous threat. It might have been a threat to the conservative mind, but as we now plainly see it was also one of the most remarkable creative phenomena of modern times—an art merging the real and the unreal with uncanny precision. I suggested that Debussy's critic might attempt, however inadequately, to emulate something of his own technique. That being so, it would be pretentious of me to emulate anything more than the eloquent silences that gleam in the music of Mélisande.

E. L.

London, 1944.

PREFACE TO FIRST EDITION

DEBUSSY once said that at the age of sixty he would write his memoirs. But he died in 1918 at fifty-five, and a definitive biography has not yet been written. Several authors have written an account of his life, but they have dealt mainly with exterior facts. One of these accounts, by M. Louis Laloy, has special value as having been written with Debussy's approval. It is an early work, however, and necessarily incomplete. Following this, the most authoritative French study that has appeared is M. Léon Vallas's *Claude Debussy et son temps*. Yet here again, as M. Vallas states in his preface, 'the personal life, rich in piquant anecdotes, of a great artist whose extreme and unrestrained sensibility forced him into certain positions which it is not our business to judge,' is intentionally left aside.

The task of writing Debussy's intimate life has therefore been largely work on virgin soil. I am deeply indebted to the work of M. Vallas, which all students must now take as their starting-point, but I have gone chiefly to Debussy's published letters, a list of which, scattered in journals and reviews, will be found in Appendix D. Many of these have not been used in any previous biography and appear here, in English, for the first time.

I have to thank Debussy's pupil and stepson, M. Raoul Bardac, for allowing me to publish the letters addressed to him and for the photographs facing pages 87 and 106; Debussy's sister, Mlle Adèle Debussy, and his friends, M. Nicholas G. Coronio, the late Paul Dukas, MM. Robert Godet, Louis Laloy and Gabriel Pierné, for valuable conversations; Count Bennigsen for searching his family records concerning Debussy's visits to Russia; Countess Bennigsen for the translations of the correspondence of Mme von Meck on pages 12–15; M. Gilaiev for information concerning Debussy's early unfinished Symphony; the committee and secretary of the Royal Philharmonic Society for communicating the letters in Appendix E; and Henry Prunières for the illustration facing page 111.

I have, however, reserved the right to interpret any information that has been given to me in my own way.

E. L.

London, 1936.

Quotations from the following works are printed by kind permission of the publishers. MM. Durand et Cie: *Mandoline, Pour ce que plaisance est morte, Ballade de Villon à s'amye, Pagodes, Reflets dans l'eau, Serenade (Children's Corner),* String Quartet, Cello Sonata, *La Damoiselle élue, Pelléas et Mélisande.* M. Jean Jobert: *C'est l'extase, Le Tombeau des naïades.* Éditions de la Sirène Musicale: *Paysage sentimental.*

CONTENTS

LIFE

Contents

ILLUSTRATIONS

J'ai la fureur d'aimer. Qu'y faire? Ah, laisser faire!
PAUL VERLAINE.

There is no canon by which a dream may be criticized ... we do not know the laws of that country.
CHARLES LAMB.

LIFE

CHAPTER I

'SEE how easily they are mistaken,' Debussy once said to a journalist in Vienna. 'Some think I'm a melancholy northerner, others that I'm from the south, from Provence, the country of Daudet—*tireli, tirela!* Well, I'm just a native of Saint-Germain, half an hour from Paris.'

Until Léon Vallas published his researches this was virtually all that was known of Debussy's ancestry. It now appears that through a line of farmers, small landowners and labourers his family goes back to one Valentin de Bussy, born in the village of Courcelles-sous-Grignon in Burgundy at the end of the seventeenth century. Five miles from this village, at Bussy-le-Grand, is the ancient Burgundian seat of the Counts de Bussy. No definite link between Debussy's ancestors and their neighbours of noble blood is known to exist, although one fact in support of a possible relationship between them may be mentioned. Roger de Rabutin, Count de Bussy, the distinguished soldier and writer, better known as Bussy-Rabutin, the cousin of Mme de Sévigné, was said to have had that prominent forehead which was one of Debussy's most striking features. He lived at Bussy-le-Grand during the second half of the seventeenth century and was notorious for his exploits with women.

Debussy's ancestors left Burgundy at the time of the Revolution and settled near Paris. His grandfather was a carpenter. His father, Manuel-Achille, was born at Montrouge in 1836, tried his hand at a number of things, and eventually settled

3

down as an accountant in a firm in Paris. On 30th November 1861 he married, at Levallois, then a village on the outskirts of Paris, a Parisian, Victorine Manoury,[1] six months his junior. The next day the young couple moved into a little brown-faced house, number 38 rue au Pain, at Saint-Germain-en-Laye, taking over the china shop on the ground floor.

Little is known of this modest couple. From one or two stray remarks of Debussy's boyhood friends we gather that Manuel Debussy was fond of music, particularly of *opéra comique*, and appears to have had a brother who was a conductor, possibly of a military band, somewhere in the provinces. Henry Prunières writes that Manuel Debussy boasted 'of only the most superficial education,' yet 'pretended to the widest interests. He frequented playhouse galleries, saw all the most successful pieces, read the most popular books, talked of them at length, and fancied himself as a musical connoisseur.' His son, however, used to refer to him as 'le vieux galvaudeux' (the old waster). Of Mme Debussy we are told that she was highly emotional. One fact is certain: the first eight years of their married life were passed under great financial strain.

The year after they were married, on 22nd August 1862, was born their first child, named after his father and paternal grandfather, Achille-Claude. Our information concerning his early childhood is still scanty; but there is one matter which I am able to elucidate. Vallas mentions that he was not baptized until 31st July 1864, that is, almost two years after his birth, and adds:

His baptismal certificate bears two names which he declared later were unknown to him: those of his godfather, Achille-Antoine Arosa, and his godmother, Octavie de la Ferronnière. The identity of the financier, Arosa, will be disclosed some day, and Octavie de

---

[1] Mlle Adèle Debussy, the composer's sister, has informed me that her maternal grandmother was likewise from Burgundy.

la Ferronnière will be despoiled of the high-sounding name she assumed; we shall ascertain what relationships, legal or otherwise, united the two people who held Achille-Claude at the baptismal font: then only shall we know the exact circumstances of his childhood. We do not propose to reveal here any further particulars on the subject.[1]

It is hardly to be wondered at that this mysterious reference caused some people to doubt the legitimacy of Debussy's birth. To counteract the conjectures that arose from this statement Vallas subsequently stated that no such idea was ever in his mind and that there existed absolutely no foundation for questioning that Achille was the son of Manuel and Victorine Debussy. The truth of the matter is that 'Octavie de la Ferronnière' was Manuel's sister, her real name being Mme Roustan (*née* Debussy). The benefactress of the Debussy family, she was able to secure through her relationship with Arosa, then a fairly well-to-do bachelor, material support and guidance for a child whose parents were living almost in misery. To this poor, struggling couple Arosa, a man of taste and distinction, appeared, in fact, to be almost a fairy godfather.[2]

Achille was the eldest of five children. Within two years a girl, Adèle, was born, and the Debussys, not having made a success of the china business, gave up their shop and moved first to Clichy and then to Paris, where they lived in the rue Pigalle. Three boys were born within a short time and Mme Debussy, doubtless for financial reasons, entrusted all her children, except Achille, to the care of her sister-in-law.

Achille—it was only in later years that, finding this name quite ridiculous, he reversed the order of his Christian names and was known to his friends as Claude—stayed with his mother. She was, we are told, 'passionately fond of him.' He never went to school. She taught him to read and write,

[1] Translation by Maire and Grace O'Brien.

[2] Information kindly supplied by M. Paul Arosa.

but such elementary education as he received from her was far from complete, and his spelling was faulty even at the age of thirty. According to his sister, he was (at about the age of eight) 'uncommunicative and closed in upon himself, liking neither his lessons nor his games. . . . He would spend whole days sitting on a chair thinking, no one knew of what.' He was much attracted by tiny ornaments and engravings and had a passion for collecting brilliantly coloured butterflies, which he arranged in zigzags on the walls of his room. At one time, it is said, he thought of becoming a painter.

Of a few years later we have these illuminating glimpses from Gabriel Pierné:

He was a gourmet, but not a gourmand. He loved good things to eat and the quantity mattered little. I remember very well how he used to delight in a cup of chocolate which my mother invited him to take at the Café Prévost, and how, at Bourbonneux's [a famous *pâtisserie*], he used to choose some delicate little pastry from a case specially reserved for the *produits de luxe*, while his friends were more likely to be content with something more substantial. This poor boy, who had come from a most ordinary class of society, had in everything the taste of an aristocrat. He was particularly attracted to minute objects and delicate and sensitive things. My father had a beautifully bound set of *Le Monde illustré*. When Achille came to the house we used to look at the pictures with delight. He preferred those which took up little space and were surrounded by a huge margin. One day he persuaded me to help him cut out these pictures to put on our walls. The crime was soon committed, and I remember that Debussy went off with reproductions of famous pictures, by Meissonier in particular, surrounded by these huge margins.

When Achille was seven, his brother Eugène died of meningitis and he and his sister were taken to Cannes by their aunt. He wrote to Jacques Durand in 1908:

I remember the railway passing in front of the house and the sea stretching out to the horizon. You sometimes had the impression that the railway came out of the sea or went into it—whichever you like. Then there was the Route d'Antibes, where there were so many roses. I never saw so many all together in my life. I hope the railway is still there, so that you will be able to come back, and also the roses, because there is no better way of decorating streets. With a Norwegian carpenter who used to sing—Grieg, perhaps— from morning till night I close my memoirs.

In Cannes it was Mme Roustan who first had the idea that her nephew should be taught music and accordingly arranged for him to take piano lessons from an old Italian teacher named Cerutti. Of these early lessons we know nothing beyond this bare fact mentioned in the early biography of Louis Laloy. It seems that his career was determined by a meeting in Paris some time later. Through Charles de Sivry he came into contact with Mme Mauté de Fleurville, a former pupil of Chopin, and the mother of Mathilde Mauté, the unfortunate wife of Paul Verlaine. 'He must become a musician,' she said, having heard him strum on an old piano; and she offered herself as a pianoforte teacher. Manuel Debussy, who up till this time had thought of sending his son into the navy, decided thereupon that he should become a virtuoso, and in the traditional manner of fathers of promising musicians imposed on him long hours of daily practice.

In his correspondence with Durand, Debussy twice mentions Mme Mauté de Fleurville. On 27th January 1915, when he was working on an edition of Chopin, he wrote: 'It is a pity that Madame Mauté de Fleurville, to whom I owe the little I know about the piano, is dead. She knew many things about Chopin.' And on 1st September of the same year:

With all respect to his great age, what Saint-Saëns says about the pedal in Chopin is not quite right, for I remember very well what Madame Mauté de Fleurville told me. Chopin wanted his pupils to study without using the pedal and only to use it sparingly when performing.   It was this use of the pedal as a kind of breathing that I noticed in Liszt, when I heard him in Rome.[1]

Such are the available facts of Debussy's childhood.   Living apart from his brothers and sister, never having gone to school and continually in the company of his mother, he was not a happy child and had little opportunity of acquiring any sense of sociability.   His father was not the kind of man to deal with such introspection as this upbringing tended to breed; and the narrowness of his mother's mind soon became apparent.   When at the age of ten he was admitted to the Conservatoire, his awkward and unsociable manner, not to mention his poor education, hardly made him attractive to his fellow students.

[1] In her *Mémoires* Mathilde Verlaine tells that her mother frequented the highest circles of Paris society.   She was an extremely kind-hearted woman, often engaged in charity work, and she had known intimately the greatest artistic celebrities of her day, among them Balzac, de Musset and Wagner.   Mathilde, to whom Verlaine dedicated *La Bonne Chanson*, was a child of her second marriage with Mauté, 'de Fleurville' being an assumed part of the name.

CHAPTER II

AT THE CONSERVATOIRE—1872–1884

DEBUSSY entered the Paris Conservatoire in October 1872 and remained there almost twelve years.

The first class in which he was enrolled was the so-called *solfège* class for which this school is famous. At no other institution is the course in ear-training so rigorous. Students are required not merely to sing at sight and to transpose easily, but to analyse and to reproduce any harmonic or contrapuntal texture before they acquire, in the study of harmony, the rule-of-thumb methods of putting parts together. Lavignac, the master, was an erudite musician who incidentally introduced Debussy to the music of Wagner by playing over to him, one winter evening, the overture to *Tannhäuser*. Whatever it meant to the young boy, he must have been completely unaware of the great conflict that Wagner was later to cause in his musical development, a conflict that was to go far to promote and to define the new Debussyan world of music. Debussy remained in Lavignac's class four years and at the annual examinations was awarded the third, second, and finally the first prize.

In the piano class which he attended at the same time the teacher was Marmontel. Debussy was not, in his opinion, one of the best pupils of his class. 'He doesn't like the piano much, but he does like music,' Marmontel once said. In 1877, however, Debussy won the second prize with the first movement of Schumann's G minor Sonata, and his parents were still able to hope for the career of a virtuoso. But the following two years were disappointing. He received no

9

award at either of the annual examinations, and all such hopes were abandoned.

Debussy's first musical leanings, as recorded by his friend Paul Vidal, reveal the almost forgotten Paris musical world of the eighteen-seventies as dominated by *opéra comique*. Offenbach, Pessard and Delibes—such were the composers who were then in vogue. In Marmontel's class they played a great deal of Chopin and Schumann and various works of Stephen Heller and Alkan. Debussy as a boy showed a preference for Berlioz and also for Lalo, whose *Namouna* brought from him such a manifestation of enthusiasm at the Opéra that he was ordered to leave the theatre. He was attracted to Ernest Guiraud, his future teacher of composition; to Pessard, whose *Capitaine Fracasse,* a popular light opera, delighted him; to Delibes and Saint-Saëns. César Franck he liked to a certain extent. Beethoven he abhorred—but only, as he said, for the reason that Marmontel had given the sentimental words: 'O mère, douleur amère,' to the rondo of the 'Pathetic' Sonata.

In the harmony class the teacher was Émile Durand. According to Maurice Emmanuel, who is the authority for Debussy's studies at the Conservatoire, his instruction in harmony was 'second-rate.' Durand, writes this author, 'liked neither music, teaching, nor his pupils. . . . If, when the class was over, one of the pupils would play over to his friends some composition he had attempted, Durand would slam the lid of the piano on his fingers and say: "You'd do better to work at your progressions!"' However, from the four years, 1876 to 1880, that Debussy spent in this class date his first known compositions. They consist of several songs on poems of Théodore de Banville and two unpublished songs entitled *Madrid, princesse des Espagnes* and *Ballade à la lune.* Of these we might possibly form some idea from the following anecdote told by Vidal, which at least throws an interesting light on his early musical taste:

First Compositions—Mme von Meck

As I kept on worrying him to play me his new works, which he
hadn't the time or the inclination to write down, he played the joke on
me of making me learn by heart a set of songs by Pessard, *Les Joyeusetés
de bonne compagnie,* which he sang to me pretending they were his.

Chanson d'un fou, a song recently published under Debussy's
name, is actually not by Debussy at all, but a song of this set
by Pessard.[1]

By 1880 he had received no awards in Durand's class, and
without some recommendation in harmony it was not allowed
to proceed to one of the composition classes. The first prize
in Auguste Bazille's score-reading class which he obtained
in the summer of 1880 enabled him, however, to do this.
But here we must interrupt the account of his studies at the
Conservatoire to relate an important episode of his early life.
During the summer of 1880, when he was first assured of
following the career of a composer, he made the acquaintance
of the patroness of Tchaikovsky, Nadezhda von Meck.

Let us picture the young Debussy, shy and clumsy, as his
friends remember him then, in the company of this Russian
grande dame. She was a woman of fifty and a multi-
millionaire. Her husband had died in 1876, leaving her with
eleven children. In the same year she developed that strange
passion for the personality of Tchaikovsky which forbade her
ever to make his acquaintance and which she sublimated in
the love-letters she incessantly wrote him over a period of
sixteen years. She was an accomplished pianist, cultured and
widely read. She had known the Rubinsteins well and
several of her children had taken lessons from Liszt. After
the death of her husband she retired almost completely from
society, giving herself up to a passionate cult of the music
of Tchaikovsky, whom she maintained with a handsome
allowance.

[1] See Catalogue of Works (Appendix B), page 260.

Debussy

Here, in her letters, is the first reference to Debussy. It is dated 10th July 1880, from Interlaken:

Two days ago a young pianist arrived from Paris, where he has just graduated at the Conservatoire with the first prize in the class of M. Marmontel.[1] I engaged him for the summer to give lessons to the children, accompany Julia's singing and play four hands with myself. This young man plays well, his technique is brilliant, but he lacks any personal expression. He is yet too young, says he is twenty, but looks sixteen.

He was, in fact, eighteen. At the end of July Mme von Meck travelled with Debussy and five or six of her children from Interlaken through the south of France to Arcachon. On 17th August she writes:

Yesterday for the first time I played our Symphony [i.e. Tchaikovsky's No. 4] with my little Frenchman. So to-day I am in a terrible state of nerves. I cannot play it without a fever penetrating all the fibres of my being and for a whole day I cannot recover from the impression. My partner did not play it well, though he read it splendidly. That is his only, though very important, merit. He reads a score, yours even, à livre ouvert. He has another merit, which is that he is delighted with your music. Theoretically he is Massenet's pupil and naturally considers Massenet the great luminary. But yesterday I also played your suite with him and he was enchanted with the fugue, saying: 'Dans les fugues modernes je n'ai jamais rien vu de si beau. M. Massenet ne pourrait jamais rien faire de pareil.' He does not care for the Germans and says: 'Ils ne sont pas de notre tempérament, ils sont si lourds, pas clairs.' On the whole he is a typical Parisian boulevard product. It seems he is eighteen and has already graduated at the Conservatoire avec premier prix. Blessed are those who study at the Paris Conservatoire. He composes very nicely, but here too he is the true Frenchman.

---

[1] As we have seen, the first prize he received in 1880 was from the score-reading class of Bazille. Either Debussy had misinformed her or she was misled by the fact that Marmontel had recommended him.

In the Service of Mme von Meck

Debussy was never, as far as is known, a pupil of Massenet. He might have been an *auditeur* in Massenet's class or, what is more likely, he might have learnt to consider Massenet as the 'great luminary' in the harmony class of Émile Durand. Massenet was the most popular master at the Conservatoire and, as the songs, *Nuit d'étoiles, Beau soir* and *Fleur des blés,* clearly show, Debussy in his younger days was certainly one of his disciples.

At the beginning of September we find the von Mecks and Debussy in Florence. The earliest mention of Debussy's compositions is in a letter of 8th September from the Villa Oppenheim:

I shall send you for your appreciation a little composition—one of many—by my little pianist, Bussy [writes Madame von Meck to Tchaikovsky]. This youth intends to become a composer and writes very nice things, but they are all echoes of his professor, Massenet. He is now writing a trio. It is very nice but it is again reminiscent of Massenet. He score-reads and accompanies singing perfectly. . . .

Many of these early pieces passed into the hands of members of the von Meck family and either disappeared at the time of the Revolution or have otherwise remained unpublished. The little composition sent to Tchaikovsky was the recently discovered *Danse bohémienne* published by Schott. Tchaikovsky remarked that it was 'a very nice little thing, but altogether too short. Not a single thought is developed to the end, the form is bungled and there is no unity.' An accurate criticism, though no doubt disheartening for Debussy, who might have shared some of his hostess's feelings for Tchaikovsky.

It appears that in Florence Debussy was required to play in the household trio with the violinist Pachulsky and the cellist Danilchenko.[1] We gather that they were on intimate

[1] On seeing a photograph of this household triumvirate, Tchaikovsky remarked: 'Bussy has something in the face and hands that vaguely recalls Anton Rubinstein in his youth. God grant that his

13

terms with the children. A song called *Rondeau* on words of Alfred de Musset that Debussy wrote in 1882 bears the dedication: 'Pour mon ami Alexandre de Meck. Souvenir bien affectueux.' Pachulsky married Julia and Maximilian de Meck remembers that Debussy fell in love with his sister, Sophie, and asked her to marry him. She was then aged sixteen and flatly refused.

On 29th September Mme von Meck informs Tchaikovsky that her 'little Frenchman' has finished his Trio. 'I am sorry not to be able to send it to you for your criticism, but he is leaving shortly and would not have the time to copy it out.' This is no doubt the Trio in G mentioned by M. Vallas in *Claude Debussy et son temps*. It has remained unpublished and is dedicated in affectionate terms to his harmony master, Émile Durand. His earliest publication seems to have been an arrangement, made at his hostess's request, of the Spanish, Italian and Russian dances from Tchaikovsky's ballet *The Swan Lake*.

No doubt the eighteen-year-old Debussy fully appreciated the agreeable duties of his post and the opportunities to work at the Villa Oppenheim. 'Just imagine, that boy cried bitterly when he left me,' writes Mme von Meck on 31st October. 'Naturally I was deeply touched—he has a very faithful heart. He would not have gone at all were it not that his masters at the Conservatoire disapproved of his request for a prolongation of leave.'

The following spring he sought to renew his engagement. Mme von Meck was then in Russia. On 12th May 1881 she wrote to Tchaikovsky from Brailov in the Ukraine: 'My

lot be as happy as that of the "king of pianists."' It was the presence of these musicians at her house that first caused Mme von Meck to suggest to Tchaikovsky that he should write a trio. 'Why have you never written a single trio?' she writes on 18th October 1880. 'Every day I regret it, for every day trios are played to me and I always complain that you have not written one.'

DEBUSSY AT EIGHTEEN, DURING HIS
STAY AT FLORENCE WITH MADAME VON MECK

little Frenchman is anxious to come here. I shall not have the heart to refuse him though I have a pianist, the elder Pachulsky.' Here, then, we are able to elucidate some of the mystery of Debussy's early visit to Russia—an episode which, until the publication of the Tchaikovsky–von Meck corre‑ spondence, had given rise to much conjecture.

We know now the circumstances and the date. Debussy arrived in Russia early in July 1881. It is not clear whether he first went to Brailov and from there journeyed with Mme von Meck to Moscow, or whether he met her in Moscow. At all events she was in Moscow from the middle of July till the end of September, and at least part of this time he was with her.

Unfortunately the references to Debussy in her corre‑ spondence of these months are few. There is mention of his having played certain scores of Tchaikovsky's, but the letters of this period deal almost entirely with family matters and business worries and give little indication of the life Debussy led in Moscow or the music he heard. From a letter of 11th September 1881 we learn of a journey that he made with Nicholas von Meck to Gurievo near Moscow to play Tchaikovsky's fourth Symphony at the house of Countess Alexandra Bennigsen (*née* von Meck). How long he stayed in Russia after this visit cannot be ascertained. The next and last mention of him is in a letter of 24th November 1881 from Florence, in which Mme von Meck says:

When Bussy was with me I often translated [the words] for him, so that he should better grasp the significance of the music. I gave him the score of the *Maid of Orleans* and he also asked me for your overture, *Romeo and Juliet*. I miss him awfully, he played me so much of your music.

Such is the information to be gained from Mme von Meck's correspondence. Her last surviving son, Maximilian de Meck, has informed me that Debussy spent three summers with his family, and it may well be that more details will be found in volumes of this correspondence, to be published later. We might then hear about the *Symphonie en si* which Debussy dedicated to his hostess, a movement of which, for piano duet, was discovered before the war in a Moscow market and pub/ lished by the Soviet State Publishing Company.[1]

Debussy's acquaintance with Russian music other than that of Tchaikovsky would appear, from this correspondence, to have been very limited. Balakirev was the only member of the 'Kutchka' whom Mme von Meck admired. Rimsky/ Korsakov she found 'lifeless,' Cui 'perverted' and Mus/ sorgsky 'quite finished.' Borodin 'never had much brains and overstepped his mark.' But she loved Napravnik and loved Anton Rubinstein 'very much,' and her love for Tchaikovsky was in her 'flesh and blood.'

Raymond Bonheur, a student at the Paris Conservatoire, remembers, however, that Debussy brought back from Russia an old opera of Rimsky/Korsakov and some songs of Borodin. The song, *Paysage sentimental,* written by Debussy in 1880, the year of his visit to Florence, shows even then an acquaintance with Borodin. And there are passages reminiscent of Borodin and Rimsky/Korsakov in other works of his belonging to this period (notably in *La Belle au bois dormant* and *Le Triomphe de Bacchus,* both written between 1880 and 1883). But not of Tchaikovsky! According to M. Laloy's biography Debussy

[1] In a private collection in Leningrad there are two unpublished pieces signed: 'Debussy, Moscow 1884.' The third volume of the Tchaikovsky–von Meck correspondence (Moscow, 1936) gives in/ formation on Debussy's visit to Russia, not in 1884, but in 1882. He was with Madame von Meck at Plechtchevo near Podolsk in August, in Moscow in September and in Vienna and Paris from October to November. See the article 'Claude Debussy dans la correspondance de Tchaikovsky et de Madame von Meck' in *La Revue musicale,* October 1937.

became well acquainted with the Tsigansky songs in the Moscow cabarets though the extent to which his early musical development was affected by them has been somewhat exaggerated.[1] On this Mme von Meck says nothing. Jean Lépine mentions that in 1880 Mme von Meck introduced Debussy to Wagner at Venice. According to the same author, in Moscow he knew Borodin. Paul Vidal mentions that during these journeys he heard *Tristan* for the first time, at Vienna. Wagner, Borodin, the Tsigansky folksongs in Moscow—here was indeed music that might have weaned him from his devotion to Massenet. Can it be that Mme von Meck, with her infatuation for Tchaikovsky, concealed from him any preference for such music that Debussy might have shown? The scarcity of references to him during his visit to Moscow would thus have some significance.

Meanwhile, at the Conservatoire, after a brief venture into the class of César Franck, with whom he was quite unable to agree, he had enrolled in the composition class of Ernest Guiraud.

Guiraud had been a great friend of Bizet and had known Berlioz. He had written a number of operas, classed in style with those of Massenet, and a treatise on orchestration which in spite of its age is still considered a work of great value. To judge from certain accounts of M. Emmanuel, Debussy at this time was beginning to see the insufficiency of the music of Massenet and Delibes and was attracted to Guiraud, not because this master was in any way opposed to the aesthetic of Massenet—for he was not—but because of a certain liberalmindedness and tolerance.

[1] According to Count Bennigsen, a grandson of Mme von Meck, Debussy might have been initiated into Moscow cabaret life by Vladimir von Meck, Mme von Meck's eldest son. A popular man in Moscow society in the eighties, it was he who played such havoc with his mother's fortune that in 1892 she was brought to the brink of ruin and saw herself forced to discontinue Tchaikovsky's allowance.

Debussy

One winter evening of 1883 [M. Emmanuel recounts] Debussy went to the piano to imitate the sound of the buses going down the Faubourg Poissonière. He played a sort of chromatic groaning, to which his friends and a few people who had stayed on from other classes listened mockingly. 'Look at them,' Debussy said, turning round. 'Can't you listen to chords without knowing their names? ... Listen, and if you can't make it out go and tell the director I am ruining your ears.'

At the piano we heard groups of consecutive fifths and octaves; sevenths which instead of being resolved in the proper way actually led to the note above or weren't resolved at all; shameful 'false relations'; chords of the ninth on all degrees of the scale; chords of the eleventh and thirteenth; all the notes of the diatonic scale heard at once in fantastic arrangements. ... And all this Claude called 'le régal de l'ouie' [a feast for the ear]. Delibes's class [of which M. Emmanuel was a member] shook with amazement and fear.

His reputation as an 'eccentric' and a 'troublesome propagandist' was investigated by the registrar.

This austere gentleman, Émile Réty, wondered how Guiraud could have any esteem for such a pupil. To Claude, caught in the very act of abusing the harmony treatise, he said one day: 'So you imagine that dissonant chords do not have to be resolved? What rule do you follow?' 'Mon plaisir!' Debussy replied. ... And Réty turned away, pale with indignation.

The history of music, it has been said, is the history of the infraction of the rule; and the terrifying though heartening gesture of genius flouting the academic canons of his art is not unfamiliar. But what we may notice here are the exact words of Debussy's reply to Réty: 'Mon plaisir,' and the description of his improvisations as 'le régal de l'ouie.' For they provide the first indication of the important element of sensualism in Debussy's art, an element of which he was becoming increasingly conscious, gradually revealing to the student-composer the shortcomings of his models from the school of Massenet.

The years 1881–4 were spent in preparation for the Grand Prix de Rome. Of his life outside the Conservatoire during these years we know that he was the accompanist to a choral society, *La Concordia*, and became intimately associated with its president, Charles Gounod. This post he received through the recommendation of Vidal. Vidal also recommended him as accompanist to the singing teacher, Mme Moreau-Sainti, through whom he met Mme Vasnier, an accomplished singer and a very beautiful young woman, who becomes another important figure in his early life.

Mme Vasnier was the wife of a civil servant eleven years older than herself. Their flat in the rue de Constantinople and their summer house at Ville d'Avray provided just that intellectual background that Debussy missed in his home. M. Vasnier suggested books that he should read and became his guide in matters literary and artistic. From Théodore de Banville and Paul Bourget, favourite poets of his earlier days, he progressed to Verlaine and Mallarmé. From this time dates the first version of *Fêtes galantes*, on the poems of Verlaine, a *Chanson espagnole* for two voices, sung by Debussy and Mme Vasnier at a fancy-dress ball, a *Rondel chinois*, 'from contemporary manuscripts,' and a *Nocturne* and *Scherzo* for piano and violin (played at a concert of the violinist Maurice Thiéberg in 1882 'with the gracious aid of Mme Vasnier and Monsieur Achille de Bussy'). Besides these, which have all disappeared except the *Fêtes galantes*, there is, in a private collection, an album of songs bearing the following dedication:

To MADAME VASNIER

These songs which she alone has made live and which will lose their enchanting grace if they are never again to come from her singing fairy lips.

The eternally grateful author.

M. Prunières, who writes authoritatively on this period,

has spoken of Mme Vasnier as Debussy's 'first great love.' It appears that her husband, older than herself, regarded the affair as one that could not come to much harm. Whether he knew that, as according to Prunières, Mme Vasnier became Debussy's mistress, we do not know. At any rate, Debussy seems to have been absolutely guileless in the matter and later, when he was at Rome, wrote him the most sincere and affectionate letters.

Let us here quote from an article on Debussy by Mlle Marguerite Vasnier:

Debussy at eighteen was a big beardless boy with clearly marked features and thick black curly hair which he wore flat on his forehead. In the evening when his hair was untidy, suiting him much better, my parents said he was like a type of medieval Florentine. His face was very interesting. His eyes especially were striking. His personality made itself felt. His hands were strong and bony and his fingers square. His playing at the piano was powerful but it could be extremely tender. . . .[1]

As he had little support [from his family] he asked my parents if he could come and work at our house, and thenceforth he was admitted as one of the family. I can still see him in the little *salon* in our flat on the fifth floor of the rue de Constantinople,

---

[1] It is curious to note how Debussy's youthful playing struck his contemporaries. As we have seen, Mme von Meck found that he lacked 'any personal expression.' Gabriel Pierné has described his playing in Marmontel's class as 'very strange. I don't know whether it was because of his clumsiness or his shyness, but he used literally to throw himself on the keyboard and exaggerate his effects. He seemed to be in a rage with the instrument—ill-treating it with his impulsive movements and breathing nervously when he came to the difficult passages. These faults gradually became less noticeable and there were moments when he produced surprising effects of sweetness. With all its faults his playing was very individual.'

M. Emmanuel says that he played Beethoven 'heavily'—hardly the word one would have expected.

where for five years he wrote most of his compositions. He used to come nearly every evening and often in the afternoon, leaving the music he wrote on a little table. He composed sometimes at the piano, on a curious old Blondel, and sometimes walking about. He would improvise for a long time and then walk up and down the room humming, either with a cigarette in his mouth or rolling one in preparation. Then, when he was sure, he wrote. He made few corrections but he spent a long time getting it right in his head or at the piano before writing. He was not easily satisfied with his work.

Then there is this interesting glimpse:

He was very quick to take offence and extremely sensitive. The slightest thing put him in good humour or made him sullen or angry. He was very unsociable and never hid his displeasure when my parents invited friends, for he did not often allow himself to be with strangers. If people dropped in and were fortunate enough to please him, he could be amiable and would play and sing Wagner or he would imitate or caricature some modern composer. But when he didn't like any one he showed it. He was original though rather unpolished, but very charming with people he liked.

Of his visits to the Vasniers at Ville d'Avray Mlle Vasnier writes:

The singing-classes were over and Debussy used to come every morning and leave at night by the last train. He worked a lot and sometimes we would take long walks in the Parc de Saint-Cloud or have endless games of croquet. He was quite skilful but he was a bad loser. . . . In the evening he would accompany my mother. Generally they went over his songs, which they studied together. . . . On rainy days we played cards. He was always a bad player and when he lost he got into a terrible humour, particularly as any money he won had often to be spent on the train journey home. To get him into good spirits we used to put a packet of tobacco under his serviette at the dinner table—and then he was so pleased! But of course he was only nineteen or twenty.

The Premier Grand Prix de Rome was awarded to Debussy in 1884 for his cantata *L'Enfant prodigue*. That he stayed on at the Conservatoire after gaining only the second prize at the competition of 1883 was largely due to the Vasniers' influence. Of the twenty-two out of twenty-eight academicians who voted in favour of *L'Enfant prodigue* the principal voice was that of Gounod. He did not hesitate to express the opinion that it was the work of a genius.

Many years later Debussy recalled his impressions:

I was on the Pont des Arts awaiting the result of the competition and watching with delight the scurrying of the little Seine steamers. I was quite calm, having forgotten all emotion due to anything Roman, so seductive was the charm of the gay sunshine playing on the ripples, a charm which keeps those delightful idlers, who are the envy of Europe, hour after hour on the bridges.

Suddenly someone tapped me on the shoulder and said breath-lessly: 'You 've won the prize !' Believe me or not, I can assure you that all my pleasure vanished ! I saw in a flash the boredom, the vexations inevitably incident to the slightest official recognition. Besides, I felt I was no longer free.[1]

In those words may be seen the saturnine recluse fleeing the tawdriness of public life, from which in later years he was never able quite successfully to escape. And little by little, as is often the way with intensely warm-hearted people, he obscured himself from the outside world by a screen of bristling irony. Here is perhaps one of the keys to Debussy's personality—irony and sensuousness, the one eating into or attempting to override the other. He was a hedonist—like Verlaine and like Wagner. And the life of a hedonist is either a short one or it demands great sacrifice and suffering until the conceptions of pleasure and gratification in art are gradually transfigured into idealistic visions, personal and at the same time impersonal—the miraculous and terrifying visions of a new world.

[1] *Monsieur Croche the Dilettante-hater.* Anonymous translation. (London, 1927.)

CHAPTER III

ROME—1885–1887

ON 27th January 1885, in accordance with the regulations for holders of the Prix de Rome, Debussy, much against his will, left for the three years' sojourn at the Villa Medici in Rome. His life here is told for us in his letters, chiefly to M. Vasnier.[1] The following is the first, written on the way to Rome, from Marseilles:

DEAR MONSIEUR VASNIER,

I have not much to say to you because I don't want to tell you how sad I am. I'm trying to show courage and even, if necessary, to forget you. No, it's not ingratitude; besides, I wouldn't be able to. I shall write to you at greater length from Rome. Believe me to be your sincere friend,

ACH. DEBUSSY.

Give my regards to Madame Vasnier and kiss Marguerite and Maurice for me.

---

[1] Significantly, the letters to Mme Vasnier have been destroyed. Concerning Debussy's relationship with her during his stay in Rome see the article 'Souvenirs de Claude Debussy' in *La Revue des deux mondes*, Paris, May 1938. Rollo H. Myers quotes a letter of 1885, published in this article, in which Debussy says: 'As I have told you before, I have been too accustomed only to want things and to conceive them *through her*. . . . I know this is not following the advice you gave me to try to reduce this passion, which I know is mad, to a lasting friendship; but it's because it's so mad that it prevents me from being reasonable. Thinking seriously about it not only makes it worse, but almost convinces me that I have not sacrificed enough to this love.'

Debussy

A few days later we have a long letter to M. Vasnier giving his first impressions:

Here I am in this abominable Villa. I can tell you that my first impressions are not very favourable. It's awful weather—rainy and windy. There was no need to come to Rome to have the same weather as in Paris, especially for any one with such a grudge against Rome as I have.

My friends came to meet me at Monte Rotondo, where the six of us slept in one dirty little room. If only you knew how changed they are! None of their good-hearted friendly ways of Paris. They're stiff and impressed with their own importance—too much Prix de Rome about them.

In the evening when I arrived at the Villa I played my cantata, which was well received by some, but not by the musicians.

I don't mind. This artistic atmosphere and camaraderie that we are told about seem to me very exaggerated. With one or two exceptions, it is difficult to talk to the people here, and when I hear their ordinary conversation I cannot help thinking of the fine talks we used to have which opened my mind to so many things. Then the people here are so very egoistic. I've heard the musicians demolishing each other—Marty and Pierné against Vidal, Pierné and Vidal against Marty, and so on.

Ah! When I got back to my enormous room, where you have to walk a league from one piece of furniture to another, I felt so lonely that I cried! I'm so used to your friendship and to your asking me about my work. I shall never forget all you have done for me and the place I had in your family. I shall do all I can to prove to you that I am not ungrateful. So please don't forget me, for I feel I am going to need you.

I've tried to work but I can't. You know how much I love music and how much this state of mind annoys me. This is not the life for me. Their happiness isn't mine. It's not pride that makes me hate this life. I can't get used to it. I have no feeling for it and I haven't the necessary indifference.

Yes, I fear that I shall have to return to Paris earlier than you think. It may appear silly, but what is there to do? I don't want to make you cross and I should be very sorry to try your friendship.

But whatever you think, you can't accuse me of lacking courage. I'm rather unwell—Rome again—my beastly heart doesn't seem to be working properly. I rack my brain to work, but nothing comes of it except a fever which knocks me down completely.

I was so pleased to get your letter, and if I'm not asking too much, I know how little time you have, send me a long letter to remind me of the pleasant talks we used to have.

Very affectionately,

Your devoted

ACH. DEBUSSY.

Give my best regards to Madame Vasnier. How is Marguerite? Is she still working at my songs? I like Marguerite very much and I would like her to become an accomplished musician. That would please you and me too, for at least I should have done something worth while. A kiss for her and also for that silly little Maurice.

Here he paints himself as very desolate. But before long he began to work and for a time his correspondence is mainly concerned with projects for compositions which he was required to send periodically to Paris. The first of these was *Zuléima,* a work for chorus and orchestra on a text from Heine's *Almanzor.* Some work was done on it but it was quickly put aside. The subject is 'too old and fusty,' he wrote in a letter of 4th June 1885.

These great silly verses, which are only great in their length, bore me, and my music would be stifled by them. Then there's another thing: I don't think I shall ever be able to put music into a strict mould. I'm not speaking of musical form; it's a literary question. I shall always prefer a subject where, somehow, action is sacrificed to feeling. It seems to me that music thus becomes more human and real and one can then discover and refine upon a means of expression.

A very interesting glimpse of the musician's development. Shortly after, he intends to send to Paris a stage work, *Diane au bois,* on a comedy by Théodore de Banville, which he had

begun in Paris and which Guiraud had advised him 'to
keep for later' or 'he would never have the Prix de Rome.' He
explains to M. Vasnier his particular liking for Banville:

Diane isn't a bit like the poems that are generally used for these
envois, which are really only highly polished cantatas. Thank God!
I had enough of one of them and I think I should take advantage—
as you would say—of the only good thing there is at the Villa, the
liberty to work and do something original instead of always keeping
to the old paths. I 'm sure that the Institut won't be of my opinion.
Their way, of course, will be the only right one! But I 'm too fond
of my freedom. At least if they don't allow me to go where I like,
I can think and do what I like. All I can say is that I can't write
the kind of music they would approve. Now, I don't know if
I 'm big enough to do what I have in mind. Anyhow, I 'll do all
I can to make some of them content, the rest can go hang.

That explosive manifestation of freedom is followed by a
request to have a long letter from M. Vasnier 'to enlarge the
doors of my prison.' 'I think it is very good,' he concludes,
'for such an unpractical fellow as myself to have stuck it here
these few months.'

The arrival of a new director at the Villa Medici gives us
occasion to quote a remark illuminating Debussy's early attitude to Wagner. The new director, Hébert, was an able
painter, a disciple of Ingres and a good amateur violinist.
'He loved music passionately,' Debussy recollects some twenty
years later,

but Wagner's music not at all. At that time I was a Wagnerian
to the pitch of forgetting the simple rules of courtesy, nor did I
imagine that I could ever come almost to agree with this enthusiastic
old man who had travelled through all these emotions with his eyes
open, whereas we hardly grasped their meaning or how to use them.[1]

'A Wagnerian to the pitch of forgetting the simple rules
of courtesy'! Debussy's early acquaintance with Wagner has

[1] *Monsieur Croche the Dilettante-hater.*

26

not been, and probably cannot now be, fully investigated. It is often held that his great *engouement* for Wagner came at the time of his visits to Bayreuth in 1888 and 1889. But apparently he was very well acquainted with Wagner in Rome and as ardent a Wagnerian then as ever. Augustin Savard, a friend at the Villa Medici, recollects his living apart, 'playing the score of *Tristan* in his room,' and Vidal has recorded a performance they heard together of *Lohengrin* at the Teatro Apollo. But whatever the extent of his admiration he realized from the first the distance that lay between the Wagnerian conceptions and his own. Referring in a letter of 19th October 1886 to *Diane au bois,* he points out to M. Vasnier that it would be 'ridiculous' to take Wagner as a model. 'I should like to keep the melodic line lyrical,' he explains, 'and not allow the orchestra to predominate.' Those are words which might have been written by Berlioz.

In the summer of 1885 Debussy was invited to spend a short time in Fiumicino at the seaside villa of Count Primoli. 'There weren't any people or casinos,' he writes. 'I was able to be by myself as much as I wanted, knowing no one and only speaking when I wanted something to eat—which was nuisance enough. . . . I worked I should almost say well.' But such contentedness lasted only a short time. The following month M. Vasnier is implored to sanction a return to Paris:

> I really believe that to make me stay here a second year would be doing me no good whatever. It would only make me dislike the place more and I should no longer be able to work with the ease I once had. You can't say, I hope, that I haven't tried to settle down here. This year has been lost. So I intend to leave at the end of the year and I ask you, Monsieur Vasnier, knowing that I can count on you as a friend, not to think that I am acting unwisely, for I am not doing this for myself but for my future.

Beyond the grant of the Prix de Rome Debussy had, as far as we know, no means of support. Doubtless M. Vasnier

Debussy

pointed this out in his reply, for the next letter, of 24th November, although full of resentment against his 'life of a non-commissioned officer with full pay,' makes no mention of leaving.

I went to hear two masses [he says in this letter], one of Palestrina, the other of Orlandus Lassus, in a church called S. Maria dell' Anima. I don't know if you know it—it is stuck away among some awful little streets. I like it very much, as it is very simple and pure in style, unlike so many others with their array of sculptures, pictures and mosaics all so theatrical. The statue of Christ in these churches looks like a lost skeleton that wonders how it got there. The Anima is the only place to hear such music, which is the only church music there is for me. That of Gounod and company seems to come from some kind of hysterical mysticism and has the effect of a sinister farce.

The two above-named people are masters, especially Orlandus, who is more decorative and more human than Palestrina. The effects he gets from his great knowledge of counterpoint are amazing. You perhaps don't know that counterpoint can be the nastiest thing in music, but in their work it is beautiful.

Beyond this sixteenth-century music and *Lohengrin*, mentioned previously, we know that Debussy heard the first performance in Italy of Beethoven's second Symphony and the 'Emperor' Concerto, played by Sgambati. He also made careful studies of the ninth Symphony and of the organ works of Bach.

In the course of his stay he travelled to other towns in Italy and became acquainted with certain of his older Italian contemporaries. Leoncavallo, whom he knew slightly, introduced him to Boito in Milan. From the account of their meeting by Andrew de Ternant,[1] Boito appeared to Debussy to be more of a literary man than a musician. His study,

[1] See footnote regarding Andrew de Ternant's articles on Debussy on page 43.

littered with magazines, books and newspaper cuttings, showed
no sign of any musical activity, and when at length Boito
came in he explained to his visitor that he had been giving
a lecture on the English Lake Poets. He talked of his own
music, with which he was generally displeased, and of the
possibility of adapting opera librettos from the plays of Shakespeare and Goethe, which he thought afforded excellent
material. His belief, however, was that it was most worthy to
write, not for the theatre or the church, but for the concert-room.

With an introduction from Boito Debussy set out to meet
Verdi at Sant' Agata. 'He found Verdi in his shirt-sleeves,'
M. de Ternant writes, 'busy planting salads with the assistance
of a small boy.' He was a jovial and good-natured man and
knew France well. But he had no inclination to discuss his
contemporaries. He felt he had made enough enemies. He
passed a few remarks about Ambroise Thomas, Gounod and
Wagner, but was careful to conceal his own feelings. After
lunch Verdi returned to his garden, in which he was seemingly
more interested than in talking about music.

Then there was Liszt, who came often to the Villa Medici
and knew Pierné and Vidal well. Debussy met him at the
house of Sgambati.

The great Hungarian musician [writes M. de Ternant] was
accompanied by his intimate friend, Cardinal von Hohenlohe, who
was a generous patron of classical concerts in Rome. The prince-
cardinal, after being introduced to Debussy, graciously requested, in
honour of the young holder of the Grand Prix de Rome and as a
compliment to French musical art, that Liszt and Sgambati should
play Saint-Saëns's Variations for two pianos on a theme of Beethoven
(Op. 35). This was the last time Liszt touched a piano in Rome.
He left the Eternal City on the following day, and never returned to
Italy. Debussy said it was the greatest musical treat of his life, and
when he related the incident to Saint-Saëns, the French composer
was much affected and warmly embraced him.

On another occasion Debussy and Vidal played to Liszt the *Valses romantiques* for two pianos by Chabrier. Liszt died the following year and may conceivably have only just missed counting Debussy as the last of his discoveries.

At the beginning of 1886 Debussy became very weary of life at the Villa, and one day burst out crying, threw himself at Hébert's feet, threatening to kill himself if he were not allowed to leave. Questioning the genuineness of this scene, M. Prunières tells us that old friends of Debussy remember how he used to play the *commediante-tragediante.* 'Do you want me to cry?' he would say. Whereupon he would pour forth a flood of tears followed by a burst of laughter. 'Furthermore,' M. Prunières pertinently remarks, 'we know that he had been reading with fervour the memoirs of Berlioz.'

However, he left, and in February he suddenly appeared in Paris. M. Vasnier apparently convinced him of good reasons to return, for in April he was back in Rome; but with the same distaste for the Villa and still feeling 'that majestic ennui which is part of the air one breathes.' He had been coun-selled to visit the museums. 'Well, I shall go to see them,' he wrote. 'I know you won't like the "well." It is that of a desperate man dragged to the Sistine Chapel as to the scaffold.' The museums in Italy meant little to him. He liked best the frescoes of Signorelli in the cathedral at Orvieto, and in architecture the less imposing things like the delightful Villa Pia in the gardens of the Vatican. Michelangelo's 'Last Judgment' in the Sistine Chapel, when finally he did see it, he abhorred.

In a letter shortly after his return he mentions a visit of Gounod, who knew Hébert well and was at the Villa Medici as a 'Prix de Rome' during the directorship of Ingres. Here is Debussy's comment:

Hébert told me that he [Gounod] is coming to Rome this winter. Together they will not be at all funny. What with Hébert pontificating almost as much as Gounod, you can imagine the grandiose ideas and hollow speeches we shall hear! By the way, the interest the Héberts show in me is a nuisance. They wish to make things more pleasant for me but actually they are making them more disagreeable. I suppose you 'll say that I haven't changed, but if they were in Paris I should probably like them very well; here they are nothing more than jailers.

And so the second year passed. By October 1886 all he had written was one scene of *Diane au bois* and the beginning of *Zuléima*. With *Diane* he was poorly satisfied and *Zuléima*, he wrote, was 'too much like Verdi and Meyerbeer.' Towards the end of 1886 we have a series of letters to a certain Émile Baron, a stationer and bookseller in the rue de Rome in Paris. These are at first of a rather different tone. Debussy tells him of the Roman men and women who pass before his window and of the long processions of priests, 'some of whom, dressed in black, are like curious black radishes, and others, in red, like roguish pimentos.' The winter was particularly cold. 'You mentioned in your letter how much you wanted to go to a town where it was always spring,' he wrote.

Well, don't come to Rome, because at present this town, reputed to be so sunny, is like Moscow, all covered with snow and freezing cold. The Romans don't seem to be able to make it out. The coats they wear are too short in any case, and they don't seem to be able to get used to proper overcoats. But the snow gives a very pretty colour to the ruins. It shows up their severe contours and makes them look clean. They are a thousand times better than with that perpetual blue sky and their usual pipeclay colour.

But before long he confides his difficulties to Émile Baron as previously to M. Vasnier. He is unable to write music 'to order'; and it is now Émile Baron who is 'about the only one' to whom he can 'speak of such things, feeling sure of being understood.' 'I have had enough of music and of the sameness of this scene,' he says, exasperated. 'I want to see

31

some Manet and hear some Offenbach. That may sound paradoxical, but I must tell you that breathing the air of this place puts the most ridiculous ideas into one's head.'

By February of the following year a new work, *Printemps*, was well advanced. He writes of this to Émile Baron:

The work I have to send to Paris is giving me a lot of trouble and causes me to lead a life compared to which convicts have a leisurely time. The idea I had was to compose a work in a very special colour which should cover a great range of feelings. It is to be called *Printemps,* not a descriptive *Printemps,* but a human one.

I should like to express the slow and miserable birth of beings and things in nature, their gradual blossoming and finally the joy of being born into some new life. All this is without a programme, for I despise all music that has to follow some literary text that one happens to have got hold of.[1] So you will understand how very suggestive the music will have to be—I am doubtful if I shall be able to do it as I wish.

Printemps and *Zuléïma* were the works he finally chose as his *envois*. *Zuléïma* has been lost. *Diane au bois* he never finished. Although he chose the text of Banville himself, he subsequently found it unsuitable. Possibly he had outgrown this favourite poet of his Conservatoire days, for his acquaintance with literature had grown. He knew the Goncourts, was very much attracted to Flaubert and had taken parts, with Vidal and Xavier Leroux, in reading the plays of Shakespeare. It was in Rome, furthermore, that he first became acquainted with the new Symbolist magazines, *La Revue indépendante* and *Vogue,* sent to him by Émile Baron, from whom, too, he received the newly published works of Jean Moréas and Rabbe's translation of Shelley. In the new spirit that was breaking through, music, he felt, had not found its level. He tells Émile Baron:

---

[1] An opinion that he would certainly not have held later.

I believe that the public, apart from the shopkeepers who form the larger part of it, have had enough of cavatinas and *pantalonnades* which show up the singer's fine voice and form. It is curious that the literary movement has found such support—the new forms of the Russian novelists, for instance (I wonder they haven't placed Tolstoy higher than Flaubert), while there is no sign of music changing at all. A dissonant chord would almost cause a revolution.

This letter, hinting at the revolution in music that Debussy himself was shortly to bring about, belongs to the early part of 1887. Before the spring, after only two years at the Villa Medici, instead of the statutory three, Debussy returned definitely to Paris. To M. Vasnier, two days before his departure, he wrote his final decision:

You know when I work how doubtful I am of myself. . . . When something of mine pleased you it gave me courage. Here I should never have that. My friends make fun of my sadness and I should never get any encouragement from them. If things don't go better I know that many people will give me up. But I'd rather do twice as much work in Paris than drag out this life here. . . .

I am leaving on Saturday and shall arrive in Paris on Monday morning. Don't, I beg of you, be too hard with me. Your friendship will be all I have.

> Believe me,
>
> A. DEBUSSY.

But his friendship with the Vasniers after his return was gradually to fade.

When he finally came back [writes Mlle Vasnier] the former intimacy was no longer the same. He had evolved and so had we. We had moved and had made new acquaintances. Reticent and unsociable as he was, he no longer felt at home. However, he often used to come in the evening and play what he had written away from us. . . . He would come to ask advice and even material aid, for, not living with his family and not yet known, he

33

had somehow to live.... Then, little by little, having made new acquaintances himself, he no longer came and we never saw him again.

That is the last record of Debussy's relations with the Vasniers.

CHAPTER IV

WITH Debussy's return to Paris in the spring of 1887 we enter upon a period of approximately five years where comparatively few facts concerning his private life are available. His published correspondence of these years amounts to no more than two or three letters; recollections of his friends are now curiously vague; and where we should expect to find a glimpse of some psychological value—from the members of certain literary circles he soon began to frequent—we are offered little more than the bare facts of his relations with them. These are lacunae, however, of which we may well take advantage; for it is just at this period that a view of the changing artistic ideals of the Paris world will tell us most about the elements in Debussy's musical formation.

The first thing to be noticed in that Paris world of 1887 is the swing away from the cold observation of fact that characterized the output of all those—Naturalists, Realists, *Parnassiens*—who proceeded from the philosophy of Auguste Comte. In much the same way as the first world war brought a craving for sound and colour in their more sensuous and primitive appeals, the Franco-Prussian war had annihilated, for the time being, all desire on the part of artists and thinkers to approach the world in any calculating, scientific manner. 'In face of the unknown,' wrote M. André Barre, 'let us rather have a poet than a scientist.' That might have been the slogan of the new idealism. Flaubert, Taine and Renan were dethroned in favour of Edgar Allan Poe (first translated

by Baudelaire), the English Pre-Raphaelites and certain of
the Russian novelists. A translation of *Is Life Worth Living?*
by William Hurrell Mallock, a penetrating English writer on
religion and philosophy, ran into a great number of editions
and preceded a vogue for spiritualism. In face of these influences the Age of Reason seemed imperilled. 'Jeune homme,'
said Renan to Déroulède, 'la France se meurt, ne troublez pas
son agonie.' A death-blow was threatened with the popularization in Paris of Wagner's music.

The new art was a sensuous, hedonistic art, and as such
sought expression most naturally in music. I will here mention an illuminating anecdote. Once at a gathering of poets
Debussy heard the line of Jean Moréas:

> Et toi, son cou, qui pour la fête tu te pares?

'Cou qui—te tu te,' he repeated. The assonance he thought
ugly. 'Musicien!' shouted Moréas derisively. 'Et vous jouez
aussi de la flûte?' For this Moréas might well have been
hounded out as a cretin. For the days were over when a
literary critic could baldly declare: 'La musique est un bruit
désagréable que l'on fait exprès.' That could be said in the
days of Berlioz, but not of Debussy. Paul Valéry, writing of
his contemporaries in the eighties, emphasizes that 'poetry felt
itself insufficient before the power and resources of the orchestra.'

What has been called Symbolism [he explains] can be quite
simply resumed in the desire common to several families of poets
... to take back from music what they had given it. The secret
of this movement is nothing other than this. . . . We were fed on
music and our literary minds only dreamt of extracting from language
almost the same effects that music caused on our nervous beings.
. . . Certain people who had preserved the traditional forms of
French verse endeavoured to eliminate descriptions, judgments,
morals and arbitrary definitions; they purged their poetry of almost
all those intellectual elements which are outside the sphere of music.
Others gave to all objects infinite meanings, implying some hidden

metaphysic. Their means of expression was delightfully ambiguous.
. . . Everything was allusion. Nothing was content to be. In
those mirrored realms everything thought, or at least everything
appeared to think. . . . Further, some magicians, more self-willed
and disputatious, challenged the old prosody. For some, coloured
hearing and the art of alliteration appeared to have no secrets. They
deliberately transposed orchestral timbres into their verse. . . .
Others cleverly sought out the naïvety and spontaneous grace of old
folk-verse. . . . It was a time of theories and inquiries, of interpretations and excited explanations. A ruthless youth discarded the
scientific dogma that was beginning to go out of fashion. They
saw order and perhaps truth in the cult of a unification of the arts.
It would have needed little more for some kind of religion to have
become established.[1]

This cult of music was not a cult of Massenet or Gounod.
It was the cult of Wagner. Wagner fell upon the Paris of
the eighties, dominating the entire world of literature and art.
He even penetrated spheres of religious and intellectual thought.

The craze began with the Wagnerian concerts of Charles
Lamoureux in 1882. The curious fact is that Wagner was
at first more appreciated in literary than in musical circles.
The *Revue wagnérienne*, a monthly journal that appeared
between 1885 and 1888, far from containing any musical
analyses, was almost exclusively devoted to studies of Wagner
by literary men. The editor, Édouard Dujardin, was a writer
who was also the editor of the Symbolist magazine, *La Revue
indépendante*. Victor Wilder wrote on the ritual of the *Meistersinger*, Huysmans on the overture to *Tannhäuser*, Swinburne on
the death of Wagner and Téodor de Wyzewa on Wagnerian
painting. This was not, as might be imagined, painting for
the scenery of Wagner's dramas, but painting such as that of
Degas, G. Moreau, Odilon Redon, Fantin-Latour, supposedly
inspired by the ideals of Bayreuth. In the number for January

[1] Paul Valéry, Preface to *La Connaissance de la Déesse,* by Lucien
Fabre. (Paris, 1920.)

1886 six sonnets in praise of Wagner appeared by the foremost Symbolist poets, among them René Ghil, Paul Verlaine and Stéphane Mallarmé. The extent to which the musicians were as yet untouched by this Wagnerian cult is seen in the fact that during these years, 1885-8, Gounod was engaged on his last sacred works while Massenet was writing *Werther*.

The outstanding example of this literary Wagnerism—by which Debussy was as much affected as by the music of Wagner itself—is the poetry of Stéphane Mallarmé.[1] Here, in a translation by A. I. Ellis, is his sonnet to Wagner:

> This silence now is death's fast gathering gloom, whose pall
> Blots out our 'household gods' with fold on silken fold,
> And they, as sink in gloom the walls that them uphold,
> Suddenly shall to utter dark's extinction fall.
> Triumphant play of word that held us once in thrall,
> Dead hieroglyphs, wherein they feel, the herd unsoul'd,
> As with a pulse of wing the thrill they crave from old—
> In inmost cupboard-void let us entomb them all.
> From out the glorious stress of powers contending flung
> And primal clash of splendour, lo! there hath upsprung
> To yon slope fore-ordained to be their imag'd shrine
> Trumpets of blaring gold on page eterne aswoon—
> Wagner, his path to heav'n with his own radiance strewn,
> That ev'n the ink finds speech in breath's sobs sibylline.

It is obvious, from this abdication of poetry in favour of music, that Mallarmé was as much concerned with the musical

[1] André Cœuroy traces the first sign of Wagnerism in French literature to a tale of provincial life by George Sand. Basing her argument on an article by Wagner on *Freischütz,* published in the *Gazette musicale* about the time of his visit to Paris in 1839, she doubts the success in France of any popular mysticism. Other writers who were attracted to Wagner before the Symbolists were Théophile Gautier, who wrote on *Tannhäuser* in 1857, and Gérard de Nerval, Champfleury and Baudelaire, who wrote on *Lohengrin* in 1859.

STÉPHANE MALLARMÉ
From the Portrait by Manet

rhythm and euphonic interrelation of words as with their actual significance. Hence his abstruseness (which makes him almost untranslatable) and his conception of Symbolism: 'To evoke in a deliberate shadow the unmentioned object by allusive words.' We are surely here very near Debussy's shadowy Mélisande.

Not all the Symbolists, however, were so directly concerned with Wagner as Mallarmé, although in Symbolist poetry as a whole there is an almost abnormal craving for the sensuousness of sound as also for the sensuousness of colour. Verlaine in his *Art poétique* demands:

> De la musique avant toute chose.

Colour, he specifies, should be represented by 'rien que la nuance,' for

> . . . la nuance seule fiance
> Le rêve au rêve et la flûte au cor !

René Ghil, inspired by Rimbaud's famous sonnet, *Les Voyelles*, beginning:

> A noir, E blanc, I rouge, U vert, O bleu,

worked out an elaborate system of 'verbal orchestration.' Flutes approximated to the sound *ou*, piccolos to *û*, trombones to *ô*, horns to *eu* and *eur*, and so on. A whole group of young poets considered that by this means poetry and music could be fused into one. Music of colour, music of words—such were the slogans of the day. The character of Jean des Esseintes, in Huysmans's *A rebours*, with his curious hankering after orange (the colour of 'men of a hectic, over-stimulated constitution') and his 'mouth-organ'—a liqueur-chest in which each liqueur corresponded in taste with the sound of a particular instrument —was perhaps less of a satire on the intellectuals of that age than is generally supposed.

So much for the literary movements. When Wagner

opened the eyes of the musicians—and it is curious that before
the later eighties the Wagnerian influence in French music
is hardly discernible—their enthusiasm bordered on delirium.
At Bayreuth during the prelude to *Tristan,* Chabrier burst
into tears and Guillaume Lekeu was carried out fainting.
French opera as Massenet or Chabrier had conceived it gave
way to such pseudo-Wagnerian works as Bruneau's *Le Rêve*
(1888), Magnard's *Yolande* (1890), d'Indy's *Fervaal* (1896) and
Chausson's *Le Roi Arthus* (1899). The most pitiful example
of them all is *Gwendoline.* It is by that most jovial of French
composers, Chabrier.

But there was another world of curiosity. In the *Revue
wagnérienne* of 8th February 1886 there appeared a letter from
St. Petersburg by one Wladimir Iznoskow,[1] who had been
asked to write about the Wagnerian movement in Russia.
He gave instead an account of the Russian 'nationalist' composers who wished to reform opera but whose ideals, he pointed
out, differed from those of Wagner in that they did not write
their own librettos nor did they believe in keeping the main
musical interest in the orchestra pit instead of on the stage.
He then went on to explain the differences between the Russian
and the Wagnerian conception of opera with a few not very
enthusiastic words about the champion of Wagner in Russia,
Serov. That, if we except César Cui's *La Musique en Russie,*
published in 1881 (without any intention to proselytize), was
the first instance of the coming conflict between the interests
of Wagner and of the Russians.

It was not long before this conflict became apparent. At
the Exposition Universelle of 1889 singers, dancers and national
orchestras from Africa, Arabia, the Orient, Scandinavia and
Russia introduced their primitive and exotic musics. The
dancing of the Javanese Bedayas to the music of their national
gamelang incited comparisons with the flower-maidens of

[1] A pseudonym of Téodor de Wyzewa.

Parsifal! Concerts were given by Hungarian gipsies and Rumanian laouters. Spanish folk music vied with choirs from Finland, the music of Norway and tribal dances of African Negroes. In the summer of this year the whole musical universe passed through Paris.

At this exhibition, rather appropriately, Rimsky-Korsakov conducted two historical concerts of Russian music. One or two short works of the Russian 'nationalists' had already been played in France, but virtually nothing had been heard of Balakirev, Rimsky-Korsakov or Mussorgsky. 'The young French and Russian schools,' wrote Julien Tiersot in *Le Ménestrel,* 'straight away greeted each other and fraternized.' And, he added significantly, 'I believe that the future belongs to them both.' From this year dates what has been called the Franco-Russian musical alliance.

Such was the background of Debussy's life in Paris from his return from Rome until the beginning in 1892 of *L'Après-midi d'un faune* and *Pelléas et Mélisande.*

The action of these various movements is told in his works. The passing vogue for the Pre-Raphaelites is reflected in *La Damoiselle élue* (1888); in the *Cinq Poèmes de Baudelaire* (1887–9) the fight against Wagner is at its keenest; the Russians are the real heroes of such compositions of about the year 1891 as the *Ballade,* the *Mazurka* and the *Rêverie*; and in 1893 oriental elements from the Javanese *gamelang* take root in the Quartet. Then suddenly, under the impact of all these extraneous influences, there was to emerge, in *L'Après-midi d'un faune,* one of the most beautiful of all French creations. A new spirit, a new world was magically revealed. Yet its novelty consisted, then, as still to-day, in revivifying the age-long French traditions. It was a world that was inevitably to be born to prove the very continuity of these traditions, whose sweet and powerful renascence was now evident to give the lie to Déroulède's pessimistic vision of his country in decline.

CHAPTER V

DEBUSSY, on his return from Rome, made many acquaintances in the literary circles of Paris, but approached terms of intimacy with few. One would have thought that at the bookshop of the *Revue indépendante,* or at the gatherings of Mallarmé, where he met Whistler and Verlaine, Stuart Merrill and Jules Laforgue, Henri de Régnier and Pierre Louÿs, he would have found just that support and understanding he had missed at the Villa Medici. But the reason he did not one may well imagine. Once in later years he was invited to the house of Marcel Proust. He declined, but with a strange explanation: 'Vous savez, moi, je suis un ours.' From this description of himself, given with such charming frankness, one suspects that he was more conscious of the shortcomings of his early education than his friends have given us to believe; and a certain sensitiveness on this point must have prevented him from frequenting the company of Mallarmé and his admirers, to whose sensibility he was instinctively drawn. Alone among these poets, Pierre Louÿs, several years later, became an intimate friend; and it is significant that in speaking of this friendship Paul Valéry should have remarked that Louÿs was 'the director of Debussy's literary conscience.'

His relations with the musicians were scarcely more fortunate. Some deep emotional support in spite of (or possibly because of) his reclusion was in any case necessary to him at all times of his life. An intimate friendship with Paul Dukas and Raymond Bonheur, both students at the Conservatoire, lasted only a short time. With Gounod he parted company in disagreement, it appears, over *Lohengrin*, a work which Gounod could not abide. 'Pour toi, pour toi, pour toi!' he angrily replied as his young friend spoke of it admiringly. With Chabrier, whom Debussy knew only slightly, there must have been great disappointment. Chabrier's capitulation to Wagner in *Gwendoline* and the establishment among his friends of 'Le Petit Bayreuth' could hardly have met with the approval of one who had taken such delight in the real, sprightly Chabrier. Somewhere between the attitudes to Wagner of Chabrier and Gounod Debussy felt his own to lie. But before attempting to discover this we must follow him again on his journeys abroad.

In 1887, the year of his return to Paris, he set out for Vienna to meet Brahms.[1] Debussy and Brahms—the very juxtaposition of these names evokes the conflicting boundaries of

[1] This information is derived from three articles by Andrew de Ternant published in the *Musical Times* in 1924. The authenticity of the facts contained in these articles has been widely questioned: the meetings with Brahms in Vienna, with Boito and Verdi in Italy, and the early journey to London, where Debussy is said to have met Parry and to have approached Novello's in the hope of their publishing *La Damoiselle élue,* are biographical data which have so far lacked corroboration from any other source and which, if not entirely discredited, still remain to be verified. I find it difficult to believe, as some writers have contended, that de Ternant might have invented these facts, particularly as they are in no way either chronologically, or even humanly, incredible. Moreover, a piece of circumstantial evidence may here be offered in support of the Vienna meeting with Brahms. We know that Brahms was acquainted with *La Damoiselle élue,* which had not been performed nor published until 1893, that is four years before Brahms's death. This information is contained in a letter from Sir Charles Stanford to W. S. Hannam of 21st October 1909 and published in Plunket Greene's book on Stanford. Stanford is recommending works for the 1910 Leeds Festival and,

two musical civilizations. A meeting between the musical lion of Vienna, austere and unapproachable, and the twenty-five-year-old Debussy, 'passionate and turned in upon himself, with something feline and something of the gipsy about him,' as Henri de Régnier remembers him, was not to pass off easily. Here is the account of their meeting by A. de Ternant:

Debussy wrote a letter to Brahms and received no reply. He called twice at his house. On the first occasion he was informed that the Master was unwell and on the other that he was engaged. At last the wife of one of the secretaries of the French embassy promised to help him in his difficulty. She was a Hungarian by birth, though married to a French diplomat, and had been in her younger days to some extent a pupil of Brahms. . . . It was not long before Debussy received an invitation to luncheon from the lady and she stated that there would be only three persons present, viz. the Master, Claude Debussy and herself.

After the introduction Brahms growled out: 'Are you the young Frenchman who wrote to me and called twice at my house?' Debussy bowed graciously. 'Well, I will forgive you this time,' exclaimed Brahms, 'but don't do it again.' During the luncheon Brahms did not utter a single word, but after drinking several glasses of French champagne at the end, he said it was the 'most glorious wine in the world,' and quoted the lines from Goethe's *Faust*:

> 'One cannot always do without the foreigner
> But give him to me in the shape of wine.

---

including among his recommendations *La Damoiselle élue,* refers to it as 'a lovely thing which curiously enough much delighted Brahms himself.' When could Brahms have seen or heard it? It seems unlikely that he would have seen the 1893 score (printed in a limited edition of 160 copies) and he certainly could not have heard the work, the only performance of which, before Brahms's death, had been given in Paris. The inference, therefore, is that he probably became acquainted with it, possibly in draft form, at the time of Debussy's supposed visit to Vienna.

Meeting with Brahms

A true-born German hates with all his heart
A Frenchman—but their wines are excellent.'[1]

This portrayal of Brahms in one of his grosser moods is
contrasted by de Ternant with a somewhat sentimental picture
of the German composer. Brahms told Debussy of his great
admiration for Bizet, whom 'he would have gone to the end of
the earth to embrace,' and that he had heard *Carmen* twenty
times. The following day Debussy was invited to dine with
him in town and to a performance of the favourite *Carmen*.
Together they visited the Conservatorium and the graves of
Beethoven and Schubert. 'Before leaving Vienna,' M. de
Ternant's account concludes, 'Debussy called at the house of
Brahms. He was "at home" this time, and wishing Claude
bon voyage and a successful career, the great German master
embraced the young Frenchman like a son. He said a
"crusty" old bachelor has quite as much fatherly feeling as a
more fortunate married man.'

After Vienna, Bayreuth. In 1888 and 1889 Debussy
attended the Bayreuth Festival performances of *Parsifal, Meistersinger* and *Tristan und Isolde*. In conversation with his old
master, Guiraud, after the second of these visits he recounted
his impressions. He argued that Wagner was less of an
innovator than he was generally considered to be; that Berlioz
was less strictly tonal than Wagner; that Wagner's harmony
was an amplification of Mozart's; that his music was very
moving, 'mais que ça chante trop.' 'So you are a liberal
Wagnerian,' said Guiraud. Debussy pointed out that he
saw no reason to imitate what he admired—which was the

[1] This is not a very accurate translation, at least of the second line
Brander's lines (in Auerbach's cellar) are:

'Man kann nicht stets das Fremde meiden,
Das Gute liegt uns oft so fern.
Ein echter deutscher Mann mag keinen Franzen leiden,
Doch ihre Weine trinkt er gern.'

45

point of that letter to M. Vasnier from Rome in which he spoke of maintaining the lyrical atmosphere and not allowing the orchestra to predominate. In truth the earnest sensuousness of Wagner's music corresponded very nearly to his own ideal, yet there arose the problem of reconciling this sensuousness with that lyrical clarity which French composers have always trea-sured. Guiraud questioned him on his own choice of a libretto. 'I would seek a poet,' he said, 'who would merely hint at things and would allow me to graft my thought on his; whose characters belong to no time or place and who would allow me, here and there, to show more art than he.' An extra-ordinary prediction of his choice of Maeterlinck's *Pelléas et Mélisande*. Meanwhile the *Cinq Poèmes de Baudelaire,* written between 1887 and 1889, reveal a potent Wagnerian influence on Debussy's musical language.

Another approach to the aesthetic problems that beset him during these years is worth following in his relationship with one of the most singular and original of French composers— Erik Satie. During his lifetime, Satie, by reason of the eccen-tricities, both in his music and in his personal life, earned the reputation of a musical exhibitionist. But by many of his pert little compositions he kept alive the breeziness of the *opéra comique* at a time when the very foundations of French music were threatened by the Wagnerian tidal wave. He went on, in fact, where Chabrier gave in.[1]

[1] The artistic relationship between Chabrier, Satie and Debussy has been searchingly investigated by Rollo H. Myers in his *Erik Satie* (London, 1948), which also demonstrates the influence of this anomalous composer on Ravel, Poulenc, Milhaud and Stravinsky. Debussy's own esteem for Satie is illustrated in a touching dedication of 1892 on a copy of the *Poèmes de Baudelaire*: 'For Erik Satie, the sweet medieval musician who has strayed into this century for the joy of his very friendly Claude Debussy.' The fascinating 'cas Satie' has not yet emerged from controversy. Perhaps he was either born

Erik Satie

Satie, when Debussy met him in 1891, was employed as a pianist at the 'Auberge du Clou' in Montmartre. In his jocular style he once gave in a lecture an account of their early relations:

When I first met Debussy he was full of Mussorgsky and was very deliberately seeking a way that wasn't very easy to find. In this problem I was well in advance of him. I was not weighed down with the Prix de Rome, nor any other prize, for I am a man like Adam (of Paradise) who never won any prizes—a lazy fellow, no doubt.

I was writing at that time *Le Fils des étoiles* on a libretto by Joseph Péladan, and I explained to Debussy the need a Frenchman has to free himself from the Wagnerian venture, which didn't respond to our natural aspirations. I also pointed out that I was in no way anti-Wagnerian but that we should have a music of our own—if possible without any *Sauerkraut*.

Why could we not use the means that Claude Monet, Cézanne, Toulouse-Lautrec and others had made known? Why could we not transpose these means into music? Nothing simpler. . . .

That was the origin of a departure which brought results that were safe enough and even fruitful. Who was to show him examples? To reveal new treasures? To suggest the ground to be explored? To give him the benefit of previous considerations? Who? I shan't reply, for I no longer care.

There is a slight suggestion in those last words that Satie

---

too late—much too late, for, as Debussy was among the first to acknowledge, he was able to rediscover, during the *fin-de-siècle* period, a genuine medieval guilelessness and innocence; or too early and—for all his specifically French qualities—in the wrong civilization. That pathetic terror, dictating the pattern of both his personal life and much of his achievement, and finding in so much of his work nothing more than an impotent expression of extravagant clownery—that terror of the soul was precisely the *Angst*, I am inclined to think, that finds its most noble expression, in the music of our age, in the works of Alban Berg.

was imperfectly briefed to prove his case. At any rate no one knows what 'new treasures' he revealed to Debussy nor what ground he suggested to be explored. As for there being 'nothing simpler' than to transpose into music the painting technique of Claude Monet, Cézanne and Toulouse-Lautrec, that is an abstract consideration by which, as far as we know, Debussy was never consciously affected.

Their relationship, which lasted nearly thirty years, shows, both musically and psychologically, the conflicting claims of admiration and envy. It has long been established that Satie's *Sarabandes*, written in 1887, contain the first examples of certain harmonic procedures (unresolved ninths in particular) which later became associated with Debussy. But I think it would be wrong to argue from this isolated example that Satie's influence on Debussy was more significant than that of Field on Chopin. For a view of their personal and musical relationship, the following account by Louis Laloy is the most convincing that I have come across:

Debussy introduced me to him, and we sometimes met at his table, exchanging a few cattish remarks and side-glances which rather amused Debussy. In his relationship with Satie there were violent outbursts of temper, yet their friendship remained indis-soluble. It was like one of those family hatreds, where all patience is lost by the continual grating of each other's faults, but where there nevertheless remains an underlying sympathy. They might have been two brothers placed by circumstances in different positions, the one rich and the other poor: the former gracious and open-hearted, but conscious of his superiority and always ready to make it felt, the other sadly appearing as a wag, paying his share by cracking jokes for the entertainment of his host, and hiding his humiliation. They were always on their guard, but they couldn't help loving each other dearly.

Satie himself endorsed this when he once wrote: 'If I didn't have Debussy . . . I don't know what I'd do to express my wretched thoughts—if I am still able to express them.' And through this remark one can see the truth of another state-ment of Laloy's: that 'Satie's great admiration for Debussy compelled him to lie low, and when he did venture into composition, to give his work the appearance of a joke.'

Satie's reference to Mussorgsky brings us to the very con-troversial question of Debussy's acquaintance with *Boris Godunov*. In 1909 Debussy supplied the information to his biographer, M. Laloy, that he had been introduced to the score of *Boris* by an old gentleman whose name, we have since come to know, was Jules de Brayer, at one time the organist at Chartres Cathedral. In the following year Debussy returned, according to M. Laloy, to Bayreuth, but came back 'undeceived.' He then 'endeavoured to explain to his old friend that one could not admire at the same time two such opposed forms of art. Being an ardent Wagnerian, this friend would hear nothing of it; and they parted.' From this account there has grown up the legend that *Boris Godunov* revealed to Debussy, in a flash, the fallibility of Wagner and delivered him, so to speak, from the clutches of Klingsor.

In the first place, as we have seen, Debussy was perfectly aware of the danger of his attraction to Wagner long before he had known *Boris*. But even if he had not been, *Boris* was not the work to wean him from a devotion to Wagner—as certain French critics have supposed it did. In a letter of 6th February 1911 he says: 'I do not consider the *placage* in *Boris* any more satisfactory than the persistent counterpoint in the *Meistersinger* finale'; by which he clearly implies that the rough-hewn, brusque qualities of Mussorgsky are as far from French lyrical ideals as any Wagnerian ponderousness.

In point of fact, the score of *Boris* that Debussy saw had passed into the hands of Jules de Brayer from Saint-Saëns, who had brought it back from his journey to Russia in 1874, the year it was first played at the Maryinsky Theatre in St.

Petersburg. Brayer admitted, in a letter of 1895 to Pierre
d'Alheim, that the only person in Paris beyond himself on
whom this score (the only one then in France) had made a
favourable impression was Debussy's intimate friend, the
Swiss journalist Robert Godet. Debussy's name is not even
mentioned in this letter, yet the score had been lent to him as
long ago as 1889. This is not to say that Debussy did not
find much to admire in Mussorgsky. But according to
M. Godet his full appreciation of *Boris* did not come until
the Mussorgsky concerts of Pierre d'Alheim in 1896—that
is, four years after *Pelléas* was begun. We know now that
the great impression of 1889 was not of *Boris*, but of the
pentatonic music of the Javanese *gamelang*, the dancing of the
Bedayas and the Annamite theatre at the Exposition Universelle.

It is unfortunate that the work in which we might best study
Debussy's state of musical development, immediately before
the composition of *L'Après-midi d'un faune* and *Pelléas et
Mélisande*, is not available. About 1890 Debussy began an
opera entitled *Rodrigue et Chimène*. The libretto, based on *Las
Mocedades del Cid* by Guillem de Castro, was prepared for him
by Catulle Mendès, the librettist of Chabrier's *Gwendoline*.
Three scenes were drafted, but they have remained unpublished
and were in the private collection of Alfred Cortot. In January
1892 Debussy wrote to Robert Godet: 'I'm anxious to let you
hear the two acts that are finished, for I fear that I have been
victorious over myself.' Victorious over himself! From the
descriptions of the style of these sketches given by Léon Vallas
and Gustave Samazeuilh (in *Musiciens de mon temps*, Paris 1947)
recalling, according to these writers, *Tristan*, *Götterdämmerung*
and *Parsifal*, Debussy would seem temporarily to have suc-
cumbed to the dreaded Wagnerian influence.

Rodrigue et Chimène was abandoned like *Diane au bois*.
Debussy was thirty, and nothing of his had been heard beyond
one or two songs or pianoforte pieces and the compulsory

performance of the Prix de Rome cantata, *L'Enfant prodigue*
Of the music he wrote during the five years following his return
from Rome, he was satisfied with very little. *La Damoiselle
élue* (on the translation by Gabriel Sarrazin of Rossetti's *The
Blessed Damozel*) was finished in 1888 and constituted the
last of the *envois de Rome.* The *envois,* with *Zuléima* and
Printemps, were then ready for the traditional concert of the
works of each holder of the Prix de Rome at the Salle du
Conservatoire. But that concert never took place. Behind
the reasons given for its abandonment one can see that Debussy
was not in the least anxious to present to the public works that
he considered experimental or transitional. Alone of the
envois de Rome, La Damoiselle élue achieved some success later.
Printemps was forgotten for seventeen years; *Zuléima* was
destroyed. The *Fantaisie* for piano and orchestra, of the year
1889, was to have been played at a concert of the Société
Nationale in 1890. But at one of the rehearsals Debussy
removed the parts from the stands himself and wrote to the
conductor, Vincent d'Indy, that it had been withdrawn. At
about the same time he wrote to his friend, Robert Godet:

> Such music as mine has no other aim than to become part of
> things and people. That you have accepted it is a more lovely
> glory than any approval from the elegant people who kow-tow
> to the Wagnerian Monsieur Lamoureux with his eyeglasses and
> hieratic forefinger. . . .[1]

And in 1893 to Ernest Chausson:

> Here I am, just turned thirty-one and not quite sure of my

---

[1] The correspondence between Debussy and Robert Godet is
published in *Lettres à deux amis* (Paris, 1942) which also contains the
correspondence with G. Jean-Aubry. This correspondence is preceded by an introduction in the form of a dialogue between Robert
Godet and G. Jean-Aubry in which the two friends of Debussy recall
the composer's associations with many contemporary figures.

aesthetic. There are still things that I am not able to do—create masterpieces, for instance, or be really responsible—for I have the fault of thinking too much about myself and only seeing reality when it is forced upon me and then unsurmountable. Perhaps I am rather to be pitied than blamed. In any case I am writing you this expecting your pardon and your patience.

Chausson replied that in his opinion Debussy knew perfectly well what he wanted; the truth of which we shall immediately see.

Cher Ami

C'est la faute à Mélisande !
et pardonnez nous a tous les deux ?

J'ai fini de fournir a la poursuite de ce
"rien" dont elle est fait (Mélisande) et je manquais
parfois de courage pour vous raconter tout cela,
au seul d'ailleurs des luttes que vous connaissez
mais, je ne sais pas si vous êtes console comme
moi, avec une vague envie de pleurer, un peu
comme si on avait, pour peu voir dans la
fournir quelqu'un de bien aimé

Maintenant c'est Arkel qui me tourmente
celui là, il est d'outre-tombe, et il a cette
tendresse désintéressée et prophétique de ceux qui
vont bientôt disparaître et il faut dire tout cela
avec, do, ré, mi, fa, sol, la, si, do,,!!! Quel métier ?

Je vous écrirai plus longuement demain aujourd'hui
c'est un simple bonjour, et pour vous dire
que je pense bien à vous,

Claude Debussy

LETTER TO ERNEST CHAUSSON

CHAPTER VI

THE YEARS OF 'PELLÉAS'—1893–1902

ONE summer evening of 1892 Debussy bought, on the
Boulevard des Italiens, the newly published drama of Maeterlinck, *Pelléas et Mélisande*. The thought of setting to music
certain scenes soon occurred to him, and within a short time he
had communicated to his friend Godet a number of sketches
and themes. The following May, a performance of the play
at the Théâtre des Bouffes-Parisiens decided him to take it as
a text for an opera.

Pelléas occupied Debussy over a period of nine years,
between the ages of thirty-one and forty. The creations of a
great artist are easily, too easily perhaps, classified by 'periods,'
and although (as we shall see in later chapters, devoted to
analyses of Debussy's works) these periods often overlap and
intertwine, *Pelléas et Mélisande* does stand out as the central
work of his life for which his earlier works served as experiments and which, once it had been brought into being, encouraged the composer not to rest content with success but to
intensify his pursuit of the ultimately unattainable ideal.

We will follow its composition in the delightful series of
letters to Earnest Chausson. The first reference is in a postscript to a letter of 6th September 1893:

LATEST NEWS

.   .   .   .   .   .

C. A. Debussy finishes a scene of *Pelléas et Mélisande* (' A fountain
in the park,' Act IV, scene iv), on which he would like to have

53

the opinion of E. Chausson. It has been suggested to run excursion trains between Paris and Royan [where Chausson was staying], in view of this event, of which there is no further need to mention the importance.

But the following month he discovered he had been too hasty. On 2nd October:

I was in too great a hurry to crow about *Pelléas et Mélisande,* for after a sleepless night, in which I began to see things clearly, I had to admit that what I had got wasn't right at all. It's like a duet by Mr. Anybody-you-like; and then the ghost of old Klingsor, alias R. Wagner, appeared at a turning of one of the bars, so I tore the whole thing up and struck off on a new line with a little com-pound of phrases I thought more characteristic—trying to be both Pelléas and Mélisande. There is music behind all those veils by which she hides herself from even her most ardent worshippers. I've got something which will please you perhaps—the others I don't care about. Quite spontaneously I have used silence as a means of expression (don't laugh). It is perhaps the only means of bringing into relief the emotional value of a phrase. If Wagner used silence, I should say it was only in an extremely dramatic way, rather as it is used in certain other dubious dramas in the style of Bouchardy, d'Ennery [1] and others!

At about this stage, permission being required for use of the libretto, Henri de Régnier wrote to Maeterlinck:

My friend, Achille Debussy, who is a musician of the most clever and delicate talent, has begun some charming music for *Pelléas et Mélisande,* which deliciously garlands the text while scrupulously respecting it. Before going further with this work, which is not inconsiderable, he would like authorization to continue. [2]

And, with Pierre Louÿs, Debussy set out to meet Maeterlinck at Ghent. On the way they stopped at Brussels.

[1] Joseph Bouchardy (1810–70) and Adolphe Philippe d'Ennery (1811–99), popular dramatists known for the facile effectiveness of their technique. D'Ennery was the librettist of Massenet's *Le Cid.*
[2] Translation by Janet Flanner.

'Pelleas' Begun—Meeting with Ysaÿe and Maeterlinck

The person I was most interested to see there [runs an undated letter of 1893 to Chausson] was Ysaÿe, whom I called on first. You won't be very surprised to hear that he actually shrieked with joy on seeing me, hugging me against his big chest and treating me as if I were his little brother. After which reception I had to give him news of everyone and particularly of you, of whom, unfortunately, my only knowledge was from letters. And then music, and music till we went mad with it. That memorable evening I played in succession the *Cinq Poèmes* [of Baudelaire], *La Damoiselle élue* and *Pelléas et Mélisande*. I got as hoarse as if I had been selling newspapers on the street. *Pelléas* softened the hearts of certain young people, English, I believe; as for Ysaÿe, he became delirious. I really can't repeat what he told me! He liked your Quartet too and is getting some people to work at it.

I saw Maeterlinck, with whom I spent a day in Ghent. At first he assumed the airs of a young girl being introduced to her future husband, but after some time he thawed and was charming. When he spoke of the theatre he seemed a very remarkable man. As for *Pelléas*, he authorized me to make any cuts I like and even suggested some very important and useful ones himself. He says he knows nothing about music and when he comes to a Beethoven symphony he is like a blind man in a museum. But really he is a very fine man and speaks of extraordinary things in a delightfully simple way. When I thanked him for entrusting me with *Pelléas* he insisted that it was he who should be grateful to me for setting it to music. As my opinion was the very opposite I had to use what little diplomacy I am endowed with.

So, you see, it was a more profitable journey than the journey of Urien.[1]

We hear nothing more of *Pelléas* until the following year, when, probably from the first days of 1894, we have this charming glimpse:

DEAR FRIEND,

It's Mélisande's fault—so will you forgive us both? I have spent days in pursuit of those fancies of which she is made. I had no

---

[1] Allusion to *Le Voyage d'Urien* (published in 1893), one of the first works of André Gide.

55

courage to tell you of it all—besides, you know what such struggles
are. I don't know if you have ever gone to bed, as I have, with a
strange desire to cry, feeling as if you had not been able to see during
the day some greatly loved friend. Just now I am worried about
Arkel. He is from the other side of the grave and has that fond
love, disinterested and far-seeing, of those who will soon disappear
—all of which has to be said with *do ré mi fa sol la si do.* What a
job!

I shall write to you at greater length to-morrow. This is just
for you to know that I am thinking of you and to wish you good day.

The letter of 8th January is probably of the following day
and here it is all gloom: 'The colour of my soul is iron-grey
and sad bats wheel about the steeple of my dreams. My only
hope is in *Pelléas et Mélisande*, and God only knows if that
won't end in smoke.'

Meanwhile he was making some reputation as a Wagnerian
pianist. On 3rd) May 1893 his former collaborator, Catulle
Mendès, gave a lecture at the Opéra on *Rheingold* and *Walküre*,
illustrated at two pianos by Debussy and Raoul Pugno. A
letter to Chausson of 21st May reveals a barbed tongue:

I'm rid of the *Rheingold.* This is a nuisance so far as the gold is
concerned, but it is good to have done with the Rhine. The last
performance was a terrible bore. Catulle Mendès spoke on the
Walküre in such a way that the mothers who had naïvely brought
their daughters were frightened away by the wicked priest's fiery
words. The month of May, it appears, is henceforth to be the
month of the *Walküre,* for some simple-minded people believe that
this work announces the spring of a new music and the death of
the old worn-out formulae. It's not what I think, but that doesn't
seem to matter.[1]

---

[1] Debussy could be equally sarcastic about the Russian composers.
In a letter of 1893 to Chausson he says: 'I suppose we shall hear a
lot of the Russians now because of patriotic feeling. When Admiral
Avellan was here it's a pity they didn't invite him to a concert.
The bard Tiersot [i.e. Julien Tiersot] would certainly have said a few

The Wagnerian Pianist

At the very time he was struggling to liberate himself from the domination of Wagner in *Pelléas* he received engagements to play *Tristan* and *Parsifal* at the piano in Paris society. It appears that Chausson put this work in his way to supplement his meagre income from lessons and transcriptions for publishers. Robert Godet has said that in the art of rendering the difficult Wagnerian scores at the keyboard he was unsurpassed even by Mottl. In illustration of this talent I will quote an illuminating passage from a letter of 5th February 1894 to Chausson from his brother-in-law, Henri Lerolle:

Debussy played the first act of *Parsifal*. It went off very well and I think the people liked it, although some of them said they couldn't hear the words. I'm not surprised! You know how he articulates. We consider ourselves fortunate if he sings anything but *tra ta ra ta ta*. *Parsifal* is very lovely, especially the religious part. But poor Debussy came to the end of his tether. I thought he'd never go through with it. Directly it was over I took him aside in a room at the back and gave him something warm. I thought he'd collapse. The fact is that he plays and sings with such energy! He assured me that if I hadn't been there to turn over the pages, at a certain moment he would have closed up the score and gone off. The next time there will be an interval for a cigarette in the middle, before the second scene, and then everyone will be happy. Our good Debussy does this playing for the same reason that a man carries a trunk—to earn a few coppers. But I believe he is happy to think that we were able to get about a thousand francs for him.[2]

One day in the spring of 1895 Debussy told Godet that *Pelléas* was finished—'this morning, to be historical.' But

---

words of welcome.' Admiral Avellan was an admiral of the Russian fleet who made an important visit to Paris in 1893 at the time of the Franco-Russian Alliance.

[2] For the correspondence between Debussy and Henri Lerolle see Oscar Thompson's *Debussy, Man and Artist* (New York, 1940).

within a short time it was taken up again, pondered afresh, revised and altered. The following year Ysaÿe, having attempted to get the work produced at the Théâtre de la Monnaie at Brussels, suggested a concert performance of certain parts. Debussy was opposed to this in much the same way that Wagner would have opposed a concert performance of *Tristan*. A letter of 13th October 1896 to Ysaÿe begins:

DEAR GREAT FRIEND,

I was most touched by your kind letter and your friendly anxiety for *Pelléas et Mélisande*. The poor little creatures are so difficult to introduce into the world, for with a godfather like you the world doesn't want to have anything to do with them.

Now I must humbly tell you why I am not of your opinion about a performance of *Pelléas* in part. Firstly, if this work has any merit, it is in the connection between the drama and the music. It is quite obvious that at a concert performance this connection would dis- appear and no one could be blamed for seeing nothing in those eloquent 'silences' with which this work is starred. Moreover, as the simplicity of the work only gains significance on the stage, at a concert performance they would throw in my face the American wealth of Wagner and I'd be like some poor fellow who couldn't afford to pay for 'contra-bass tubas'! In my opinion Pelléas and Mélisande must be given *as they are,* and then it will be a matter of taking them or leaving them, and if we have to fight, it will be worth while.

In 1897 a second version was finished which Pierre Louÿs had the greatest difficulty in persuading his friend not to destroy. The same year it was accepted by Albert Carré for performance at the Opéra-Comique. But it was not given until five years later. It was not only that the management, although they had accepted it, were diffident about producing a work of such novelty (Carré, with as little success as Ysaÿe, had at first suggested special performances in concert form); Debussy was continually taking back his score for improvement. As the opera, still in an embryonic form, was about to emerge from the composer's unconscious mind, the composer André Messager, who was to conduct the first performance, became its ardent champion and was personally initiated by Debussy into each section of the work as it was yet again rewritten. Even on the eve of the rehearsals revisions were still being made.

Let us now review Debussy's other musical activities during these years. The first time an important work of his was performed was on 8th April 1893. Gabriel Marie conducted *La Damoiselle élue* at a concert of the Société Nationale. Charles Darcours, in the *Figaro*, described it as 'very sensual and decadent,' and prophesied that 'this subcutaneous injection may possibly produce dangerous eruptions among the small fry of the future.' The same year, on 29th December, the string Quartet was played at another concert of the Société Nationale by a quartet led by Ysaÿe. Guy Ropartz, in the *Guide musical*, referred to it as 'a very interesting work in which the predominant influence is that of young Russia'; and the Belgian musician, Maurice Kufferath, remarked on the 'sustained harmonies that evoke a memory of the *gamelang*.' But on the whole the reception was not very favourable. Chausson was apparently displeased with it; and Debussy wrote to him:

I must tell you that I was for some days very grieved by what you said of my Quartet, for I felt that it had only made you like *certain things* in me which I had wished you not to see. Well, I'll write another for you, really for you, and I'll try to bring more dignity to the form.

Whatever his intentions may have been, Debussy produced only one quartet, published somewhat misleadingly as 'Ier Quatuor.'

A year later, on 22nd December 1894, came the first performance of the *Prélude à l'Après-midi d'un faune*, conducted, again at the Société Nationale, by Gustave Doret. This work, inspired by Mallarmé's eclogue, was originally to have extended beyond the *Prélude* to *Interludes* and a *Paraphrase finale*. Of these sections we know only that they were announced, but not given, at a concert in Brussels on 1st March 1894. Possibly Debussy incorporated whatever sketches he had made in other works.

Here is the interesting programme of a concert of contemporary music at which *L'Après-midi d'un faune* was first performed:

La Forêt	Glazunov
Suite serbe	J. Bordier
La Vague et la cloche	Henri Dupuis
L'Enterrement d'Ophélie	A. Bourgault-Ducoudray
Troisième Concerto pour violon	Saint-Saëns
Prélude à l'Après-midi d'un faune	C. A. Debussy
Prière	Guy Ropartz
Rédemption, fragment symphonique	César Franck

Again there was no enthusiasm in the press. In the majority of cases it was coupled with the *Prière* of Ropartz as merely 'interesting.' Nor, apparently, did it receive any more whole-hearted recognition at a subsequent performance at the Concerts Colonne the following year. On this occasion Isidore Philipp, the famous piano teacher, wrote in *Le Ménestrel*: 'The *Prélude à l'Après-midi d'un faune* of M. Debussy is finely and delicately orchestrated; but one seeks in vain any heart or any strength. It is precious, subtle and indefinite in the same way as the work of M. Mallarmé'—and he continued with a very enthusiastic account of César Franck's *Psyché*.

In a letter to G. Jean-Aubry of 25th March 1910 Debussy recalls the impressions of Mallarmé:

I used to live then in a little furnished flat in the rue de Londres. ... Mallarmé came in with his prophetic air and his Scotch plaid around him. After listening to it he remained silent for a long time; then said: 'I didn't expect anything like that. This music draws out the emotion of my poem and gives it a warmer background than colour.' And here are the lines that Mallarmé wrote on a copy of *L'Après-midi d'un faune* which he sent me after the first performance:

> 'Sylvain d'haleine première,
> Si ta flûte a réussi
> Ouïs toute la lumière
> Qu'y soufflera Debussy.'

The opinion of most musicians, however, was more akin to the caustic expression of Saint-Saëns in his *Rimes familières*:

> Je deviendrais vite aphone,
> Si j'allais en étourdi
> M'égosiller comme un faune
> Fêtant son après-midi.

Before *L'Après-midi* was completed Debussy had begun the *Nocturnes*. In its original form this was a work in three movements for violin and orchestra intended for performance by Ysaÿe. In a letter to Ysaÿe of 22nd September 1894 we read:

I am working at three *Nocturnes* for violin and orchestra. The orchestra of the first part consists of strings; of the second, flutes, four horns, three trumpets and two harps; of the third, of both of these groups. It is, in short, an experiment with the different combinations that can be obtained from one colour—like a study in grey in painting. I hope this will appeal to you, for the pleasure it might give you is what I am most concerned with. I am not forsaking *Pelléas* for this—and I must say that, the further I go, the more depressed and anxious I become. . . .

Two years later, on 13th October 1896, Ysaÿe is begged to accept, in the place of excerpts for concert performance of *Pelléas,* 'three *Nocturnes* for violin and orchestra written for Eugène Ysaÿe, a man I love and admire.' And he continues: 'Indeed, these *Nocturnes* can only be played by him. If Apollo himself were to ask me for them I should have to refuse him! What do you say to that?' The following year they were recast in the form we now know, revealing, however, no sign or suggestion that there was originally a solo violin part. Following the correspondence of 1896, the next and last published letter to Ysaÿe is of 30th December 1903, two years after the first performance of the work in Paris. Ysaÿe had decided to conduct it at Brussels. Debussy wrote: 'I needn't tell you of my joy. My only regret is that, for the most wretched reasons, I shan't be able to be there to hear what I am sure will be *the performance I have dreamt of*.'

Whilst the *Nocturnes* were being recast, Debussy again entertained a number of projects for works that never materialized. In the letter to Ysaÿe of 13th October 1896 (from which I have already quoted) we read: 'It is probable that by December I shall have finished a work I am doing [1] on a poem of D. G. Rossetti—*La Saulaie*. It is an important work and written in the light of my latest discoveries in musical chemistry.' *La Saulaie* was a translation, made by Pierre Louÿs, of Rossetti's *Willowwood*. Of the music nothing beyond a single manuscript page is known.

He also planned to write a stage work on a libretto of Pierre Louÿs called *Cendrelune*. But he suggested so many alterations in Louÿs's text that Louÿs finally gave up all hope of collaboration. He wrote to Debussy in May 1895:

Write *Cendrelune* yourself. You are perfectly capable of it. You have made so many changes in the little thing that it has become quite foreign to me. As it stands I can't go on with it. The religiousness, the triumph of the lily over the rose and of Chastity over Love—all that means nothing to me. I can't do anything at all along a direction where I have no idea of my bearings. . . .

Several projects were discussed, often at length and over a number of years, between the poet and the musician, but apart from the *Chansons de Bilitis* and the *Six Épigraphes antiques* they

---

[1] In the original, 'une chose que j'ai faite,' meaning, no doubt, the piano score.

were never brought into reality. At most a manuscript page or two of Debussy's music has survived. Among these projects was the ballet on the scenario by Louÿs, *Daphnis et Chloé*. Early in 1896 Louÿs sketches out the plan, taunting his friend with advice on the type of themes he should use:

In the first section we must have a theme constructed like the first phrase of *Parsifal*. . . . The score should begin with a theme for the flute, and so that we shouldn't lose time, couldn't you pinch something from the *Faun's Afternoon* [in English in the original] by a certain Debussy?

And he signs his letter, 'Houst! Ton Chamberlain' (Hey! Your Chamberlain), the pun being on the name of Houston Stewart Chamberlain, the well-known Wagnerian champion. Debussy replies, in a letter of 17th January 1896, in the same ironical tone:

MY DEAR PIERRE,

I have received from Mr. Houston Chamberlain an offer to write a ballet on *Daphnis et Chloé*. Although this man has given his name to a filter, his ideas appear to me confused.[1] Ask him to come with you to-morrow, I really need more details. He doesn't even mention how or where the ballet is to be given. Is it to be for xylophone, banjo or Russian bassoon? And then just imagine that he's no farther than Wagner and still believes in the recipes of that old poisoner!

Your invulnerable
CLAUDE.[2]

It is perhaps significant that at the time these projects were being abandoned Debussy was sufficiently interested in the *Deux Gymnopédies* of his friend Erik Satie to make an orchestral

[1] Allusion to the *Filtre Chamberland,* a filter for water.
[2] *Correspondance de Claude Debussy et Pierre Louÿs (1893–1904)* (Paris, 1945.) The excellent annotations of this correspondence by Henri Borgeaud provide many biographical details of Debussy's life during this period.

version of them, performed at the Société Nationale on 20th February 1897. From the spring of the same year date the three songs on texts from Louÿs's book, *Chansons de Bilitis*. Bilitis, 'born at the beginning of the sixth century preceding our era, in a mountain village on the banks of the Melas forming the eastern boundary of Pamphylia,' was the perfect hedonist. Here, in an anonymous translation (published by the Fortune Press), is the text of the second of Debussy's songs, *La Chevelure*:

He told me: 'To-night I dreamed. I had your hair around my neck. I had your locks, like a black necklace, round my neck and over my breast. I caressed them, and they were mine, and we were tied for ever thus by the same hair with mouth upon mouth, like two laurels, which have but a single root. And little by little it seemed to me that our limbs were so melted together that I became you and you entered, like a dream, into me.' When he had finished he laid his hands softly on my shoulders and looked at me with a look so tender that I lowered my eyes, trembling.

For some time Debussy appears to have been peculiarly loath to allow the performance of these songs. On 16th October 1898 he wrote to Louÿs:

So M. A. Ségard is going to give a lecture on the *Chansons de Bilitis*. Therein, in beautiful language, is all that is ardently tender and cruel'in acts of passion; so true, in fact, is this that the most craftily voluptuous of people are obliged to admit the childishness of their play by the side of this terrible, fascinating Bilitis.

Now will you tell me what my three little bits of music can bring to a straightforward reading of your poems? Nothing. My dear fellow, I will even say that my music, blundering in, would divide the listeners' excitement. Really, what is the point of harmonizing the voice of Bilitis in major or minor, since she is the possessor of the most persuasive voice in the world? You will ask me why I wrote the music. Aha! old fellow, that's another point. . . . The music is for other occasions. Now you must listen to me— when Bilitis appears, let her speak unaided.

I needn't mention other, quite material difficulties, such as finding some young person who, out of consideration for our pale aesthetic figures, would be willing to consume herself in the study of these songs for a mere thank you. Then there's that shameful habit I have of scattering whole handfuls of wrong notes about whenever I play before more than two people.

Well, I have said all; and I hope you will understand. I don't wish to shirk, but to help you.

With all my affection,

CLAUDE DEBUSSY.

The *Chansons de Bilitis* were first sung by Blanche Marot at the Société Nationale on 17th March 1900. The same year, on 9th December, the Concerts Lamoureux gave the first and second parts of the *Nocturnes* and on 27th October of the following year the complete triptych. The reception was most enthusiastic. Meanwhile, at the Exposition Universelle of 1900, official performances had been given of *La Damoiselle élue*, the Quartet and the *Chansons de Bilitis*. Debussy at last gained recognition. On 1st April 1901 he accepted, for a period of six months, the post of music critic to the *Revue blanche*. An important landmark was reached, so far as public recognition was concerned, when in 1902 it was decided to give *Pelléas et Mélisande* at the Opéra-Comique.

In these ten years Debussy's unobtrusive emergence was to change the whole face of French music, and gradually the almost unbelievable results of his explorations were to become a source of fresh vitality for composers throughout Europe. Modesty and a spirit of humble inquiry were predominant traits of his disciplined character and, as we have seen, his work was achieved with the least possible personal display. During these formative years his methods of self-discovery were slow, almost imperceptible. In the composition of each of his works he assimilated, discarded and reorganized, his superior artistic integrity demanding a ceaseless repetition of the process before the unconscious ideal could begin to approach definition. In the end, as each work finally took some living form, a beginning, too, was announced of yet a further province of discovery. This Debussyan influence was to extend not only to music's future evolution. As his independence became more clearly established, the discernible figures who had contributed to his formation—Massenet and Wagner and the Russian composers—became, not dwarfed by his conquests, as some of Debussy's contemporaries were inclined to judge, but themselves endowed with a new spirit and significance. The Debussyan art opened new realms of music's infinity.

Yet at the close of the century his achievement was by no means fully appreciated. In a report on French music in 1900 presented to the Minister of Fine Arts, Alfred Bruneau praised the *Nocturnes* and *L'Après-midi d'un faune*, but considered that a more valuable achievement was Charpentier's opera *Louise*. Debussy's opinion of *Louise,* as expressed in a vituperative letter of 5th February 1900 to Pierre Louÿs, reveals, beyond the out-burst of intolerance, a confident sense of security in his own judgment and mission:

DEAR PIERRE,

I have been to the show of the Charpentier family, so that I am in just the right state of mind to appreciate the forcefulness of your letter. It seems to me that this work had to be. It supplies only too well the need for that cheap beauty and idotic art that has such an appeal. You see what this Charpentier has done. He has taken the cries of Paris which are so delightfully human and pic-turesque and, like a rotten 'Prix de Rome,' he has turned them into sickly cantilenas with harmonies underneath that, to be polite, we will call parasitic. The sly dog! It's a thousand times more conventional than *Les Huguenots*, of which the technique, although it may not appear so, is the same. And they call this Life. Good God! I'd sooner die straight away. What you have here is some-thing of the feeling after the twentieth half-pint, and the sloppiness of the chap who comes back at four in the morning, falling all over the crossing-sweeper and the rag-and-bone man. And this man imagines he can express the soul of the poor!!! It's so silly that it's pitiful.

Of course M. Mendès discovers his Wagner in it and M. Bruneau his Zola. And they call this a real French work! There's something wrong somewhere. It's more silly than harmful. But then people don't very much like things that are beautiful—they are so far from their nasty little minds. With many more works like *Louise* any attempt to drag them out of the mud will completely fail.

I assure you that I'd very much like *Pelléas* to be played in Japan, for our fashionable eclectics might approve of it—and I can tell you that I should be ashamed.

Thank you for your kind and lovely letter, and *à bientôt,* eh?

Your

CLAUDE.

CHAPTER VII

THE HEDONIST

BEFORE proceeding to an account of the production of *Pelléas*
we may profitably pause at this juncture to consider some of the
more immediately apparent aspects of Debussy's moral and
psychological character. André Suarès, recalling his impressions of the composer about the year 1900, emphasizes the
physical sensibility evident in his appearance:

At first sight there was nothing striking about him. He was
not tall and appeared to be neither particularly robust nor delicate.
He had a certain look of solidity about him although he was rather
languid. He was well-covered, not to say stout, the lines of his
figure all merging into each other. His beard was soft and silky,
his hair thick and curly. His features were full, his cheeks plump.
He had a bantering manner, but beneath there was a subtle shrewd-
ness. He was an ironic and sensual figure, melancholy and voluptuous. His complexion was of a warm amber brown. Highly
strung, he was master of his nerves, though not of his emotions—
which must have affected him profoundly, especially as he tried
to conceal them. In love's retreat and night's inveigling sweetness
he must have known some passionate hours.

Irony was part of his nature, as indeed was his love of pleasure;
he had a mischievous sense of humour and acknowledged a love
of good living. He had a barbed tongue, a certain carelessness of
speech and something rather affected in his gestures; his enthusiasms
were controlled, his taste unfailing, and though appearance often
suggested the contrary, he was very simple. Debussy was as much
a bohemian of Montmartre as he was a man of the world. In his
reclusion there was something feline. With all his apparent sen-
suality there was no sign of brutality, though there might have been

a capacity for violence. . . . The shape of his head showed great obstinacy of mind.

All who saw him were impressed by his face and head. Casella writes: 'The enormous forehead bulged forwards, while there seemed something missing at the back of the huge skull.' Another observer, Ugo Ojetti, speaks of his 'box-like head,' and Cyril Scott of his 'somewhat Christ-like face, marred by a slightly hydrocephalic forehead.' I do not know what justification there is for saying that the shape of his forehead was due to hydrocephalus. To my knowledge, only one other person has hinted that he was afflicted with this disease. This was the playwright Georges Feydeau, who spoke of Debussy as 'a sort of dark, bearded hydrocephalic.'[1] On the occasions of his visits to England his physical resemblance to Rossetti was frequently mentioned.

Casella's recollections of his appearance about the year 1910 continue:

His colour was sallow; the eyes were small and seemed half-sunk in the fat face; the straight nose was of the purest classical Roman type; in the thick and jet-black hair and beard fifty years had here and there sown a silver thread. As always with artists of the finer sort, the hands were most beautiful. Debussy's voice was unprepossessing, being hoarse (and this was aggravated by the abuse of tobacco), and he spoke in an abnormal, nervous, jumpy way. His dress was scrupulously cared for in every detail. His walk was curious, like that of all men who have a weakness for wearing womanish footgear.[2]

By the side of this we may place a comparison of Debussy and Maeterlinck. Georgette Leblanc, observing them together, notes that they were both of a saturnine disposition, but points to interesting differences.

[1] His brother Eugène, it will be remembered, died at an early age of meningitis.

[2] Translation by Richard Capell.

69

Debussy's reserve was physical [she writes]. In him one felt a painful sensitivity and even something morbid which was biding its time. In Maeterlinck the physical and moral balance made itself felt at once. His timidity was the result of his nature and character.

The musician suffered from the little things of life. The poet refused to endure them. With him the 'Do not enter' sign meant 'Do not disturb me.' . . . With Debussy it seemed to mean 'Do not make me suffer.'

Both had an unquiet look in their eyes, but of a definitely different nature: in the poet's glance it was clear and hurriedly questioning; in Debussy's it took on a fixed intensity that awaited no answer. What was most noticeable in the musician was his body, built for strength and yet apparently uninhabited by it.[1]

Intensity of perception and an overwhelmingly acute sensitiveness were part of his nature, so that some degree of suffering was inevitably and continuously produced not only by the calamities and horrors of life, but by almost every manifestation of human experience—and particularly life's joys and ecstasies. Solitude is therefore imposed upon such passionate souls as a defence against exacerbation—solitude, or paradoxically speaking, the intimacy of identification. Delicately tinged with irony are these intimate confessions of Debussy, selected from his letters in the 1890s, in which we may glimpse, beyond the banter and the unashamed sentiment, the mechanism of a self-imposed moral discipline.

To Robert Godet

25th December 1889.

I am so glad, dear friend—just allow my little sensibility to speak awhile—yes, I am so glad of our friendship, over which thoughtless pride had cast its shadow—and I am glad too that such pain as we have known has been shared. All this is perhaps an old-fashioned way of looking at life. But then, fortunately, we are not 'modern'!

---

[1] Translation by Janet Flanner.

Moral and Emotional Character

13th February 1891.

I am sorry not to have been near you, but recently I have been so afraid of myself that all you might have seen was a soul in distress. Silence, I thought was preferable, though if we had been able to have a heart-to-heart talk I should have told you about my troubles and my sufferings. To tell you about it all using the right adjectives would either be rather meaningless or unnecessarily bombastic. But I did miss you! So do please forgive this silence on my part which was not in itself real, for I was bursting to say everything. In truth I am still much distressed, for the unexpected and sorry end of the episode I told you about brought some bad words between us. I had the strange experience then, as those hard words fell from her lips, of hearing too, at that very moment, the most touching and beautiful things she had said. The result was that I felt powerless and torn to pieces by the discord of reality tending to obliterate the ringing memory of her voice living still within me. I had to face reality in the end, but I have left much behind me and it will be some time before I can find salvation in work. . . . Though I still don't know whether she possessed what really I was looking for—Nothingness, possibly, in the end—I am nevertheless mourning the disappearance of the dream of a dream. . . .

TO ERNEST CHAUSSON

4th June 1893.

Ah, my dear friend! What a Sunday! A joyless Sunday it was without you. Had you been here the atmosphere would have been a delight to breathe, for I must tell you that if I had already loved you very much, the few days I spent in your company have made me ever your devoted friend. But I will not try to express my emotions here. However lyrical I might become I should not do myself justice.

Yet this is not so laughable as you might think. It was so good to feel that I belonged somehow to your family and that I was part of you all. But am I not going too far, and won't you feel my friendship to be rather a nuisance? I wish so much to please you that sometimes I imagine things that, decidedly, are crazy.

71

Debussy

TO PIERRE LOUŸS

(? *April*) 1898.

I really do need your affection, I feel so lonely and helpless.
Nothing has changed in the black background of my life and I
hardly know where I am going if it is not towards suicide—a senseless
ending to something that might have turned out better. I've got
into this state of mind from continually fighting against silly and
despicable impossibilities. You know me better than any one and
you alone can take it upon yourself to tell me that I am not altogether
an old fool . . .

It would be an over-simplification to say that Debussy was an
atheist. As a boy at the Conservatoire he told his friends that
he lacked the necessary religious feeling to set to music Lamar-
tine's *Invocation,* required of him at a preliminary examination
for the Prix de Rome. He might at one time have taken part in
the spiritualist séances at Bailly's offices of *La Revue indépendante,*
but rather because it was a fashion than to find some form of
religious expression. To quote Jean Lépine: 'His atheism was
sensual and instinctive. To find support for his lack of belief
there was no question of devoting himself to any serious study as
Voltaire, Renan and Anatole France did. Nor did he seek
any philosophic system to defend himself. Quite simply he
experienced no desire for a religion.' And what interests us
particularly: 'It is unlikely that these problems presented
themselves with sufficient force for him to seek a satisfactory
solution.' (It is impossible not to suspect that it was this lack
of any religious feeling that drove him away from César
Franck's class at the Conservatoire.) His young friend, René
Peter, tells us that he was very superstitious and 'would not go
to bed without first thoroughly blowing his nose and then
placing his slippers so that the toes pointed outwards. (Not
to do this was to tempt Providence.)'

René Peter has also written about Debussy's reactions to
certain political movements. At the end of the last century

the Dreyfus affair divided the whole of France. Debussy was only mildly interested. In keeping with most of his friends, he instinctively took sides with the nationalists. Peter persuaded him to hear Anatole France and Jean Jaurès speak in favour of Dreyfus at the meetings in Montparnasse; but he was little impressed. Yet at this period of his life he was anything but the fierce chauvinist he is generally thought to have been. In 1897 *Messidor*, an opera by Alfred Bruneau on a libretto by Zola, Dreyfus's most ardent supporter, was produced at the Opéra. Partly for political reasons, it was a failure. In a letter to Louÿs Debussy leaves no doubt as to his feelings on the intermingling of politics and art:

I haven't got any further than you with the score of *Messidor*, for life is short and I'd rather go to a café or look at pictures. How do you expect people so ugly as Zola and Bruneau to be capable of anything but the second-rate? Have you noticed, in their two articles, the deplorable use they make of patriotism? It might be bad, but in any case it's French!!! *Saint-Georges!* We've only got one musician who's really French, and that's Paul Delmet. He's the only one who has caught the melancholy atmosphere of the faubourgs and the whole-hearted sentimentality round where that burnt grass is by the fortifications.[1] The best disciple of this master is Massenet.[2] The others with their social preoccupations and their claim to put life into chords of the seventh are just a lot of dreary fatheads. If, indeed, they have any view of life at all, it is through their last laundry bill.

Until the production of *Pelléas* Debussy's material position was always insecure. On his return from Rome he contrived to make a living as a pianoforte teacher and by making transcriptions for the publishers Fromont and Durand. His compositions were a source of revenue for only a short time. About

[1] Meaning the outlying, poorer districts of Paris.
[2] The point here is that the chansonnier Paul Delmet (1861–1904) was a pupil of Massenet.

1895 Georges Hartmann, a publisher later associated with Fromont, secured the rights on all his work for five hundred francs a month. But Hartmann died in 1900, leaving him without any hope of securing a similar contract from another publisher. 'He was sent to me by Providence,' he told Pierre Louÿs, 'and played his part with a grace and charm quite rare among the philanthropists of art.' In 1893 he contemplated taking a post as a conductor at Royan, and on two occasions he attempted to establish connections in London.

On the sole authority of Andrew de Ternant Debussy first came to London when a young boy and heard *H.M.S. Pinafore* at the Strand Opera Comique. He paid another visit on his return from Rome in 1887, this time to investigate the rights of *The Blessed Damozel*. Berthold Tours introduced him to Novello's, but to no material advantage. In 1895 he came again and stayed for three weeks near Belsize Road at the house of a French professor. On the way over he met Saint-Saëns, who introduced him to Parry at the Royal College of Music. But again, as one might in this case well imagine, to no avail. Debussy could hope for even less success in London than in Paris. It was long before he could reap any material benefit from his works. His royalties amounted to less than £10 a month, even when he was over forty.

He had, however, an extravagant way of living and seemingly an unfortunate lack of practical sense in financial matters from which he was frequently to suffer in his later life. In his thirties he was once known to leave his home with his last twenty francs hoping to borrow from his friends, only to return penniless and with a porcelain cat he had seen in a shop window. Still, this was a far cry from the stupendous extravagances of Wagner. And the difference between the ways of living of the two musicians was characteristic in other respects. A predominant trait of both men was their love of sensual pleasure. But while Wagner collected forty silk dressing-gowns, the French musician was content to steal a friend's tie because it was of his favourite green. Let us imagine that in their amorous relationships too there was something of the difference between the gorging Tristan and the more hesitant Pelléas.

Mention has been made in earlier chapters of Debussy's adolescent attractions to Sophie von Meck and Mme Vasnier. About 1888 he decided to share his life with Gabrielle Dupont, known to his friends and mentioned in his correspondence as Gaby.

The most remarkable thing about the appearance of this pretty blonde [writes René Peter] was the strikingly green colour of her eyes. I don't know where Claude met her; scandalmongers— but we shan't listen to them—said in some frivolous place. She was certainly the least frivolous blonde I ever came across. Her chin was forceful, she was strongly built and looked at you as resolutely as a cat.

Beyond this our knowledge of her relations with Debussy is limited. During this period of about ten years that they lived together in the rue de Londres and the rue Gustave-Doré, Debussy inscribed to her a sketch for *L'Après-midi d'un faune* and his unfinished opera, *Roderigue et Chimène*. But she did not hold his whole affection during this time. About 1893 he was engaged for a short time to a young singer, Thérèse Roger. And about five years later he had a violent romantic affair with a young society woman. This gives us occasion to quote an illuminating passage from a letter of 9th February 1897 which Debussy sent to Louÿs, then in Algeria:

I 've had some troublesome business in which Bourget seems to have joined forces with Xavier de Montepin [1]—which may not be altogether impossible. Gaby, with her steely eyes, found a letter in my pocket which left no doubt as to the advanced state of a love affair with all the romantic trappings to move the most hardened

[1] Xavier de Montépin (1826–1902), popular author of serial stories and melodramas.

heart. Whereupon—tears, drama, a real revolver and a report in the *Petit Journal*. Ah! my dear fellow, why weren't you here to help me out of this nasty mess? It was all barbarous, useless and will change absolutely nothing. Kisses and caresses can't be effaced with an india-rubber. They might perhaps think of something to do this and call it The Adulterer's India-Rubber!

On top of it all poor little Gaby lost her father—an occurrence which for the time being has straightened things out.

I was, all the same, very upset and again very sad to feel you so far away, so hopelessly far away that I hadn't the strength to pick up my pen and write to you. I didn't think I could give you the right feeling of the thing. For writing is not the same as looking into the face of a friend. You will think perhaps: 'It's his own fault.' Well, there you are. I am sometimes as sentimental as a *modiste* who might have been Chopin's mistress. I must say that my heart is still capable of fluttering instead of getting on quietly with its own business. . . . Now don't let us speak of this any more, and believe me to be still your fine strong Claude.

Slightly before this he had made the acquaintance of Rosalie Texier.

She had come from the department of Yonne [writes René Peter], a pretty girl, pale complexion, a small mouth and her hair then rather dark brown. She came to earn her living at a Paris dressmaker's. Her first meeting with Debussy, brought about by friends of whom I was one, brought little sign of affection from either of them. Claude found her pretty but peevish; he even used to imitate her little ways. But she was a charming girl and took it very good-naturedly. Gaby, however, liked her very much. Then we lost sight of the three of them. No one could have foreseen that what, in the eyes of us all, was hardly the beginning of a relationship, was one day to come to a formal and happy ending.

For on 19th October 1899 they were married, the witnesses to the ceremony being Pierre Louÿs, Erik Satie and Lucien Fontaine; and the impecunious bridegroom, according to one account, having had to give a piano lesson in the morning in

DEBUSSY WITH HIS FIRST WIFE, PAUL POUJAUD (*left*), PAUL
DUKAS (*right*) AND PIERRE LALO (*seated*), ABOUT 1902

order to pay for the wedding breakfast at the Brasserie Pousset. From a letter to wrote to Godet on 5th January 1900 he certainly appeared to have no illusions about his wife's intellectual capacities:

I must tell you straight away of what has happened. Two things: I 've moved and I 'm married. Yes, my dear friend, and please remain seated. Mlle Lily Texier has changed her disharmonious name to Lily Debussy, much more pleasant-sounding, as every one will agree. She is unbelievably fair and pretty, like some character from an old legend. Also she is not in the least 'modern-style.' She has no taste for the music that Willy [1] approves, but has a taste of her own. Her favourite song is a roundelay about a grenadier with a red face who wears his hat on one side like an old campaigner —not very provoking aesthetically.

A year later we may judge of his feelings from an inscription on the manuscript of the *Nocturnes*:

This manuscript belongs to my little Lily-Lilo. All rights reserved. It is proof of the deep and passionate joy I have in being her husband. Claude Debussy. At the peep of January 1901.

Finally there is a glimpse of the unaffected person she must have been in an unfinished play, *Les Frères en art,* which Debussy wrote with René Peter. Here Maltravers, impersonating Debussy, says to a character impersonating Lily:

You don't pretend to be a Muse who frightens the sparrows away. You don't do your hair like the women in the frescoes. You have a lovely perfume and you are as sweet as a peach without ever reminding me of the latest success from Houbigant's. You dress up very little, which gives you so much more time, but which is also rather my fault.

The marriage to Lily Texier, this simple, good and unaffected girl of the people, was the natural result of the genuinely simple and unsophisticated life led by Debussy during the nineties,

[1] i.e. Henri Gauthier-Villars, the critic.

moving among the ordinary honest folk of Paris, sharing with them an occasional visit to the music-hall or the circus, an evening on the café terrace, or a summer afternoon in the city's surrounding woods, and discovering in life's common and daily animation a new and intense poetry—a poetry of the senses and of sensations whose endless associations were to be caught and finally held in the music he was slowly able to exteriorize.

CHAPTER VIII

TWO YEARS—1902–1904

IT was decided to give *Pelléas* at the Opéra-Comique in 1902, and rehearsals began on 13th January. But it was only in March that the date of the dress rehearsal was fixed for 27th April and the first public performance for three days later. Debussy was taken by surprise, for during the rehearsals a number of revisions were recommended and orchestral interludes were seen to be necessary to allow time for the scenery to be changed. Many passages were thus not completed until the last moment. Robert Godet mentions that during these months he had 'to settle affairs with the legatee of one of his patrons [i.e. Georges Hartmann] and this exposed him to daily summonses for debts he could not repay.' To complicate matters still further a quarrel broke out between Debussy and Maeterlinck. For a time it was thought that the whole production would be wrecked.

The unfortunate publicity and gossip to which this quarrel gave rise makes it difficult, even now, to reconstruct the episode without distortion. Here is, I think, the most authoritative version, by Georgette Leblanc, Maeterlinck's wife, around whom the affair centred. The scene is in the rue Raynouard at Passy at the end of 1901:

Debussy came to play his score. The position of the piano forced him to turn his back to us and permitted Maeterlinck to make desperate signs to me. Not understanding music in the least the time seemed long to him. Several times he wanted to escape, but I held him back. Resigned, he lit his pipe.

79

Debussy

At this first hearing of *Pelléas* many of its beauties escaped me, but with the prelude for the death of Mélisande I felt that special, that unique emotion we undergo in the presence of a masterpiece. . . . It was late. Two candles outlined Debussy's silhouette. Maeterlinck was half asleep in his arm-chair. Before my eyes the high windows framed the soft blue of growing night.

Just before he left we talked of the casting. I longed to play the part. Maeterlinck urged it. Debussy said he would be delighted. It was decided that I should begin to study Mélisande immediately. We arranged for the first rehearsal.

There were two or three rehearsals at my house and two at his, the fifth floor in the rue Cardinet, where he lived in an extremely modest apartment. . . .

My work with Debussy was progressing, when one day Maeterlinck read in a paper that another artist had been engaged to create Mélisande and that she was rehearsing with him. That Debussy should do such a thing surprised me, as he was not a man to pay meaningless compliments. My enunciation gave him a pleasure that he constantly commented upon. Was it not the poem of *Pelléas* that had inspired him? Had he not followed it word for word as no other composer had ever done before? No, certainly the quarrel was not between him and me. It came from the Opéra-Comique and my disagreeable adventure connected with *Carmen*. . . .

Maeterlinck, thus betrayed by Debussy, referred the case to the Society of Authors, thinking that he was legally within his rights. He was mistaken, first because the law gives precedence to the musician rather than to the author, and furthermore because in his preliminary authorization he had added a gracious clause: 'The piece may be played where, how and when you like.'

Justly annoyed to find himself stripped before the law, Maeterlinck brandished his cane and announced to me that he was going to 'give Debussy a drubbing to teach him what was what.'

My love had none of the stoic quality of the heroines of antiquity. This threat of a beating terrified me, and I clung to Maeterlinck who jumped briskly out of the window. (Our ground-floor flat in the rue Raynouard was half-way up the slope of the street.

We had to go down through the garden in order to reach the *porte cochère* and then climb the hill. We often went out through the window.) I waited in agony, convinced of disaster. I did not picture Debussy with his tragic mask of a face taking kindly to a reprimand.

I watched the deserted street for Maeterlinck's return. Finally he appeared at the top of the hill, brandishing his cane to heaven with comic gestures.

The story was pitiable. As soon as he entered the *salon* he had threatened Debussy, who dropped into a chair while Mme Debussy distractedly ran towards her husband with a bottle of smelling salts. She had begged the poet to go away and, my word! there was nothing else to do.

Maeterlinck, who did not like musicians any more than music, kept saying as he laughed: 'They're all crazy, all off their heads, these musicians!'

This scarcely reassured me. I thought that after Maeterlinck had left Debussy would arise from his chair in terrible wrath. Perhaps his seconds would call on us the next day.

As for Maeterlinck, he found it only just to attack the management of the Opéra-Comique.[1]

Whereupon Maeterlinck wrote a letter, dated 14th April 1902, to *Le Figaro*, in which, besides opposing the substitution of another singer for Georgette Leblanc in the part of Mélisande, he says:

They have managed to exclude me from my work, and from now on it is in the hands of the enemy. Arbitrary and absurd cuts have made it incomprehensible. They have retained passages that I wished to suppress or improve as I did in the libretto which has just appeared and from which it will be seen how far the text adopted by the Opéra-Comique differs from the authentic version. In a word, the *Pelléas* in question is a work which is strange and almost hostile to me; and deprived of all control over my work, I can only wish for its immediate and decided failure.

M. MAETERLINCK.

---

[1] Translation by Janet Flanner.

The question of a duel did arise, possibly as the result of this letter, and Albert Carré and Robert de Flers both offered to take the place of Debussy. But eventually the affair blew over, although Maeterlinck was for a long time deeply hurt by the way in which he considered his wife had been slighted. He heard only one act of Debussy's work, many years later, in New York.

The part of Mélisande was thus given to Mary Garden, a young Scottish-American girl who, ironically enough, had made a romantic début some years previously in the opera which was an object of Debussy's special hatred—*Louise*. Here is the cast of the first performance:

Mélisande	Mary Garden
Geneviève	J. Gerville-Réache
Pelléas	Jean Périer
Golaud	Hector Dufranne
Arkel	Félix Vieuille
Yniold	Blondin

Scenery painted by Jusseaume and Ronson

Conductor   André Messager

Several matters combined to make the dress rehearsal a painful experience. At the doors a 'Select Programme' was sold, in which the plot was maliciously ridiculed. Maeterlinck's letter had afforded just the opportunity to laugh a new work off that a certain section of the Paris musical public always awaits, and during the performance there was the uproar that, ever since Victor Hugo's *Hernani,* traditionally accompanies the first production of a great work in France. The storm broke forth in the second act at the words of Mélisande, 'Je ne suis pas heureuse.' At mention of the words 'petit père,' in the scene between Golaud and Yniold, the house set up peals of laughter. At one point in this scene the uproar almost brought the curtain down. 'Sont-ils près du lit?' asks Golaud; and with the sweetest innocence Yniold replies: 'Je ne vois pas le lit.' This passage, as well as Yniold's scene with the sheep in the same act, was cut at the first public performance.

The reception in the press was divided. Romain Rolland in the Berlin paper, *Morgen,* had no hesitation in proclaiming that *Pelléas* was 'one of the three or four outstanding achievements in French musical history.' Gaston Carraud in *La Liberté* made a pertinent comparison when he spoke of Debussy taking his place 'more definitely even than Wagner among the sensualists in music of whom Mozart was the greatest.' Some weeks later he enlarged on the connection with Mozart in the journal *Minerva*:

M. Debussy is really a classical composer. I am not speaking paradoxically. After the unbridled romanticism to which music has fallen a prey, he has the lucidity, the tact, the restraint and the sense of proportion that characterize the classical composers. He has the same controlled emotion as they; he has their charm and dignity of expression, their scorn of emphasis, exaggeration and mere effect.[1]

The notice in *Le Journal,* typical of the complete incomprehension of the masterpiece on the part of many critics, was by Catulle Mendès, whose co-operation as librettist with Debussy in *Rodrigue et Chimène* had proved so signal a failure. Nonsensically declaring his desire to hear the score without the singers or alternatively the play without the music, Mendès wrote:

Every artist has noted the collaboration [of Debussy and Maeterlinck] with great pleasure. By their delicate and subtle sensibility, the similarity of their emotions and dreams, their fraternity, one might say, they seem as well matched as possible. One expected —what is so rare in an opera-house—a really homogeneous work, as if inspired by one man and in which the spoken drama would of itself develop into a musical drama.

---

[1] Translation by Maire and Grace O'Brien.

If our hope was not always deceived, it was too seldom realized. There was often disagreement, sometimes divorcement, just when we expected that perfect concord more indispensable in this work than in any other.

Debussy's own feelings at the performance, finely expressed in an article which appeared in *Musica* six years later, show how the process of creation, however satisfying and inevitable, must at the same time condemn an artist to relinquish his command over the limitless world of the imagination. As dream and fantasy cross the borderline from the unconscious mind into life and reality, not only is the artist aware of the victory of achievement; he is aware too of the corresponding impoverishment of his inner world, temporarily abandoned by the very fact that his phantom-like visions are taking some earthly, material form.

The scenic realization of a work of art [Debussy wrote], no matter how beautiful, is always contrary to the inner vision which drew it in turns from its alternatives of doubt and enthusiasm. Think of the charming life in which your characters and you yourself dwelt for so long, when it sometimes seemed that they were about to rise, tangible, from the silent pages of the manuscript. Is it any wonder if you are bewildered on seeing them come to life before your eyes through the intervention of such and such an artist? It is almost fear that is experienced; and one hardly dares to speak to them. In truth, they are like phantoms.

From this moment, nothing remains of the old dream. The mind of another interposes between you and it. The setting materializes under the deft movements of scene shifters, and the birds of the forest find their nests in the orchestral woodwind. The lights are turned on. The play of the curtain curtails or prolongs emotion. Applause —aggressive noises resembling the sounds of a distant fête where you are but the parasite of a glory which does not always prove to be what you desired.[1]

Nevertheless he was not disillusioned by the interpretation of the characters, in particular by the singing of Mary Garden in

[1] Translation by Maire and Grace O'Brien.

the part of Mélisande. Her rendering of the death scene left
him indescribably amazed. 'Here was, indeed, the gentle
voice I had heard in my inmost soul, with its faltering tender-
ness, the captivating charm which I had hardly dared to hope
for.'

Within a short time *Pelléas* became a great box-office
success. But one performance was dissatisfying, and Debussy,
temporarily disheartened, wrote to Messager:

I suppose I had to expect the consequences of such excitement
—I fell into an awful state of depression. The performance last
Saturday didn't go off very well. All sorts of silly little things
happened which really had nothing to do with me. There 'll be
another performance next Thursday unless something unfortunate
happens in the meantime. I am quite incapable of putting a good
face on things when I am discouraged, as you know.

The following performance was again a success and a curious
suggestion was made, though it was never adopted, of giving
the part of Pelléas to a woman. Debussy commented in a
letter to Messager:

It may seem strange, but it 's not altogether silly. Pelléas has not
the ways of making love of a hussar, and when he finally does resolve
upon something his plans are so quickly checked by the sword of
Golaud that the idea might be worth considering. I must admit that
I would rather like to see . . . Without speaking of the change in
sex there would be a change in the scheme of timbres which worries
me rather. Perhaps I am more curious about it than genuinely
interested. I will await your advice.

In the course of the year, the musical historian Jules Com-
barieu, then an official at the Ministry of Education, proposed
Debussy for the decoration of the Croix d'Honneur. He
accepted it, but only, as he told Louis Laloy, 'for the joy it will
give my old parents and all those who love me.'[1] He soon

[1] Paul Valéry's comment in a letter of congratulation was: 'Every
real artist has the power, some day, to decorate the government.'

found life in the public eye, which the success of his opera had brought him, distasteful. In June, at the end of the Paris season, he wrote to Godet:

> It is I, Claude Debussy, and I am none the prouder for being he. You will never know what remorse I feel for this unmentionable behaviour to you—you whom I love with all my heart! Truth to tell, I am tired out. It is like neurasthenia—a fashionable illness to which I thought I was immune. Apparently the mental and nervous strain of these last months has got the better of me, for I couldn't even think of writing to Godet. I have just now a moment when I feel less fagged and I beg you not to think too badly of me and to believe that there's nothing rotten in the state of Denmark. As for your article, I can hardly thank you, it would almost be an insult. Besides, I did not need to be reminded of your sensitive understanding and your scrupulously loyal love of beauty. . . . To come back to the story, I must tell you that the dress rehearsal has given me the most wretched trouble. What I foresee is that I shall continually be pushed into public life. I am not really made for that kind of thing and all I shall be is my clumsy self. . . .
>
> Well, I am anxious to see these performances of *Pelléas* over. It's time they were. They are beginning to take it for one of the repertory works. The singers are beginning to improvise and the orchestra is getting heavy. They'll soon be thinking more of *La Dame blanche*. . . . But I think I've got some way of getting the orchestral score published.
>
> I will write to you shortly when I am in less of a hurry. I want this to reach you as soon as possible.

Then he retired for the summer to the home of his parentsinlaw at Bichain in Burgundy. *Pelléas* was given in the autumn and again during the following year. The OpéraComique, he told Durand in 1903, 'is absurdly taking up all my time, and this life of the theatre disgusts me and deadens me.' The two years from the summer of 1902 to the summer of 1904 were, however, remarkably fruitful. They saw the

DEBUSSY AND HIS SECOND WIFE, EMMA BARDAC

appearance of a number of piano works—the *Estampes*, *D'un cahier d'esquisses* and *L'Isle joyeuse*, the second series of the *Fêtes galantes* on the poems of Verlaine, the *Danse sacrée et danse profane* for harp and orchestra, and the beginning of the second large orchestral triptych, *La Mer*.

The first mention of the last work is in a letter to Durand of 12th September 1903. Its three movements are here referred to as *Mer belle aux îles sanguinaires*, *Jeux de vagues* and *Le Vent fait danser la mer*. In a letter to Messager of the same date he alludes to certain boyhood memories revealing that the poetry and mystery of the sea which he had earlier evoked in *Sirènes* and in *Pelléas* were not only still predominant in his mind, but were crystallizing now into concrete ideas for the greatest of the Debussyan seascapes.

You perhaps do not know [he writes] that I was destined for the fine life of a sailor and that it was only by chance that I was led away from it. But I still have a great passion for the sea. You will say that the ocean doesn't wash the hills of Burgundy and that what I am doing might be like painting a landscape in a studio. But I have endless memories and, in my opinion, they are worth more than reality, which generally weighs down one's thoughts too heavily.

At the beginning of 1903 Debussy was appointed music critic to the daily paper *Gil Blas*, and in April came to London to notice the *Ring* at Covent Garden. The rest of the year passed without any noteworthy happenings. Performances took place and his reputation seemed assured. If there was no great improvement in his material position, it at least promised to be more secure. Then, in the summer of 1904, came a turning-point in his private life. Debussy left his wife for Mme Bardac. Lily Debussy shot herself and was taken to a nursing home severely wounded near the heart. The Paris world flamed with scandal. On all sides Debussy was accused of having crudely sold himself to a rich woman. Several of his friends deserted him.

Debussy

It is difficult to reconstruct the episode without being influenced by the views of one party or another. Emma Bardac, *née* Moyse, was a Jewess and the wife of a prominent financier. She was a woman of the world, a brilliant talker and a delightful singer. Debussy had become intimate with her shortly after his marriage with Rosalie Texier and had considered abandoning his wife for her many times before the final rupture. What decided him is not clear. He told Robert Godet that the sound of Lily's voice 'made his blood run cold.' On the other hand, we know nothing of his love for Mme Bardac. The life she offered was certainly alluring, and it has been argued that Debussy, always susceptible to the luxuries of life (and in particular to fine cooking), foresaw, principally, freedom from material worries. As Lily bluntly said of her successor: 'Elle l'a pris par la gueule.' But we know as yet too little of the inner history of the affair to form any judgment of Debussy's action. So far as the material side of the question is concerned his new alliance involved him in endless complications.

In the autumn of 1905 a girl was born. She was named Claude-Emma. Debussy and Mme Bardac had both petitioned for divorce and were married some time later.

On 19th September 1904 Debussy sent the following letter to Messager:

My life during the last few months has been strange and bizarre, much more so than I could have wished. It is not easy to give you particulars, it would be rather embarrassing. I would rather wait and tell you over some of that excellent whisky of the old days. I have been working . . . but not as I should have liked. . . . Perhaps I was over-anxious or perhaps I was aiming too high. Whatever the cause, I have had many a fall, and have hurt myself so much that I have felt utterly exhausted for hours afterwards. There are numerous reasons for this of which I will tell you some day . . . if I have the courage, for it is all very sad. There are times when one spends one's days mourning for the past, and I have been mourning the Claude Debussy who worked so joyfully at *Pelléas*, for, between ourselves, I have not been able to recapture him, and that is one of my many sorrows.[1]

---

[1] Translation by Maire and Grace O'Brien. The grim trials of Debussy's personal life during this period are fairly presented both by Oscar Thompson in Chapter XIII of his *Debussy, Man and Artist* and by Rollo H. Myers in Chapter VI of his *Debussy* (Great Lives series). Mr. Thompson's account has the merit of embodying all the available published details, while the more concise account of Mr. Myers is perhaps more judiciously attuned to the motives of Debussy's actions. Observing that Lily was far from being her husband's intellectual equal, Mr. Myers concludes that Debussy was attracted to Emma Bardac not only as a woman but also as an artist. 'A new world seemed to open up before his eyes—a world in which the woman he loved would also be able to share his thoughts and aspirations and interpret his musical creations.'

CHAPTER IX

THE YEARS OF 'DEBUSSYISM'—1904–1913

AT the time of his separation from Lily, Debussy was engaged on some incidental music to *King Lear*, which was about to be produced at the Odéon by Antoine, the great producer of the Théâtre Libre. In January 1904 Debussy promised to have several short pieces ready by October. But at the time of the rehearsals they were far from complete, and *Lear* was given with the music of one Edmond Missa. Of these troubled months we have an illuminating document in a letter of 14th April 1905 to a new friend, the critic Louis Laloy.

You should know how people have deserted me! It is enough to make one sick of every one called a man. I shan't tell you of all that I have gone through. It's ugly and tragic and ironically reminds one of a novel a concierge might read. Morally I have suffered terribly. Have I some forgotten debt to pay to life? I don't know; but often I've had to smile so that no one should see that I was going to cry. So, my dear friend, be assured of my joy on seeing you again. I shall try to bring up the old Claude Debussy you knew. If he is rather care-ridden don't mind, for his affection for you is unshaken.

His new alliance did not begin under very auspicious circumstances. A series of lawsuits started which continued until the end of his life, and indeed long after. In the summer of 1905 he came to England. On 28th August, from the Grand Hotel at Eastbourne, he wrote to Laloy:

It would have been unpardonable to leave Paris without seeing you if my departure had not been a flight. I fled from all that tedious fuss. I fled from myself, who was finally only allowed to think by permission of the usher. I've been here a month. It's a little English seaside place, silly as these places sometimes are. I shall have to go because there are too many draughts and too much music—but I don't quite know where. . . . I am trying somehow to get back to myself. I have written a certain amount of music as I have not done for quite a time.

After the birth of his daughter in October, Debussy and his family moved into a little house at the end of the Avenue du Bois de Boulogne (now the Avenue Foch), where he lived for the rest of his life. Laloy speaks of the arrival of Claude-Emma, alias Chouchou, as 'the fulfilment of one of his most cherished hopes.' Four years later, on the score of the piano pieces, *Children's Corner,* three appeared the dedication: 'To my dear little Chouchou, with her father's affectionate apologies for what follows.' But one is not to assume that she was an infant prodigy. 'Chouchou' only took piano lessons (from 'a lady in black who looks like a drawing by Odilon Redon') at the age of nine. She died in 1919.[1]

On 15th October *La Mer,* finished in March 1905, was conducted by Chevillard at the Concerts Lamoureux. 'The work was awaited in Paris with an impatience that was not kindly disposed,' writes M. Laloy. 'Prudish indignation had not yet been appeased, and on all sides people were ready to make the artist pay dearly for the wrongs that were imputed to the man.' A fierce controversy broke out in the press. A number of critics took advantage of the fact that the work marked a new phase in Debussy's development to maintain an attitude that was definitely hostile. Pierre Lalo, in *Le Temps,* concluded his derogatory report with the words: 'I neither hear, nor see, nor feel the sea.' And Gaston Carraud wrote in *La Liberté:* 'It is certainly genuine Debussy—that is to say, the most individual, the most precious, and the most

[1] Lily Debussy died in 1932 and Emma Debussy in 1934.

Debussy

subtle expression of our art—but it almost suggests the possibility that some day we may have an Americanized Debussy.' On the other side the chief praise came from Louis Laloy and M. D. Calvocoressi. Debussy was again mercilessly held in the limelight. Émile Vuillermoz whipped up an excited controversy between the followers of Debussy and those of Vincent d'Indy, the director of the Schola Cantorum and champion of César Franck and the German Romantic composers. The very different art of Ravel was dragged into the discussions and opposed to 'Debussyism' and 'd'Indyism.'[1] In 1907 the performance of Paul Dukas's opera, *Ariane et Barbe-bleue,* on a libretto of Maeterlinck, provided a fresh opportunity to attack *Pelléas.*

All this bickering created in Debussy nothing but a feeling of disgust. His admirers, who made a cult of 'Debussyism' as previously they had of 'Wagnerism,' regarded him as their *chef d'école,* a function he never wished to perform and for which he was singularly unsuited. In 1908, on the occasion of the twenty-fifth anniversary of the death of Wagner, he declared to a journalist, Maurice Leclercq: 'There are no more schools of music. The main business of musicians to-day is to avoid any kind of outside influence.' A climax to the controversies came when the interview in which this statement was made was published against Debussy's wishes, and a questionnaire sent to a number of noted people in France and abroad by the *Revue du temps présent.* 'Is Debussy the leader of a school?' the questionnaire said. 'Should he form a school? Is he an original personality or an accidental phenomenon?'—and so forth. The replies, together with the interview with Maurice

[1] Some time in the nineties Edmond Bailly predicted to René Peter: 'You will see, one day they will speak of the Debussyists and the d'Indyists as once they spoke of the Gluckists and the Piccinnists.' Debussy, on being informed of this, said simply: 'I only hope no one will ever speak of "d'Indyists."'

Leclercq, were published in a little book called *Le Cas Debussy* by C. Francis Caillard and José de Bérys. It will be sufficient to quote the sarcastic reply of Romain Rolland, signed 'Jean-Christophe':

I don't like all your modern French music very much and I am not mad about your M. Debussy. But what I can't understand is that, being so poor in artists, you have to quarrel about the greatest one you have.

As for the question of whether he is the leader of a school, and what this school will be worth, one can simply say that every great artist has a school and that all schools are evil. It might then be better if there were no great artists?

Debussy's own feelings on the matter are to be found in a letter of March 1908 to Durand:

I find these times particularly ungracious in that a lot of noise is made about things of no importance. We have no right to poke fun at American 'bluff' whilst we cultivate this sort of artistic 'bluff' which we shall have to pay for one of these days—and very unpleasant it will be for our French vanity.

Five years later, in a conversation recorded by M. D. Calvo-coressi, 'he declared that, wishing to concentrate upon his own work, he had made it a rule to hear as little music as possible.' Of the evils of premature discussion of young composers he said:

I consider it almost a crime. The former policy of allowing artists to mature in peace was far sounder. It is wicked to unsettle them by making them the subjects of debates that are, generally, as shallow as they are prejudiced. Hardly does a composer appear than people start devoting essays to him and weighing his music down with ambitious definitions. They do far greater harm than even the fiercest detractors could do.

After *La Mer* the next important work was the series of *Images,* of which there are in all three sets. The two piano sets are of 1905 and 1907. The orchestral set, first conceived for two pianos, was begun in 1906 and finished six years later. It consists of *Ibéria* and *Rondes de printemps* (written between 1906 and 1909) and *Gigues* (written between 1909 and 1912). During these years Debussy travelled extensively, conducting his works in foreign towns.

The first journey was to England. In 1907 one T. J. Guéritte founded in England the Société des Concerts Français and organized concerts in London, Newcastle, Sheffield and Leeds. By the initiative of G. Jean-Aubry, to whom, with his brother-in-law Guéritte, Debussy's early reputation in England was largely due, the Quartet received its first English performance at these concerts in December 1907. In February of the following year Debussy was invited to conduct *L'Après-midi d'un faune* (which was first played in England at a ballad concert conducted by Sir Henry Wood in 1904) and *La Mer* at Queen's Hall. Here are some very strange extracts from the criticism that appeared in *The Times* of 3rd February:

As in all his maturer works, it is obvious that he renounces melody as definitely as Alberich renounces love: whether the ultimate object of that renunciation is the same we do not know as yet. . . . For perfect enjoyment of this music there is no attitude of mind more to be recommended than the passive, unintelligent rumination of the typical amateur of the mid-Victorian era. As long as actual sleep can be avoided, the hearer can derive great pleasure from the strange sounds that enter his ears, if he will only put away all idea of definite construction or logical development. . . . M. Debussy is a master of colouring, and there may be some good reason for his abandonment of that element of music which has been considered as the most essential of all from the earliest ages until now. . . . At all events the practical result of this music is to make the musician hungry for music that is merely logical and beautiful, and many regrets were expressed by those who were obliged to leave the long concert before the Unfinished Symphony.

The following year he came again to London to conduct the *Nocturnes* and was to have gone to Manchester and

Edinburgh. But he was prevented from doing so by a serious illness. In January of this year, 1909, he became afflicted with cancer. Scarcely more than a fortnight before his visit he was suffering to the extent of having to resort to morphine and cocaine. Of the concert at Queen's Hall he wrote to Durand:

Fêtes was encored and it only depended on me to get an encore for *L'Après-midi d'un faune*. But I was ready to drop—a very bad posture for conducting anything.

To-night I have to go to a reception organized by the Musicians' Club. What sort of a figure will I cut? I shall look like a man condemned to death. I can't get out of it, apparently because of the Entente Cordiale and other sentimental conceptions, most likely calculated to hasten the death of others.

On 21st May 1909 *Pelléas* was performed at Covent Garden. Debussy came to supervise the rehearsals, but did not attend the performance.

They demanded the composer for a quarter of an hour [he wrote to Durand], but he was peacefully reposing at his hotel suspecting nos uch glory. Cleofante Campanini [the conductor] was twice recalled and telephoned me that the opera had an enormous *souccès,* such as had rarely been known in England. He came to see me the next morning to tell me about it in his Punchinello manner and embraced me as if I were some medal blessed by the Pope.

The Times spoke of it as the work which had provoked the most discussion in recent times—'excepting of course the works of Richard Strauss'—and praised 'a hand almost as certain as Wagner's own.' From this time on Debussy gained great popularity in England, and English musicians began to take into serious account developments in France. The first book on Debussy was, in fact, by an Englishwoman, Mrs. Franz Liebich. It appeared in 1908.

In 1910 in Vienna and Budapest, in 1911 in Turin (where

he met Elgar [1] and Strauss) and in 1913 in Moscow and St. Petersburg, Debussy was invited to conduct his works. He undertook these tours primarily to meet financial exigencies, for conducting had little appeal for him. 'It's amusing,' he told Paul-Jean Toulet, 'while you seek out the colours with the end of the little stick; but after a time it's like an exhibition, and the greeting from the audience is not very different from the greeting a showman at a circus gets.' Nor was he an inspiring conductor. At Turin it became necessary for the Italian conductor, Vittorio Gui, to take over the rehearsals. 'At the concert,' Gui writes, 'Debussy conducted as well as he could, but without any feeling or control; and the audience remained unimpressed.' After the journey to Vienna he wrote to Durand: 'I am not the composer to take my wares abroad. You are required to have the heroism of a travelling salesman.'

In 1910 he conducted *Rondes de printemps* at the Concerts Durand in Paris. *Ibéria* had been given some days previously by Gabriel Pierné. The reception was again hostile and led to the same futile bickering among the critics. This was also the year of the first set of *Préludes* for piano and of the songs, *Le Promenoir des deux amants* and *Ballades de Villon*. Alluding to the lines of Villon:

> Ung temps viendra qui fera desseicher,
> Jaulnir, flestrir vostre espanie fleur,[2]

---

[1] There is unfortunately no record of Debussy's opinion of Elgar, whose music, in any case, he may not have heard. In a letter of 10th September 1909 to T. J. Guéritte he wrote: 'You may be assured of my greatest sympathy with your plan to establish a Society for British Music in Paris, and you may certainly make use of my name in whatever way you please.' As far as I know this society never materialized.

[2] Shall come a time when your bloom will have gone:
And sear, and dry, your beauty's flow'r turn.
From the translation by Nita Cox.

he writes in a letter of mock despair to Durand: 'To-day I received the *Ballades*. They are perfect, although I should like the parchment to have been more yellow. But a time will come when it will have withered—and the music too. Anyhow, the edition is pretty.' A week later, on 25th September, an underlying agitation is disclosed: 'I am in a period of disquietude—rather like someone waiting for a train in a dark waiting-room. I have a desire to go no matter where and at the same time a fear of going away. I need a lot of patience to put up with myself.'

On 22nd May 1911 *Le Martyre de saint Sébastien,* a new dramatic work of Debussy's, was given at the Théâtre du Châtelet. The text was a miracle-play by Gabriele d'Annunzio. Whereas the composition of *Pelléas* was spread over ten years, *Le Martyre de saint Sébastien* was written in a few weeks, the work having been commissioned for immediate production by Ida Rubinstein, who played the part of the Saint. In the circumstances the score could only be hurriedly sketched out and most of the orchestration was entrusted to the conductor, André Caplet. Moreover, during the period of its composition Debussy was in a very bad state of health. The last bars were sent to Durand a month only before the performance, with the words: 'I admit that I'm not displeased with it. But, as I've told you several times, I'm at the end of my tether.'

The Archbishop of Paris censured the production—ostensibly for the presentation of a saint on the stage, but possibly also for the incursion of Debussy into the realm of quasi-sacred music. This allowed the composer to define his attitude towards both religious and pantheistic music in statements which he made to the press, showing not only a fierce awareness of his individuality but with this awareness, and probably because of it, a growing consciousness of some identification with the infinite. 'Is it not obvious,' we read in one of these statements (reproduced in Vallas's *Life and Works*) 'that a man who sees mystery in everything will be inevitably attracted to a religious subject? . . . Even if I am not a practising Catholic nor a believer, it did not cost me much effort to rise to the mystical heights which the poet's drama attains.' And he goes on to declare that he wrote the music for *Le Martyre* as though it had been commissioned for performance in a church, and expressed the hope that in the last act he had conveyed the feelings aroused in him by the symbolism of the Ascension. Reasserting a belief to which he had given expression in his youth in Rome, that no significant sacred music had been written since the sixteenth century, he confessed that he had 'made a religion out of mysterious nature' and that his conception of prayer was the capacity 'to feel the supreme and moving beauty of the spectacle to which nature invites her ephemeral guests.' If the origin of his inspiration eludes him, he was at least able to indicate the pantheistic and psychological phenomena conducive to inspiration:

The sound of the sea, the curve of the horizon, the wind in the leaves, the cry of a bird register complex impressions within us. Then, suddenly, without any deliberate consent on our part, one of these memories issues forth to express itself in the language of music. It bears its own harmony within it. By no effort of ours can we achieve anything more truthful or accurate. In this way only does a soul destined for music discover its most beautiful ideas.

And in a spirit of primitive, child-like innocence he declares: 'I wish to write down my musical dreams in a spirit of utter self-detachment. I wish to sing of my interior visions with the naïve candour of a child.'

Though the 1911 production of *Le Martyre* was not favourably acclaimed—and little wonder since this eminently French work was written on a text by an Italian poet and provided with scenery by the Russian artist Léon Bakst—the final rehearsal of the score produced an overwhelming impression on those privileged to hear it. Émile Vuillermoz, who was partly

responsible for the training of the chorus, relates how the
artists taking part in the performance, normally indifferent on
such occasions, were profoundly moved:

> The work was so strangely imbued with a magic of its own that it
> could hardly be approached on a level of familiarity. It was un-
> folded and laid out before the composer with amazing veneration and
> respect. . . . Debussy himself, who possessed an honest sense of
> shame and modesty, was unable to maintain his normal tone of good-
> natured irony and, thus faced with a musical expression of his inner-
> most feelings, quite simply and ingenuously burst into tears. It must
> certainly have been a unique moment in his artistic life and ex-
> perience.[1]

Shortly before the composition of *Le Martyre* Maud Allan
had commissioned Debussy to write the music for an Egyptian
ballet to be called *Khamma*. Debussy sketched out the work,
but orchestrated only the first few pages, entrusting the re-
mainder of the orchestration to Charles Koechlin. It was
completed in 1913, the year too that *Gigues* (the first part of the
Images for orchestra), which had earlier been completed by
André Caplet, was given its first performance at the Concerts
Colonne, and that the ballet *Jeux* was first performed at the
Théâtre des Champs-Élysées, the scenario and choreography
of which were by Nizhinsky. The collaboration of Debussy
and Nizhinsky had been promoted by Diaghilev, but Debussy
(like Stravinsky) had no respect for Nizhinsky as a producer,
and one can only assume that he consented to collaborate with
him for material reasons. When, in 1912, Nizhinsky produced
for Diaghilev a ballet on the music of *L'Après-midi d'un faune,*
Debussy scornfully wrote to Godet:

> Nizhinsky's perverse genius is entirely devoted to peculiar mathe-
> matical processes. The man adds up demisemiquavers with his
> feet and proves the result with his arms. Then, as if suddenly

---

[1] See *Claude Debussy et Gabriele d'Annunzio : correspondance inédite.*
Edited by Guy Tosi. (Paris, 1948.)

stricken with partial paralysis, he stands listening to the music with a most baleful eye. . . . It is ugly; Dalcrozian in fact.[1]

Produced by Diaghilev's Russian Ballet two weeks before the first production of Stravinsky's *Le Sacre du printemps, Jeux,* though not one of Diaghilev's most successful productions, is a score demonstrating an important development in Debussy's style, opening a way not only to the polytonal technique of Stravinsky and Milhaud, but to the twelve-note system of Schoenberg. Less ambitious than *Jeux,* but none the less inventive and original, was the children's ballet *La Boîte à joujoux,* on a scenario by André Hellé, the piano score of which was completed by October 1913. (According to Vallas the orchestral score was only partly the work of Debussy and was completed by André Caplet.)

While the scenario of *Jeux* was not intended to provide more than a symbolical background for Debussy's complex yet lucid musical illustration, the amusing details of Hellé's children's play inspired him to compose a score full of enchanting humour and parody, developing the style of *Children's Corner.* Reflecting the innocence of his beloved daughter, he told Durand that he was amusing himself, in the course of composing the work, by 'extracting confidences from some of Chouchou's old dolls. The soul of a doll is more mysterious than even Maeterlinck

[1] Translation by Maire and Grace O'Brien. Those who are interested in the scandal that followed Nizhinsky's choreography for *L'Après-midi* (Stravinsky maintains that it was Bakst who was really responsible for this choreography) will find a detailed account in *Nizhinsky,* by Romola Nizhinsky (London, 1933). One result was that Rodin, Nizhinsky's champion, was maintained for the rest of his life in the Hôtel Biron, which after his death became the Musée Rodin. Mme Nizhinsky rather naïvely says that Debussy 'was delighted with the sensation the *Faune* created,' and that he was 'enthusiastic at the idea of collaborating with Nizhinsky on a new composition.'

imagines,' he is driven to conclude. 'It does not readily tolerate the kind of clap-trap so many human souls put up with.' The three songs on poems by Mallarmé, *Soupir, Placet futile* and *Éventail*, which appeared in the summer of 1913, provide a further example of the extraordinary variety and fecundity of Debussy's music of this period—a period in which the composer seems to be travelling in several different directions at the same time, reaching back to old associations with the poet of *L'Après-midi d'un faune*, enlarging upon the pantheistic and mystical aspects of his art and preparing the ground too for the still bolder experiments of his final years.

CHAPTER X

THE WAR—1914–1918

THE first world war broke out in the first days of August 1914. Mallarmé had been dead sixteen years; Verlaine had died a drunkard and a vagabond; Rimbaud, before his death, had become a business man; Huysmans had retreated to the Trappists. Romain Rolland's Jean-Christophe could hear 'in the distance the rumbling of cannon, coming to batter down that worn-out civilization, that moribund little Greece.' It was a civilization, however, to be perpetuated throughout the war years in the extraordinary late works of Debussy, written as he was heroically battling not only with the moral problems so acutely raised by the war, but also with the perilous inroads made on his physical health by disease.

On 8th August 1914 he sent this note to Durand:

MY DEAR JACQUES,

Your letter has reassured me and I am really glad to have got your news.

You know that I have no *sang-froid* and certainly nothing of the army spirit. I've never had a rifle in my hands. My recollections of 1870 and the anxiety of my wife, whose son and son-in-law are in the army, prevent me from becoming very enthusiastic.

All this makes my life intense and troubled. I am just a poor little atom crushed in this terrible cataclysm. What I am doing seems so wretchedly small. I've got to the state of envying Satie who, as a corporal, is really going to defend Paris.

And so, my dear Jacques, if you have any work that you can give me, do not forget me. Forgive me for counting on you, but you are really all I have.

Your devoted,

C. D.

In the next letter, of 18th August, there is more determination. 'My age and fitness allow me at most to guard a fence,' he writes, 'but if, to assure victory, they are absolutely in need of another face to be bashed in, I'll offer mine without question.'

Then began a period of unproductiveness. 'It is almost impossible to work,' he writes. 'To tell the truth one hardly dares to, for the asides of the war are more distressing than one imagines.' During the first year of the war he edited the Waltzes and the Polonaises of Chopin which Durand's brought out to replace the German editions, and published the *Six Épigraphes antiques* for piano duet. (According to a discovery of Léon Vallas these were originally sketches for certain further *Chansons de Bilitis,* written about 1900.) The only new work written between the summers of 1914 and 1915 was the *Berceuse héroïque* composed for *King Albert's Book* and inscribed to the King of the Belgians and his soldiers.

The summer of 1915 was spent at Pourville, near Dieppe. In June he was seized with a sudden determination to work and produced, in rapid succession, the *Douze Études* for piano; the pieces for two pianos entitled *En blanc et noir,* inspired by the greys of Velasquez; and two Sonatas, one for cello and piano and the other for flute, viola and harp. At the beginning of October he wrote to Durand:

I am enjoying these last days of liberty. I think of Paris as a sort of prison where one has not even the right to think and where even the walls have ears. . . . I am writing down all the music that comes into my head—like a madman, and rather sadly too. Now the curtains have gone from the windows and when I see a trunk it makes me feel as sad as a cat. . . .

Earlier he had written: 'I want to work, not so much for myself, but to give proof, however small it may be, that even if there were thirty million Boches French thought will not be destroyed.' On the title-page of the Sonatas, under the composer's name, appeared, as an assertion of pride, the words *musicien français*.

On his return to Paris his cancer took a turn for the worse. At the very end of 1915 one further composition was written, the charming song, *Noël des enfants qui n'ont plus de maisons,* the words of which were suggested to Debussy by the horrible devastations in France and Belgium. Then an operation became necessary. From this time on he was a sick man. He became thinner and gradually lost strength. The following summer was spent at Le Moulleau-Arcachon and the summer of 1917 at Saint-Jean-de-Luz. His unhappy state of mind during these years may best be judged from the following extracts from his letters to Durand:

PARIS, *8th June* 1916.

The sick man again thanks you for your friendly inquiries. As the days go by I must admit that I am losing patience. I have been tried too long. I wonder whether this illness isn't incurable? I might as well be told at once. 'Alors! Oh! Alors!' as poor Golaud cries.

Life has become too hard, and Claude Debussy, writing no more music, has no longer any reason to exist. I have no hobbies. They never taught me anything but music. That wouldn't matter if I wrote a great deal; but to tap on an empty head is disrespectful.

LE MOULLEAU-ARCACHON,

16th October 1916.

Le Moulleau has not been able to help me and I shall not bring back any masterpieces. I might have a few sketches to be used later. I have never found hotel life so unpleasant. Even the walls are hostile—not to speak of this life in a numbered box.

Yesterday I had a visit from X. He made me sorry for a moment that I had ever written a sonata and made me doubtful of my own writing. Well, no doubt, there are bad musicians everywhere. But this incident very much disturbed me. It means a great deal, and I shall no longer be surprised at the lack of understanding my poor music meets with. . . . It was frightening. Why wasn't I taught to polish eye-glasses, like Spinoza? I should never have expected to earn my living by music.

SAINT-JEAN-DE-LUZ,
22nd July 1917.

Up till now I've been horribly tired. My last illness has left me with an aversion to doing anything. There are mornings when dressing is like one of the twelve labours of Hercules and I don't know what I expect—a revolution or an earthquake—so that I shan't have to go on. But without being unduly pessimistic, mine is a hard life. I have to fight against illness and against myself. I feel a nuisance to every one.

The piano and violin Sonata was completed in the early spring of 1917. It was his last work. During the previous winter a big choral work, *Ode à la France,* was sketched out on a libretto by Laloy, but was left incomplete. 'Do not be grieved,' he wrote to Godet in most beautiful terms of mingled despair and pity, 'if I no longer write to you of my plans. There is no reason to weep if music forsakes me. I cannot help it. And I have never forced any one to love me.'

On 5th May 1917 he appeared on a concert platform in Paris for the last time. With Gaston Poulet he played the piano and violin Sonata. André Suarès, who saw him at a concert a few weeks before, was struck by his absent expression and extreme lassitude.

His complexion was the colour of melted wax or of ashes [Suarès writes]. In his eyes there was no feverish flame, but the dull reflections of silent pools. There was not even bitterness in his gloomy smile. . . . His fat, plump hand, like the hand of a priest, hung from his arm, his arm from his shoulder and his head from his body. . . . As he sat down, his eyes, under their flickering lids, moved slowly round, like those of people who would see without being seen, who steal a glance at something they seem only half to see.

At the beginning of 1918 he was confined to his house.

His features became hollowed out [writes Louis Laloy] and his look grew dull. He had first to stay in his room, then in bed. 'Always in bed, in bed!' he used to say despairingly. At the Opéra they were rehearsing *Castor et Pollux*, given on 21st March in the afternoon, for in the evening there was the fear of raids. One of his last regrets was not to be able to go. 'Remember me to Monsieur Castor,' he said feebly, trying to smile as I went off.

The bombardment of Paris by long-range weapon started on Saturday, 23rd March. During those last days he heard the dreadful sound of the shells exploding in the streets. By this time he was too weak to be carried down to the cellar. He died on Monday, 25th March, at ten o'clock in the evening.

The funeral took place on the following Thursday.

I can see as in a bad dream [Laloy writes] the coffin near the piano and the musicians in their soldiers' uniforms. . . . The door kept on opening and closing and there was no more room for the flowers. The Minister of Education took his place at the head of the procession. Side by side, in front of me, the two conductors of our great philharmonic societies, Camille Chevillard and Gabriel Pierné, walked in silence. All those concerts in which they had taken care of his music were over. The sky was overcast. There was a rumbling in the distance. Was it a storm or the explosion of a shell? Along the wide avenues there was nothing to be seen but military trucks. The people on the pavements pressed ahead hurriedly. But there was still a bustle in the populous uphill streets of Montmartre. The children made way and stood in a line in the gutter and stared at us. The shopkeepers questioned each other at their doors and glanced at the streamers on the wreaths. 'Il paraît que c'était un musicien,' they said.

By the time the procession reached the cemetery of Père-Lachaise, half of the fifty odd people who had started out from the Avenue du Bois de Boulogne had made off on the way. Only one oration was made, for the grave times, it was held, made such orations superfluous. Some time later the body was removed to the cemetery at Passy.

DEBUSSY (*right*) AND LOUIS LALOY FLYING A KITE

CHAPTER XI

AFTER the production of *Pelléas* Debussy contemplated or began no fewer than five other operas. They were: *Comme il vous plaira* (*As You Like It*), which was first suggested to him at the Villa Medici and which he kept at the back of his mind till the end of his life; two stage works on tales by Edgar Allan Poe, *Le Diable dans le beffroi* (*The Devil in the Belfry*) and *La Chute de la maison Usher* (*The Fall of the House of Usher*), the librettos of which Debussy adapted himself; a *Tristan*; and an *Orpheus*. None of these materialized.

Debussy's *Tristan* was to be based on *La Légende de Tristan* by Joseph Bédier. The project dates from 1907. In a letter to Durand of 23rd August Debussy enclosed this little note:

One of the 363 themes of the ROMAN DE TRISTAN

A month later, on 25th September, he wrote: 'On Monday Mourey [1] passed the day with me. We worked and discussed and I think we have got hold of something good. You will excuse my not having come to see you on account of *Tristan*.' This is all that is known of this attempt, 'whose episodical

[1] Gabriel Mourey, who was to have arranged Bédier's *Tristan*.

107

character,' writes Vallas, 'would have been related to the
tales of chivalry' and 'diametrically opposed' to the Germanic
conception of Wagner.

The text of *Orphée-roi* was specially written by Victor
Ségalen. It would have been as different from Gluck's *Orfeo*
as the *Tristan* from Wagner's. When *Iphigénie en Aulide* was
performed at the Opéra in 1903 Debussy wrote in the paper
Gil Blas an 'Open Letter to M. le Chevalier C. W. Gluck,'
condemning Gluck in favour of Rameau and maintaining
that it was Gluck who propagated 'the germs of the Wagnerian
formulae.' Judging from a conversation with Ségalen, he
seemed to have little more regard for *Orfeo*. 'Gluck's *Orfeo*
is only the sentimental side of the legend,' he said. 'Orpheus
was not a man, nor any human being, living or dead. Orpheus
is the Desire to hear and to be heard. Orpheus is the symbol
of Power in the world of sound.' (Cannot one see in those
words, tinged as they may be by a certain prevalent chauvinism,
the composer who conceived music as an expression of 'the
naked flesh of emotion'?[1]) Victor Ségalen's *Orphée-roi* was
published in 1921, but no music by Debussy is known to
exist. According to Vallas, the work was to have been
mainly choral.

The first mention of *Comme il vous plaira* is in a letter from
Bichain, of the summer of 1902, addressed to the poet, Paul-
Jean Toulet:

I would like to have news of *Comme il vous plaira*. I'm continually thinking of it and would like to think of it with you in
my mind. I am working very hard at doing nothing. . . .

By October Toulet had submitted certain sketches.

Now let us talk of good Monsieur William [Debussy wrote
eagerly]. The second plan you sent me suits me in every way.
Don't you think we might heighten the interest of the first scene by

[1] From a letter to Robert Godet.

the introduction of a choir off-stage which would comment on the
various incidents of Orlando's wrestle? They would have exclama-
tions to sing such as 'He's down! No, he's not! Ah! He's
no coward!' But, all joking apart, I think that musically it will
be quite original. And I would like to have some of the songs
sung by a group of people. The duke is rich enough to have the
Chanteurs de Saint-Gervais [a well-known choral society] and
their conductor come to the Forest of Arden. We must find some
pretty ceremonial for the betrothal and have it all end happily.
Whenever you can replace the exact word by its lyrical counterpart
don't hesitate. That doesn't mean that the tone in which the two
scenes are written doesn't please me. Quite the contrary. I suggest
it because of your fear of being too rhythmical. . . .

I have an idea which I offer to you for what it is worth. Couldn't
we use the scene between Charles the wrestler and Oliver (Shakespeare scene i) as an introduction?

Send me everything you can before you leave. I'm convinced
we've got hold of something really admirable.

Four days later he again wrote enthusiastically of the betrothal
scene, in which 'wonderfully clothed people would appear to
clearly marked rhythms and would announce the entry of
Orlando's Rosalind—all this intermingled with chants in the
ancient style, that is to say, describing the action.' But all
these plans came to nothing. Toulet left for Tongking in
Indo-China and the project was abandoned.

Fifteen years later, in 1917, Gémier having produced *The
Merchant of Venice* at the Odéon, Debussy suggested an *As
You Like It*. But it was again Toulet who failed him. 'I
distrust Gémier,' Toulet wrote to Mme Debussy. 'I rather
think that, like Antoine, he is afflicted with "chexpyrite"
and wants a severely literal translation.' Debussy implored
him to see the play from Gémier's viewpoint.

Like poor Mélisande [he wrote], 'je ne fais pas ce que je veux,'
which is indeed the greatest punishment. You imagine Gémier
to be too much of a disciple of Shakespeare. If only you knew the

Debussy

translation of *The Merchant of Venice* you would be reassured. All
Gémier wants is to use his gifts as a producer and to make his
crowds move about. *As You Like It* will not be of much use to him
for this. But he'll find some means of doing what he wants, you
may be sure. If necessary he'll make the theatre attendants act or
have the people in the stalls go and change places with the people
in the balcony. But without any pointless jokes, I believe you could
do *As You Like It*.

From a letter to Durand of November 1917 it appears that
Toulet and Gémier came to some agreement. But, again,
nothing is known of any music by Debussy. In a private
collection there exists Toulet's manuscript version in which
Debussy has underlined every word that seemed to him too
direct and which was to be replaced by its 'lyrical equivalent.'

During that same summer of 1902 came the first ideas for
Le Diable dans le beffroi. To Messager Debussy wrote:

There's something to be got from this tale in which reality and
fantasy are so happily combined. The devil is much more ironic
and cruel than the traditional sort of red clown. I want to destroy
the idea of the devil as the spirit of evil. He is rather the spirit of
contradiction.

In 1903 the libretto was 'practically finished.'

As for the people who are so kind as to think that I'll never get
beyond *Pelléas* [he comments], they can't see farther than their
noses. They evidently don't know that if that were the case I
should immediately begin growing pine-apples. For the worst
thing one can do is to reproduce what one has already done. Most
likely these same people will find it scandalous that I should abandon
the shadowy Mélisande for the irony of the devil.

What could reveal better the saturnine recluse on the one
hand, shy and highly introspective, and on the other the cynic
labouring under a screen of bristling irony, than the choice,
first of *Pelléas et Mélisande* and then of *The Devil in the Belfry*?
The theory that a composer reveals himself in his choice of a

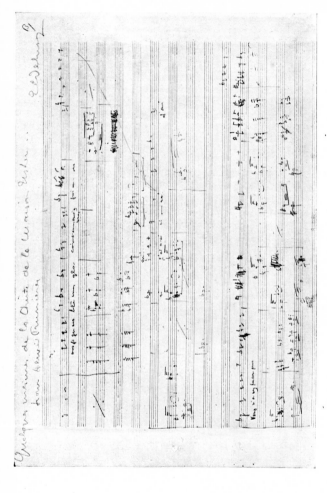

UNPUBLISHED SKETCHES FOR 'LA CHUTE DE LA MAISON USHER'

The inscription at the top is in the handwriting of Emma Debussy

libretto is nowhere so strikingly illustrated as here. In the letters to Durand *Le Diable* is referred to in 1906 and again, and for the last time, in 1911. It appears that the devil was only to have whistled, while the music of the crowd, unlike that in the *Meistersinger* or in *Boris,* was to have been very fluid. (In a letter to Godet Debussy speaks of the music he has written as a 'sly cheating of the ear.')

La Chute de la maison Usher was begun in 1908 and had not been discarded when the composer died. Here are the references in the letters to Durand.

June 1908.

These last days I have been working hard on *La Chute de la maison Usher.* . . . There are moments when I lose the feeling of things around me and if the sister of Roderick Usher were to come into my house I shouldn't be very surprised.

July 1909.

I have almost finished a long monologue of poor Roderick. It almost makes the stones weep. The mustiness is charmingly rendered by contrasting the low notes of the oboe with harmonics of the violin. . . . Don't speak of this to any one; I think a great deal of it.

July 1910.

I spend my existence in the House of Usher . . . and leave with my nerves as taut as the strings of a violin.

July 1911.

I am afraid the charms of Houlgate may not be sufficient to let me forget the Usher family.

September 1912.

Although very tired [*Jeux* was just completed] I have gone back to my old work. I like it well enough to get new strength from it. At least that is what I am hoping.

In 1916 he completely recast the libretto and the following

year sent it to Durand. In September 1917, he wrote to Godet from Paris:

This house has a curious resemblance to the House of Usher. Although I haven't the mind troubles of Roderick, nor his passion for the last thought of C. M. von Weber,[1] we are alike in our super-sensitiveness. . . . On this point I could tell you things that would make your beard fall off, which would be most unpleasant—not for your beard but for me, who don't like attracting attention.

The history of these unfinished words brings us to consider several points. There is no actual record of music having been written for *Comme il vous plaira,* nor for *Orphée-roi.* Possibly he never got as far as writing the music. But what has become of the music for the two works of Poe which, between them, occupied him during the whole of his later life? In a footnote to a letter referring to the music for *Lear,* Durand says: 'If the rest of this incidental music was written the composer must either have destroyed it or used it in other works.' Could he similarly have utilized the chorus of *Le Diable dans le beffroi* in *Le Martyre de saint Sébastien* or *Jeux?* It is unlikely—although in the practice of incorporating sketches for one work in the body of another Debussy would not have lacked precedents. (Berlioz, for all his adherence to a pro-gramme 'as the spoken text of an opera, inspiring the character and expression of the music,' thought nothing of using for the *idée fixe* of his *Symphonie fantastique* a theme borrowed from a discarded cantata written for the *Prix de Rome.* And that was the theme symbolizing Harriet Smithson!)

We know that an unpublished scene of the libretto of *La Chute de la maison Usher* is in a private collection, though nothing, apart from a few bars, is known of the music on which

[1] Allusion to this passage in *The Fall of the House of Usher:* 'Among other things I hold painfully in mind a certain singular perversion and amplification of the wild air of the last waltz of von Weber.'

he appears to have been engaged over a period of ten years. Speaking of the later unfinished works in a letter to René Peter, Albert Carré says: 'I am sure that the bitter memories Debussy had of the dress rehearsal of *Pelléas et Mélisande* were in some way accountable for the lack of courage he subsequently showed and the doubts that obsessed him.' [1] The experience of *Pelléas* may have increased his natural diffidence, but it does not account for it. It was in Debussy's nature to dwell on, and to think round, an idea, but not always to carry an idea to an end. From the two years at Rome, *Diane au bois* started the long list of un-finished or discarded works, and it is perhaps only as he would have wished that his last two big works should remain un-finished and unknown. Certainly he lacked no assurance that they would be performed, for in 1908 he sold the rights of production to Gatti-Casazza, of the Metropolitan Opera of New York. It was only with difficulty that Debussy was persuaded to sign an agreement, for there existed then barely more than the sketch of the librettos. As Gatti-Casazza left, Debussy made it quite clear that he felt under no obligation. 'Do not forget,' he said, 'that I am a lazy composer and that I sometimes require weeks to decide on one harmonious chord in preference to another. Remember also that you are the one who insisted on making this agreement and that probably you will not receive anything!'

'Define one's aims? Finish works?' we hear M. Croche, the imaginary interlocutor of Debussy's journalistic essays, sardonically querying. 'These are questions of childish vanity. . . .' [2]

[1] In this letter Carré mentions that Debussy thought of writing a *Don Juan*.

[2] Since this was written the available literary and musical manu-scripts of both *La Chute de la maison Usher* and *Le Diable dans le Beffroi* were assembled and published, many of them in fascimile, in my study, *Debussy et Edgar Poe* (Paris, 1962).

WORK

CHAPTER XII

THE SONGS

THERE are so many approaches to the Debussyan world, though hardly ever is any single one of them wholly or consistently valid, or able alone to disclose the magic of one or other of his creations. The delights of the explorer are indeed increased by the ambiguities which analysis promotes. There are the visual aspects of Debussy's hedonistic art and the auditive; the sensuous indulgence of his indefinable moods and their spiritual idealization; the psychological undertones of his portraits, the symbolical implications of his dreams, his visions and his fantasies. The complexities of music alone—the technical and material means of the artisan—cannot provide more than an initiation into the mechanism of creation, even though for a composer of music all experience is necessarily organized, transmuted and etherealized in sound. Nor can communion with the soul of Debussy be achieved merely in pursuit of the lanes and bypaths of contemporary aesthetic trends. The genius is larger than life, larger than the earthly world it is called upon to re-create. Ultimately the language of art is alone the language of understanding, and humility and faith are the surest guides to its revelations.

Poetry fertilizes the art of Debussy, and from this marriage spring the manifold images of nature whose innumerable sights and sounds are outlined with such a love of tiny detail, as the intimate union of human voice and keyboard presents a new and revitalized form of the art of song. Nymphs are brought to life from remote mythology, and ghosts from the *Fêtes galantes* ironically re-enact their courtly scenes in moonlit parks. Verlaine is followed on his vagabondage through Flanders and the age of chivalry is revived in princely castles. It is not merely the romantic, picturesque elements of such scenes that are conveyed: by means of an uncanny power of evocation they are alive again, as some long-forgotten dream brought into reality. The poets of Debussy's inspiration, from the sentimental Paul Bourget to the elliptical Mallarmé, are each endowed with the musician's novel and arresting vision which, however, is capable of the most bold transformations according to the demands of his fantasy. The empurpled style of the erotic Baudelaire songs, or the subdued pastel shades of the settings of Verlaine, the noble medieval severity of the Villon ballads or the sensuous delicacy of the *Chansons de Bilitis*—almost all the definable aspects of the rich and varied nature of the great artist are consecutively presented in this enchanting gallery.

Debussy's earliest songs, *Nuit d'étoiles, Beau soir* and *Fleur des blés,* on poems respectively by Théodore de Banville, Paul Bourget and André Girod, were written between the ages of fourteen and sixteen. Apart from their affinity with Massenet they hardly display, even in embryo, any of the recognizable features of Debussy's characteristic style of vocal writing. *Nuit d'étoiles,* originally sold for fifty francs to a publisher who was a friend of the Debussy family and later brought out in a variety of transcriptions, is a broad symmetrical song in E flat major, reflecting the more conventional associations of the poet's nocturnal landscape and his lingering memories of past loves. Unaffected in its derivativeness, too, is the coquettish *Fleur des blés,* where the poet's similes inspire a fresh and charming turn of phrase. *Beau soir,* published only a year before beginning *Pelléas,* catches, as in some vignette of the period, the feeling of repose and well-being matched by the placid image of a rose-tinted river at sunset with soft breezes running over the summer cornfields. The lyrical bond with Massenet is illustrated in this song, particularly in the nostalgic premonition of death at the close:

Car nous nous en allons
Comme s'en va cette onde
Elle à la mer—nous au tombeau

Dating from the years 1880–3, that is from the time of the
student-composer's association with Mme von Meck and his
latter years at the Conservatoire, are a series of songs revealing
a development seemingly pursued along several directions
simultaneously. *La Belle au bois dormant,* on a text by Vincent
Hypsa, the poet of the Montmartre cabaret 'Le Chat noir,' is a
ballad on the story of the sleeping beauty, nearer in spirit to
Gounod than to the music inspired by this fairy-tale by Borodin
or Ravel. Not without a touch of malice, Debussy's setting
of the sentimental story is based on the jovial popular round,
Nous n'irons plus au bois, which incidentally seems to have
haunted him over many years since he introduces it in 1903 in
his *Jardins sous la pluie* and again in 1909 in *Rondes de printemps.*
Paul Bourget is the poet of both *Paysage sentimental* and *Voici
que le printemps,* the former an attempt by the young composer to
define the emotional associations of a desolate wintry landscape,
the latter providing an early glimpse of the wonderful glorifica-
tions of spring of his later years. Reminiscences of Borodin
as in this extract from *Paysage sentimental:*

- mi   des   va - peurs   blan   -   ches,

and also of Massenet float through these early evocations of nature, the style of which is more fluent than independent. *Zephyr* and *Rondeau*, on poems respectively by Banville and Musset, show the composer experimenting, however timidly, with the form of the song presenting a prelude and an epilogue. Harmony and vocal writing are still orthodox, but there is a noticeable sensitiveness to the poetry's underlying associations. Finally, in this early group are the most significant indications of the new spirit that was about to break through, the first settings of poems by Paul Verlaine, *Pantomime, Fantoches* and *Mandoline*.

The texts are from the *Fêtes galantes*,[1] the *fin-de-siècle* poet's visions of scenes from the Italian comedy in the pictures of Watteau, Lancret and Fragonard. *Pantomime* was withheld from publication during the composer's lifetime, and reasonably enough since the melodious music hardly endows the figures of Pierrot, Cassander, Harlequin and Columbine

[1] Only *Fantoches* appears in one of the two sets of Debussy's songs published under this title. It was published in 1903 and dedicated then to Mme Lucien Fontaine, though it was originally written for Mme Vasnier. *Pantomime* belongs to a set of four songs dedicated to Mme Vasnier and published posthumously (in a supplement to *La Revue musicale*, May 1926), the others being an early setting of *Clair de lune* (Verlaine), *Pierrot* (Banville), and *Apparition* (Mallarmé). *Mandoline* was published separately.

with sufficient animation or individuality for them to step out of their miniature tableaux. In *Fantoches,* Scaramouche and Pulcinella are puppets whose evil designs, as they plot together in the moonlight, are ironically conveyed in the twanging lute-like accompaniment while, with seeming amusement at the nefarious proceedings, the voice-part periodically breaks off into nonchalant *la-la-las.* These puppets have not yet the poetic soul of the Golliwog or the Doll in *Children's Corner* but they are something more than mere cardboard figures. The humour of the little spectacle already betokens the artist's latent sensibility.

Mandoline, the most popular of the early Verlaine songs, is an amorous serenade in which courtiers and their ladies light-heartedly commit themselves to vows under the sighing branches:

The setting takes the form of a commentary, good-naturedly
mocking at so much indiscretion, a little gem in a light fantastic style which might have been inspired by the serenade
of Mephistopheles in Berlioz's *Damnation of Faust,* or even by
the still unwritten music of Ravel, notably the *Chanson à
Dulcinée.* Berlioz, Ravel and Debussy seem somehow to have
joined hands in this clever and deliberately acrid serenade, a
precursor of the *Serenade for the Doll* and the *Sérénade interrompue,*
in which the composer, no more than twenty-one, was able to
hit upon that vein of musical irony to be pursued with so much
wisdom and humanity throughout his life.

Massenet, the Russians, Berlioz, a foretaste of Ravel, and now
something of Wagner is to be incorporated into Debussy's
pregnant style of these years—the Wagner of *Tristan* which, in
the Paris of the 1880s, had almost inevitably to be associated
in the composer's mind with Baudelaire's *Fleurs du mal.* The
Cinq Poèmes de Baudelaire (1887–9), more articulately sensuous
than anything he had yet produced, were, moreover, written at
the time of the pilgrimages to Bayreuth.[1]

The first of the collection, though not the first in order of
composition, is a setting of *Le Balcon* written by Baudelaire at
the time of his desperate reunion in 1855 with Jeanne Duval,
the disastrous 'Vénus noire' of his amorous life. It is a poem of
reminiscent sadness embittered with remorse, but elevated
beyond the personal plane of mortal failings to the spiritualized

[1] Among the first to recognize the significance of the Baudelaire
songs was Gabriel Fauré who, though later estranged from Debussy
for both personal and artistic reasons, was nevertheless discerning
enough in the 1880s to declare the *Cinq Poèmes* to be the 'work of a
genius.' Vallas illustrates the older composer's attitude to Debussy
by quoting his inspiring declaration of independence—which would
certainly have received his rival's endorsement: 'Il ne faut jamais me
parler de Debussy. Je ne veux pas savoir qu'il y a Debussy. Si
j'aime Debussy, je n'aime plus Fauré. Comment alors être Fauré?'

world of the poet's imagery where good and evil are as fatally embraced as day and night in the nostalgic twilight, and where the only symbol of hope is in the implicit faith that a new dawn must rise again beyond the setting sun.[1]

From a technical point of view the setting is remarkable for the impassioned and declamatory style of the vocal writing, the ornate accompaniment creating the illusion of an orchestra and the recurrence of melodic phrases marking the repetition of lines at the opening and close of each verse. In its romantic and emotional effect, the dark, heavily laden style of the song conveys not only the indulgent pleasure of the Baudelairean *malaise* but also, with its Tristanesque suspensions and chromaticism, much of the poem's psychological anxiety.

Harmonie du soir is one of the later poems by Baudelaire, written under the influence of E. T. A. Hoffmann's *Kreisleriana*, where the theory, later developed by the French symbolist poets, is first expressed of the existence of some hidden and profound connection between colours, sounds and perfumes. The poem, constructed according to an enigmatic pattern whereby alternate lines of each verse are interlaced into the

---

[1] In her book on Baudelaire, Enid Starkie suggests that a passage from Baudelaire's *Journaux intimes* must similarly have been inspired by the reconciliation with Jeanne Duval. To my mind, this magnificent passage defines with even more potent symbolical precision the intolerable conflict of despair and hope, illustrated too by Debussy in *Le Balcon,* and through means of which he was able to identify the unconcealed eroticism of both *Les Fleurs du mal* and *Tristan*: 'Les deux êtres déchus, mais souffrant encore de leur reste de noblesse, s'enlacèrent spontanément, confondant dans la pluie de leurs larmes et de leurs baisers, les tristesses de leur passé avec leurs espérances bien incertaines d'avenir. . . . A travers la noirceur de la nuit, il avait regardé derrière lui dans les années profondes, puis il s'était jeté dans les bras de sa coupable amie pour y retrouver le pardon qu'il lui accordait.'

succeeding verse, imperceptibly glides through the worlds of the senses ('Les sons et les parfums tournent dans l'air du soir') until only memory can console the poet for his frightening vision of the emptiness of infinity. Both the form and the substance of the poem appear, however, to have set the composer problems solved with perhaps more conscientiousness than inspiration. The automatically recurring motives and the too consistently sumptuous chromaticism suggest that he may have been aware that there were still realms to explore in this particular region of the Baudelairean world, as indeed he was to show in the first book of *Préludes*. The limpid imagery of *Le Jet d'eau*, on the other hand, is more accurately defined, notably in the transparent arpeggio figures of the sparsely written accompaniment evoking the sparkling play of a fountain with its myriad bejewelled associations. A lingering influence of Borodin has been traced in the seconds of the opening bars, but to my mind these seconds are the discreet musical symbol of the forbidding closed eyes of the poet's beloved reclining alongside the fountain's 'glittering sheaf.' Consonance is, in fact, established only where an ideal of renunciation is succeeded by the pursuit of pleasure: true to the Baudelairean philosophy of disillusionment, ecstasy finds only a bland and uninhibited expression, in the open fifths and major thirds of the accompaniment's aimless chords. This singularly expressive accompaniment was orchestrated by Debussy as late as 1907, a revision, after the composer's death, having been undertaken by his disciple André Caplet from a desire (according to Vallas) to alleviate the alleged heavy instrumental texture.

It has often been observed that the opening bars of *Recueillement* strikingly recall the horns of *Tristan*. The profound, almost mystical, resignation, however, of the opening lines of this poem,

> Sois sage, ô ma Douleur, et tiens-toi plus tranquille.
> Tu réclamais le Soir; il descend; le voici,

proclaims, by the simplicity of its music and its measured cadences, the spiritual peace achieved by Baudelaire at the end of his life which, as it now appears to me, might have been more appropriately illustrated in music derived from *Parsifal*. The eloquence of the musical imagery of the setting nevertheless becomes apparent when eventually there emerges from the supple and sensitive harmonies of the accompaniment the sweet but mournful vision of Night as the ultimate consolation of poet and musician. Finally, the luxuriously imaginative *La Mort des amants,* actually the first of the group in order of composition, is a song in strophic form, revealing another dual allegiance of the young Debussy—on the one hand to Wagner, on the other to the pictorial and literary aesthetic, transposed into music, of the English Pre-Raphaelite movement.

In contrast to the articulate eroticism of the Baudelaire songs are the hushes and sighs of the contemporaneous Verlaine settings, their slender contours conceived with an almost pious respect for sensuousness, their subtle moods refined upon with so much grace, reticence and discretion. It is in these shy confessions that one is made aware of the underlying significance to the civilized French mind of *la pudeur,* that word for which there is hardly an equivalent in English, expressing an honest sense of shame with no suggestion of either priggishness or hypocrisy. The art of Verlaine, as fertilized by the music of Debussy, resides precisely in such courageous accuracy of perception— hence its disarming clarity—served by a novel technique of musical sonorities. René Chalupt in an illuminating article, 'Verlaine ou de la musique en toute chose,'[1] contends that the distinctive contribution of Verlaine was not so much his recognition of music's primacy ('de la musique avant toute chose')— so much must necessarily be admitted by any lyrical poet worthy of the name—but the revelation in his verse of new

[1] *Contrepoints,* No. 6, Paris, 1949.

rhythmic subtleties and of an unexplored world of acoustic associations.[1]

As in the songs of the Middle Ages, poet and musician are one in the Verlaine settings, embraced and interlocked. *C'est l'extase,* the first of the *Ariettes oubliées,* allows its voluptuous message to linger at the opening among gliding chords of the ninth:

---

[1] 'Sa robe rendait d'étranges musiques,' for instance; or evoking an almost Baudelairean disillusionment:

    'Sonore et gracieux baiser . . .

      Comme le vin du Rhin et comme la musique

      Tu consoles.'

Analysing Verlaine's elusive technique, René Chalupt lists the poet's allusions to instruments—violins and flutes, trumpets and horns, the fife and the harpsichord—and what is especially characteristic of both Verlaine and Debussy, the numerous reverberations of bells.

and, like the changing colours of the stream that runs through the spring woodlands of this poem, proceeds to reflect each of the infinite subtleties of nature's murmurs and shadows. The laconic writing for the voice is a manner of recitative, though occasionally, where suggestion merges into sentiment, it is allowed to describe a generous melodic curve. The song *Il pleure dans mon cœur* is prefaced by a line from a poem by Rimbaud, 'il pleut doucement sur la ville,' a line reminiscent of the poem set to music, but even more reminiscent, to my mind, of another poem by Verlaine, the pathetic *D'une prison,* written when the poet was imprisoned at Mons for his attempt on Rimbaud's life. The tragic episode must certainly have been known to Debussy particularly as, while still a boy, he had been associated with Mme Mauté, Verlaine's long-suffering mother-in-law, at the very time that Verlaine and Rimbaud made their dramatic flight to England. One may conjecture that, with the tact the young composer would still wish to use in regard to the painful affair, the quotation from Rimbaud would be intended to convey Debussy's homage to Verlaine's appalling fate. Or let us say that both song and quotation may have been a vicarious manner of setting *D'une prison* itself. However this may be, verse and music combine to create a beautiful monochrome reaching out to an immaterial world where half forgotten memories of pain, grief and regret, though dulled by the still more unbearable pangs of boredom, are ultimately accepted with resignation and placidity.

The novel and arresting modulations of *L'Ombre des arbres,* finely calculated to illustrate the poetic disparity between illusion and reality, are worth noting, in passing, as an indication of further technical independence. A prefatory quotation from Rostand's *Cyrano de Bergerac,* amusingly taunting the gleeful nightingale for its fear of drowning as it spies its reflection in the river, suggests again the irony glinting even in the more sombre

Debussy

Debussyan moods.   The joyous *Green,* on the other hand, with
its virgin freshness and tender fervour:

> Sur votre jeune sein, laissez rouler ma tête
> Toute sonore encore de vos derniers baisers,

more hedonistic though not, in my opinion, more successful in
its capturing of the ethereal quality of the poem than the setting
of *Green* by Fauré,[1] has understandably become one of the
most accessible of Debussy's songs.   *Spleen,* with its obstinately
recurring theme in the accompaniment, deriving, as Vallas
maintains, from the *Épithalame* in Chabrier's opera, *Gwendoline,*
provides another example of the new recitative style—the
impression created by the singer is of the poem most expressively
spoken; and finally *Chevaux de bois,* actually the first in order of
composition of the *Ariettes oubliées,* though the most developed
in picturesque detail, vividly displays a portrayal of hilarity at
a Flemish country fair.   The poem, a recollection of the irre-
sponsible gaiety of Verlaine during his wanderings with
Rimbaud as a happy vagabond through the villages of Flanders,
describes the lifeless wooden horses of a local merry-go-round,
ceaselessly revolving as the crude tones of oboes and cornets
emerge from the primitive band.   Whirling arpeggios and
successions of common chords outline the raucous scene as it is
filled in with an amusing series of puppet-like characters—the
rosy-cheeked child accompanied by the pale-faced mother, boys
in black and girls in pink and the slinking sneak-thief waiting
for his chance.   Oscar Thompson quotes several interpretations
of details in the realistically descriptive score—the cry of a
servant girl, the shout of a soldier and coarse hiccups on the
cornet.   An unmistakable counterpart of the early *Mandoline,*

[1] Under the title *Offrande* the same poem was set by Reynaldo Hahn
in his *Chansons grises.*   Inspired by Verlaine's idealistic love for the
adolescent Mathilde Mauté, it is only by chance that the poem does
not figure in *La Bonne Chanson.*

the song is in the form of a rondo, boisterously illustrative of the good-natured bourgeois scene until, as the contented crowd begins to disperse, the music nostalgically hints at distant chimes of a church bell and the first star of night.

Abandoning for a moment the chronological order so far pursued, this should be the point from which to explore some of the remaining lanes and bypaths of the Debussy-Verlaine retreats, beginning with the *Trois Mélodies* of 1891. *La Mer est plus belle,* the poem of which is inspired by the changing colours of the sea off the south coast of England,[1] has a florid arpeggio accompaniment, its frequent modulations skilfully attuned to the poem's indefinable moods. *Le Son du cor s'afflige* is a picturesque landscape of wintry snows, the romantic but conventional associations of which are accentuated by the mournful howls of wolves and a call of horns through the evening woods. The unemphatic setting, however, discreetly allows the imagery to make its own effect without providing what might have been a too obvious musical parallel. England again, is the inspiration of the wholly satisfying *L'Échelonnement des haies,* where the hedgerows, spaced out into infinity under the wide Lincolnshire sky, inspire a delicate water-colour of rural peace.[2] The harmony is here consistently tonal. Both the vocal line and the accompaniment are designed to convey the cool clarity of the scene, deliberately avoiding any hint of symbolical detail, until at the close the song allows itself to be diffused into the musical vision of a watered sky:

> Des cloches comme des flûtes
> Dans le ciel comme du lait.

---

[1] Though published in the collection *Amour,* the poem was written at Bournemouth, where Verlaine was temporarily engaged as a French master in a private school.

[2] The poem was written when Verlaine was a French teacher at the grammar school of the little Lincolnshire town of Stickney.

Debussy

The two sets of *Fêtes galantes* date from 1892 and 1904, though as we have seen, *Pantomime, Mandoline* and *Fantoches* were composed much earlier. *En sourdine* is similarly said to have been written at the time of Debussy's association with the Vasniers, though its subtle workmanship rather suggests the period of *L'Après-midi d'un faune*. A flute-like theme evoking the song of the nightingale is threaded through the little idyll as the courtly lovers of the eighteenth-century scene are barely awakened from their dreamlike raptures. The orthodox form of the *Lied* would seem to emphasize the classical elegance of the scene: the melodic lines of voice and piano symbolically intertwine in the form of an instrumental duet. In *Clair de lune* the contrasts in the accompaniment between passages of modal writing and others of sensitive chromaticism throw into relief the opposition inherent in the poem between the forbidding coldness of a remote and artificial world and the spontaneous and natural joys of its human inhabitants. Happiness cannot endure; therefore it must leave humanity to turn the play of the moonlit fountains into tears of ecstasy. A ghost-like evocation of the rhythm of the minuet accompanies the lovers' forlorn revelry endowing the miniature song with a magic of unreality.

In the second set the wit and parody of *Les Ingénus* are conveyed with a merciless precision of observation. An endearing touch of realism is introduced by means of playful appoggiaturas marking the intrusion of a ruthless insect on what is after all the most innocent of adventures. There is malice, too, as the artlessness of the youthful lovers is made still more embarrassing by high heels and long dresses:

> En sorte que, selon le terrain et le vent,
> Parfois luisaient des bas de jambes, trop souvent
> Interceptés!

The beautifully ornate piano accompaniment is conceived as a

130

pastiche of an old dance—a sophisticated minuet reconstructed by a twentieth-century composer with the added technical and artistic experience of the intervening centuries. *Le Faune* is not meant to be more than an effigy of the voluptuous Mallarméan creation: the dancing figure in plaster of Verlaine's poem ironically presages disaster to approaching lovers while watching over his enchanted wood. Suggestions of flute and tambourine in the accompaniment again provide the illusion of an imaginary dance while the pictorial delicacy of the scene is evoked by the *ostinato* drum-like bass. Finally, the well-known *Colloque sentimental,* which has been likened to a Latin counterpart of Schubert's *Der Doppelgänger,* is a moving dialogue in the style of *Pelléas.* Two ghostly figures recall their past love. A long A flat pedal in the bass creates an obsessional impression of melancholy over which the finely nuanced harmonies are most carefully designed to illustrate each of the poet's associations. At the end the flute-like figure of *En sourdine* is almost imperceptibly introduced as the song is allowed to vanish into infinity: echo of the flutes of antiquity in *Le Faune* and *L'Après-midi,* mythological flutes of primitive gratification and desire, leaving the listener to dream upon his visions of grace and pleasure and love.

The four *Proses lyriques* of 1892–3, of which the texts in lyrical prose are by Debussy himself, are especially significant as a document of the composer's psychological evolution. They reveal both his literary and his musical allegiances during this period and—what must particularly interest us—his efforts to achieve a synthesis of words and sounds in a single creative endeavour. Just as Verlaine, Régnier and Mallarmé were constantly aware of the unattainable art of music to which their own poetic art aspired, so, contrariwise, Debussy would seem to have been anxious himself to define the poetic imagery which was the source of his inspiration. If the results of these curious experiments are less satisfying from a literary than from a musical viewpoint, they must nevertheless be considered successful since one of the purposes of such experiments was apparently to placate and exorcise such extraneous influences as were binding down the artist in the pursuit of his fantasies. So much, at any rate, one gathers from the derivative nature of the strangely precious texts, written in an attempt to emulate, according to most French critics, the styles of Mallarmé, Baudelaire, Henri de Régnier and Jules Laforgue. I should be inclined to add the influence of Maeterlinck's *Serres chaudes* (set to music, incidentally, by Chausson), particularly in the third song, *De fleurs,* with its almost surrealist vision of the sun, not as a beneficent but as an evil force, the destroyer of the poet's dreams and the life of poisonous flowers. In *De rêve* a nightmarish jostling of reminiscences produces a procession of knights who have died in quest of the Grail, and visions, too, of the delicately pretty women of the *Fêtes galantes. De grève* is a seascape in which the far-fetched simile between a windy sea, with its dancing white horses, and the gaiety of a band of schoolgirls, their skirts blown up by the wind, appears to have been inspired in Debussy's mind by an English water-colour— possibly his favourite Turner. *De Soir* is an ironic portrayal of a Parisian Sunday, pitifully descriptive of the bourgeois crowds transported in excursion trains to the surrounding countryside. The music of these four songs is similarly derivative, displaying traces of Wagner, Borodin and Massenet, a folk-song reference (*La Tour prend garde*), the style of the earlier *Arabesques* and the *Fêtes galantes* and, particularly characteristic of Debussy's preoccupations at this period, a variety of references to different chimes, bells and echoes. The *Proses lyriques* were a bold and an inevitable experiment whose rewards were to be reaped not only in the tangible results of these four unequal songs, but perhaps more profitably on the unconscious level, authorizing, many years later, the creation of such highly integrated works as the Mallarmé and the Villon songs.

In the meantime the *Chansons de Bilitis* of 1897 provide one of the most moving revelations of the hedonistic, pagan art of Debussy, a reminder that the antique grace and splendour of the earlier *Après-midi d'un faune* was not only still alive in the composer's imagination, but that it was capable of a more remote and therefore a still more poignant spiritualization. Indeed, one may go further and conjecture that Bilitis and the Mallarméan faun are in a sense the illegitimate progenitors of the ultimate glory of Debussyan paganism, *Le Martyre de saint Sébastien*. The disarming simplicity of *La Flûte de Pan* conceals an astonishing ambiguity of associations which, however, compels a minute analysis to disclose some of its magic: the contrast between the ingenuous, syrinx-like melody of the opening and the dark lower register of the mythological flute— so wonderfully suggested in the accompaniment of the persuasive line, ' Il m'apprend à jouer assise sur ses genoux, mais je suis un peu tremblante'; the melting sweetness of honey caught for a moment in the miracle of a single E major chord; the pathetic croaking of the green frogs, sardonically implying the only earthly consequence of the transitory union of Bilitis and her lover; or, at the end, the nervous flight of Bilitis whose mother will never believe that she has spent so long looking for her lost belt—all these swiftly succeeding impressions conveyed by no more than a chord, a run or a few grace-notes are built into a miniature mosaic of ineffable amorous secrets. The less reticent avowals of *La Chevelure,* declared in an undulating and flexible recitative style, recalls the eroticism of the tower scene in *Pelléas*; and the song also takes from Massenet not merely his superficial lyrical elegance, but some of the unashamed exuberance of this misjudged composer, whose spirit, as Romain Rolland has so aptly put it, will continue to slumber in the heart of every Frenchman. It is a dream of ecstatic love rendered strangely archaic by its use of reiterated notes in the vocal line which, however, is allowed to soar into an outburst

of passionate vitality as the poet touches upon the vision of Pan
and Bilitis eternally united in body and soul. *Le Tombeau des
Naïades* presents one of those glacial snowscapes like *Des pas sur
la neige,* sparkling and radiant in its evocation of the crystal
colours of drift-ice and icicles. Where do they lead, these
mysterious footsteps marked out across the snow? Bilitis is
following the lonely trail of a faun to the distant tomb of the
naiads:

Je suis la tra-ce du sa-ty - re.

Ses pe-tits   pas fourchus al-ternent comme des

trous   dans   un   man - teau   blanc

The song illustrates each stage of her slow, shivering pursuit, and the reward at the end is the sight not of any trace of the laughing naiads, but of the infinitely wide and pale expanse of a wintry sky reflected through the great blocks of ice which Pan has hewed from the naiads' tomb. The palpitating fervour of Bilitis, so voluptuously conveyed in similes of honey and gleaming tresses, is marvellously transformed in this music into a remote, icy and colourless disillusionment.

With the settings dating from 1904 of two rondels by the fifteenth-century poet Charles d'Orléans a window is opened on to the Middle Ages and the sombre grace of minstrels and jugglers. The first of these stark, primitive rondels, *Le temps a laissié son manteau,* sings of the decorative embroidery-like spring foliage and the clear shining sunlight welcomed at last after the hard, barren winters of medieval Touraine. Debussy finds the musical equivalent of this fresh and sweet vision in rolling lines of modal counterpoint, studded with bird calls and effects suggesting the luminous ripples of water in sunlit streams. The medieval fourths and fifths of the harmonies, though archaic, contrive to present a translucent brightness of atmosphere, while the lively vocal line threads its way through the sparse texture of the accompaniment like the lay of some forgotten minstrel. The second of these fifteenth-century rondels, *Pour ce que plaisance est morte,* is a forbidding dirge rendered into music by a noble pavane with intertwining arabesques of glorious delicacy and expressiveness. Both the Dorian mode and the whole-tone scale are used in the superbly wrought accompaniment which sometimes trails out into a seemingly aimless melodic line, to be drawn again into the rich formal rhythms of the stately processional dance. 'I tell thee, dead is sweet pleasure,' laments the poet, in overwhelmingly simple terms of resignation; and Debussy endows the ensuing humble elegy with a sense of mingled dignity and pity, reviving something of the faith of the saints who stand carved on the walls of medieval cathedrals:

Ce may, suis ves-tu de

noir;

Piety and profanity are indissolubly merged in this grave and unforgettable musical discourse until, at the very end, a whisper-
ing echo of regret is finally allowed to recall the heavenly music
from the skies and to hint at the sorrow of human failings.

Usually considered of the same period, though less individual
and imposing, are the *Trois Chansons de Charles d'Orléans* for
a cappella choir. They appeared in 1908 and were conducted
by Debussy at a Paris concert the following year. Declaring
that this sole example of the unaccompanied choral style in the
composer's work was prompted by the extraordinary results of
the research undertaken by Charles Bordes and Henry Expert

into the vast and forgotten realm of French Renaissance music of the fifteenth and sixteenth centuries, Léon Vallas shows that two, at any rate, of the three pieces date from the year 1898 and were written for an amateur choir which Debussy conducted at that time at the house of his friends, Mesdames Lucien and Arthur Fontaine. Despite some characteristic Debussyan harmonies, modal counterpoint is used in these somewhat scholastic settings rather in the manner of a Renaissance pastiche than for an original and compelling purpose. *Quant j'ai ouy le tabourin,* with its subtle onomatopoeic effects, has the light dancing quality of Costeley or Jannequin, while the settings of the two beautiful poems, *Dieu! qu'il la fait bon regarder!* and *Yver, vous n'estes qu'un villain,* revive something of the more severe and chaste art of Orlandus Lassus.

Sets of three songs on verses of a chosen poet present the favourite form of the miniature vocal triptych cultivated by Debussy since the appearance of the two series of *Fêtes galantes,* and of which the remaining examples are on poems of Tristan Lhermite, François Villon and Stéphane Mallarmé. The opening song, *Auprès de cette grotte sombre,* of the set entitled *Le Promenoir des deux amants* on words by the seventeenth-century poet Tristan Lhermite, was originally published with the rondels of Charles d'Orléans under the title *Trois Chansons de France.* The elegant and stylized language of Lhermite's classical ode conveys, beyond its allusions to grottoes, fountains and nymphs, a moving and almost romantic sense of melan-choly illustrated in the music with remarkable precision and purity. The persistent halting rhythm of the accompaniment maintains in the background a sombre mood of apprehension as the poet's dreams, reflected in the shaded waters of the grotto, are expressed in a slow-moving chant coiled around the text with a subtle and lingering sweetness of effect. *Crois mon conseil,* the centre-piece of the group, is a touching conceit identifying the chastity of Climène with the fragrant Zephyr:

Sa bouche d'odeur toute pleine
A soufflé sur notre chemin,
Mêlant un esprit de jasmin
A l'ambre de ta douce haleine.

The ingenuous naïvety of the delicate vision is perfectly caught in lacy, harp-like figures, made astonishingly articulate by unexpected and elusive changes of tempo. Finally, in *Je tremble en voyant ton visage,* poet and musician are in such complete harmony in presenting a momentary fusion of earthly and spiritual love that as the last liquid sounds float away beyond the song's horizon they are no longer sounds, but the pearly raindrop or diamond snowflake of the poet's hidden metaphors, captured and held in music's infinity.

The violence of the Villon songs discloses the new aesthetic of the late Debussy. Here is the hardness of outline and dramatic power that we shall find in *Le Martyre* and *Jeux,* and a mordant sense of harmony approaching Stravinsky or Bartók. But these songs are not an example of revolutionary *Zukunfts-musik* in the style of Wagner or Strauss or Schoenberg. At each conquest of Debussy's constantly advancing technique he is somehow compelled to seek the unknown not in the future nor even in the present, but in the remote past with which he is able to identify himself in a spirit of cosmic unity. And I will imagine that, compared with the ethereal Charles d'Orléans songs of only six years ago, these last, medieval ballads of Debussy have the terrifying and endurable strength of Gothic sculpture.

The *Ballade de Villon à s'amye* is a song of the disillusions of love: 'A cank'rous love eating as rust eats iron'; of 'Love like a thief that steals on one unseen'; of the hopeless despair of the debauchee: 'Where shall I turn? Where my dishonour hide?' Let us say that the austere and dignified setting, with its piercing accents of anguish,

Ha - ro, ha - ro,

le grand et le mi - neur !

provides a counterpart, from among the works of Debussy's later years, to the more indulgent Verlaine songs. The piety and simple fervour of the moving prayer to the Virgin Mary prompts a vision of Verlaine too—not the hedonistic Verlaine so frequently set by Debussy, but the repentant Verlaine of *Sagesse* which in his youth he had avoided—while the racy and ironic ballad to the women of Paris with its sly allusion to folk tunes has the extravagant humour of some fantastic gargoyle.

Civilized and sophisticated are the settings, consisting of an endless succession of tiny musical images—some no more

than a trill, an arpeggio, or an unexpected change of rhythm—
of the three poems of Mallarmé, *Soupir, Placet futile* and *Éventail*.
The still waters and pale autumn skies of *Soupir* are clearly
evoked in the music despite the poem's many abstruse allusions.
The 'futile petition' is to the painted princess adorning a Sèvres
teacup and amusingly transmitted by means of a slow minuet
with something of the character of a saraband. Edwin
Evans has suggested as a translation of some of the tantalizingly
obscure lines:

> Since I may not be your furry-bearded lapdog,
> Nor lozenge, nor stick of rouge, nor yet the
> Arch-forfeit of your games—appoint me shepherd of your smiles.

Humour is apparent, as the similes of pomp, in this searching
poem, are delineated in the agile accompaniment with correct
ironic appraisement. The enigmatic poem of the song
Éventail is shrewdly commented upon by Oscar Thompson,
who quotes Roger Fry as stating that the poem's real meaning is
to be found in its revelation of a lack of meaning. 'The fan
opens horizons and closes them. There are red lips but no one
to kiss them. Motion and incident make up a pattern, and in
the fan is symbolized futility.' The playful setting marks each of
the numerous undertones of expectation and disillusionment,
trailing off at the end into a high, gaping B natural and leaving
the listener with a series of philosophical vignettes where the
roles of poet and musician are not merely merged but virtually
exchanged.

Debussy's last song, *Noël des enfants qui n'ont plus de maison*, was
written on the eve of his first operation, in December of the first
world war. The prose text is his own, conceived as a naïve
supplication to 'Le Petit Noël' (Father Christmas) from the
child victims of the invaded territories of northern France.
The colloquial style of the words which is not meant to obscure
the brutal feelings of hate and revenge in the hearts of the

innocent victims—the children pray that there be no Christmas
for the Germans and that Christ should abandon them—is a
curious sequel to the precious lines of the earlier *Proses lyriques*:

> Ils ont brûlé l'école et notre maître aussi,
> Ils ont brûlé l'église et Monsieur Jésus-Christ
> Et le vieux pauvre qui n'a pas pu s'en aller.

The folksong character of this wry carol has the intentional
simplicity of music written for a popular occasion.

CHAPTER XIII

THE PIANO WORKS

IN the eighties and nineties Debussy published several small pieces for the piano, showing not so much a groping towards the individual conception of the keyboard of his later years as the cultivation of pastiches, neatly and elegantly turned out, though not more significant than many other contemporary echoes of Massenet, Borodin, Delibes and Chabrier. For the most part these early piano pieces, from the *Danse bohémienne* of 1880 to the *Suite bergamasque* published as late as 1905, appear to have been thrown off without facing any artistic conflict or seizing upon any element of originality. Several of them were in fact later disowned: according to Vallas, Debussy unsuccessfully attempted to stop their publication. The two *Arabesques* of 1888 are graceful reproductions of the ballet style of Delibes with perhaps a hint of the Schumann of the early *Phantasiestücke*. The *Rêverie,* an orthodox little piece of two years later, was unfortunately published after the appearance of *Pelléas,* when the shocked composer not unjustifiably protested 'En deux mots, c'est mauvais!' The *Ballade* and the *Danse,* respectively entitled in their original forms, *Ballade slave* and *Tarantelle styrienne,* show an influence of the Russian composers, notably Borodin and Rimsky-Korsakov, while the *Valse romantique* and the *Nocturne* are similarly unoriginal, displaying affinities with Chabrier and Fauré, only the shadows of whose spirits, however, pass over these unpretentious essays.

Vallas ascribes both the *Mazurka* and the *Marche écossaise,* for piano duet and later orchestrated, to the year 1891. The former toys with processes of Borodin and Chopin; the latter, commissioned by and dedicated to General Meredith Read, a descendant of the earls of Ross, makes effective use of a spirited Scottish tune supplied by the general, which was to have been orchestrated originally, so it appears, for a brass and reed band. Few of these early piano pieces are heard nowadays. Nor would they easily be identified as the work of Debussy, so studiously do they seem to avoid any of the characteristic harmony of the contemporary songs, still less any sign of the wonderful Debussyan keyboard technique that was soon to be revealed. An exception, so far as popularity is concerned, is the *Petite Suite* for piano duet of 1889 which, having been arranged for small orchestra by Henri Büsser, has an enviable place in the repertory of so-called light music. Its period prettiness recalls the earlier style of Fauré in the opening barcarolle, entitled *En bateau,* Bizet in the *Cortège,* Massenet in the elegant *Menuet* and, as Vallas suggests, something of Chabrier's *Bourrée fantasque* in the final *Ballet,* though the movement quickly reverts to the more conventional spirit of Delibes.

The *Suite bergamasque* is the first indication in these early-period piano works that the composer was willing to submit to the literary and pictorial inspiration which had been so fructifying in the spheres of vocal and orchestral music: the eighteenth century is evoked with less imagination than in the *Fêtes galantes,* though in each of the four pieces of the suite there is a distinctly personal message the stylistic origin of which is not easily discernible. Vallas refers to elements suggesting a Mediterranean Grieg, a more sentimental Saint-Saëns, a more subtle Massenet. Clearly the *Suite bergamasque,* almost alone among the pieces so far considered, may claim attention as a work of transition, if not actually as an achievement of minor emancipation, for it contains none of the conventionality which had up till then fettered the composer's efforts. The F major *Prélude* has an abundance of lyrical ideas and a freedom of form that is nevertheless wholly convincing. The diatonic harmony, despite some arresting modulations, is, however, still orthodox. The *Menuet* similarly displays much freedom and spontaneity within the accepted tonal framework. If the famous *Clair de lune,* more of a monochrome than any other of the moonlit scenes we have so far considered, defines for the first time at the keyboard something of the Debussyan atmosphere, its too satisfying popularity unfortunately appears to have damped curiosity among the uninitiate concerning any of the composer's subsequent works. The final movement, *Passepied,* is a sophisticated pastiche of an eighteenth-century dance, not dissimilar, proportionately speaking, from the more fashionable pastiches of Stravinsky's *Pulcinella.* A sidelight on the significance of this final example of the youthful piano works is provided by the fact that Debussy originally intended the *Suite bergamasque* to include the two magnificent pieces of his maturity inspired by eighteenth-century scenes, namely *Masques* and *L'Isle ioyeuse.*

The neglected *Fantaisie* for piano and orchestra of 1889 is actually a conventional concerto in three movements which was publicly performed in France and England only after the composer's death. The original performance, planned in 1890 under the conductorship of Vincent d'Indy, had been cancelled by the young composer's prompt and high-minded action in withdrawing the parts from the stands after the first rehearsal. With the finale, it appears, he was dissatisfied, and rather than allow himself to be goaded into accepting a performance of a truncated version of his work, he refused permission for the *Fantaisie* to be played either at this concert at the Société Nationale or at any other public concert during his lifetime. This finale is built in the variation form and contains many a hint of the style of the *Nocturnes.* The first movement is more or less orthodox in form, and shows affinities with both Fauré and d'Indy. The first subject of this movement serves, as the opening theme of the string Quartet, as a germinal theme for the whole work. The second movement is not far removed in structure, harmony and melodic charm from the slow movement of the string Quartet. The piano writing does not yet disclose any of the magic of the Debussyan keyboard. Indeed the *Fantaisie* is an almost exact counterpart of the Quartet in the early stages of the composer's evolution and leading, in the orchestral sphere, to *L'Après-midi* and, among the piano works, to *Pour le piano* and the *Estampes*.

The suite *Pour le piano* is generally considered to display the original elements of Debussy's keyboard style and, indeed, how alive, suggestive and interesting in detail the writing suddenly becomes! The opening *martellato* theme of the *Prélude*, reiterated with an obsessional insistence in vividly contrasted registers, the bolder harmony using the whole-tone scale and the aerial, harp-like cadenza at the close—here are unmistakable signs that the composer was no longer content to think of the stereotyped melodies, patterns or chords that fall under the ten fingers but that, like Chopin, he was beginning to imagine the evocative power of the instrument, of the music not so much heard in the ceaseless tumbling of notes out of the box of strings and hammers, but of that other music which the pianist's hands must be almost afraid to capture. The shades of Couperin and Rameau inhabit the little score, and so do memories of the Javanese *gamelang* which will remain to haunt the composer in an inexhaustible gallery of exotic mirages. Much the same may be said of the companion piece in this suite, the brilliant *Toccata*, in which the underlying classical and oriental sources of inspiration are perhaps even more artfully intertwined. The archaic *Sarabande* with its grave succession of sevenths and ninths reproduced on different degrees of the scale has provoked much discussion in regard to the origin of this procedure in the *Sarabande* of 1887 by Erik Satie. In acknowledging the innovation of Satie's earlier work, let us be content to watch it acquire an added beauty and significance under the shadow of Debussy's undoubtedly more accomplished and finely chiselled essay in archaic evocation.

The logical development of the tentative orientalism of *Pour le piano* is triumphantly displayed in *Pagodes,* an astounding musical illusion, said to have been inspired by the composer's conception, following the music he had heard played by Javanese and Cambodian musicians in Paris, of the pagodas of Juggernaut and the porcelain tower of Nanking.   The exoticism of this most imaginative piece was something entirely new in music.   It seemed then, and seems to us still to-day, far more authentic and realistic than the romantic exoticism of Rimsky-Korsakov or Strauss, and it was able to reveal the possibility of a new and potent influence in European music, the supreme example of which is Stravinsky's *Chant du Rossignol.*   The main theme of *Pagodes,* built on the oriental five-note scale,

délicatement et presque sans nuances

is ingeniously thrown into relief by a cunning manipulation of harmonies, emphasizing the dissonances of seconds and fourths, and at the close, as deep bell-like effects emerge from beneath a ceaseless tinkling of runs over the black notes, a vision appears to be built out of music of the glitter of glass palaces and of little oriental idols in crystal.

The imaginative genius of Debussy was released and, in *Soirée dans Grenade,* the second movement of the suite entitled *Estampes,* a similarly authentic fantasy is presented of scenes unknown to the composer in reality—the fantasy and illusion of Spain. As Rimbaud, while still a boy, had written some of the most beautiful poetry of the sea, which in fact he had not yet seen, and Schubert some of the most moving love music without, so far as we know, having lived through any corresponding experience in his personal life,[1] so Debussy was similarly able to give a greater intensity of life to his world of dreams than any earthly or material vision could have commanded. Debussy's knowledge of Spain was limited to a day at San Sebastian, yet this voluptuous nocturnal music, evoking the languid strumming of guitars and the sinuous rhythm of the habanera, manages to conjure up impressions so genuine and so accurate that no less an authority than Manuel de Falla declared them to represent 'the images in the moonlit waters of the *albercas* adjoining the Alhambra.' Alone among earlier works of Spanish associations, Ravel's *Habanera* appears to have prompted the seductive magic of these pages. The imagery of *Jardins sous la pluie,* into the delicate tracery of which are woven the children's songs *Do, do, l'enfant do* and *Nous n'irons plus au bois,* suggests the merging effects of light produced by the April sunshine and showers of a northern landscape—the musical equivalent, let us say, of a Pissarro or a Sisley. 'Modulations change momentarily the look of the sky,' conjectures Oscar Thompson, 'the lawn is drenched, the wind

[1] See *La Musique consolatrice* by Georges Duhamel, who amusingly quotes the remark of Massenet: 'La vie de Schubert, si remplie d'amitié, est si pauvre d'amour que l'on cherche une femme autour de soi pour la lui mettre dans son lit.'

rises, the sun comes through the mist, away goes the cloud, the grass seems jewelled in the sunlight.' And he adds, with distinguished modesty before the little masterpiece: 'It is for the listener, of course, to say whether this is what the music conveys to him and whether through it all runs a hint of regret for vanished happiness, as expresssed in the plaintive character of the children's songs; or whether here is only a lively exercise for the fingers, fashioned in what by this time had become definitely a Debussy style.'

With the *Estampes* the piano not only leaves the practice-room and the drawing-room; it even leaves the concert-hall. It becomes the poetic instrument of a wandering imaginative spirit, able to seize upon and define the soul of far-off countries and their peoples, the ever-changing beauties of nature, or the innermost aspirations of a childlike mortal observing the fresh and most moving wonders of creation. *Reflets dans l'eau,* the initial piece of the first series of *Images* (a generic title that might well be applied to nearly all Debussy's works), mirrors among its liquid sonorities and floating chords a dark mood of dismay, recalling, during its more powerful moments, the mysterious sea music of *Pelléas.* The muffled thuds of three notes, overlaid and blurred at the opening with drowsy harmonies,

are symbolically echoed throughout the score like the successive dropping of stones into the pool's unfathomable depths, the encircling and widening ripples pursued in undulating arpeggios to the water's edge, and beyond. *Hommage à Rameau,* written when the composer was engaged upon the revision of that master's *Les Fêtes de Polymnie,* is a tribute, not, as one might be led to expect, in the form of a pastiche, but of a majestic sarabande of classical proportions and development. It is transformed, however, into a thoroughly Debussyan conception by the use of augmented fifths, the repetition of common chords and, at the close, a curious sort of triangular effect, of almost geometric abstraction, produced by a figure in open octaves. In *Mouvement,* a piece of extraordinary animation in the *moto perpetuo* style, something of the gawky humour of Stravinsky or Bartók is foreshadowed. There is a marionette-like jocularity, suggesting *Petrushka,* as the pitiful little ugly themes are juggled through the running triplets until, with a masterly touch of the unexpected, the fanciful scene—a Punch and Judy show with the puppets in violent dispute?—appears to be suddenly extinguished in a few laconic bars of glinting irony.

Before approaching the later *Images,* it is worth while observing the resemblance between *Mouvement* and the exhilarating *Masques* of 1904. This impetuous toccata, inspired by the antics of Scaramouche, reveals a chain of ideas in Debussy's work originating with the early song *Mandoline* and fertile still in the slow movement of the late cello Sonata: the *Commedia dell' arte,* as illustrated in French eighteenth-century painting, seems continuously to have held a peculiar fascination for Debussy, authorizing music that was later able to divine the soul of toys and puppets in *Children's Corner* and in *La Boîte à joujoux.* Of the same period, *L'Isle joyeuse,* illustrating the picture of Watteau, *L'Embarquement pour Cythère,* is a brilliant essay in virtuoso writing, not dissimilar from the virtuoso style of Ravel and frankly suggestive of orchestral timbres. The work has, in fact, been most successfully orchestrated, with the composer's approval, by the Italian conductor Bernardo Molinari.

Three pieces constitute the second set of *Images* of 1907: *Cloches à travers les feuilles, Et la lune descend sur le temple qui fut* and *Poissons d'or.* Set out on three staves, the writing achieves both greater complexity and lucidity, the harmonic refinements are still more subtle and the arabesques still more expressive in detail. The first piece appears to be a study in the contrasts of clear and muffled sonorities, designed to convey the slumbrous atmosphere of an autumn landscape with an illusion of distant chimes emerging from beyond the screen of rustling leaves. In the second, with its faint, tenuous outlines and its gravely monotonous chant, Debussy was obviously experimenting with the maximum variety of contrast to be obtained from the softer vibrations of the piano strings—the curious title reminiscent of Chinese poetry was given by Louis Laloy after the work was written. Finally, *Poissons d'or* is a piece of rich fantasy inspired, according to Vallas, by the contemplation of a piece of oriental lacquer. The bright, sparkling sonorities of the piano are principally explored in this study—for a technical study it is, despite the poetry of its imagery—and all the effects to be obtained between contrasts of trills and tremolos with the playful clicking of grace-notes and swiftly leaping arpeggios. The

Debussy

descriptive interest of this vivacious scherzo is no less arresting: Thompson indicates in the animated scene 'the flash of sunlight and the gleam of moving fins.'

The six pieces forming *Children's Corner,* touchingly dedicated to Debussy's daughter Chouchou 'with her father's apologies for what is to follow,' are exquisite miniatures of artistic finish and sensitive psychological insight. Chouchou, whose name was Claude-Emma, as opposed to her mother's Emma-Claude, was not more than five at the time of their composition,[1] and the titles of four of the pieces were prompted by the child's toys— Jumbo the Elephant (Debussy mistakenly calls him Jimbo), the Doll, the cardboard Shepherd and the Golliwog. Chouchou's English governess, who was until recently living in London, was apparently responsible for the English titles, some of which are not a little quaint (*The Snow is dancing* and *Serenade for the Doll* which should be either *Serenade to the Doll* or *The Doll's Serenade,* for, as it has been pointed out, the doll is not the serenader but the one serenaded).

The first piece, *Doctor Gradus ad Parnassum,* is an amusing parody of Clementi, not on this composer's worthy and indispensable exercises themselves, but on a child's typically bored manner of ploughing through them, starting out with perky confidence but soon distracted, ready to yawn and to sulk, until, as practice time is almost over, the last bars are hurriedly scamped and the piano-lid shut down with a resounding bang. The stuffed elephant which is being put to sleep in *Jimbo's Lullaby* is obviously being told a fairy tale. '*The Thousand and One Nights,*' says Léon Oleginni,[2] and, with no apparent reason for doubt, he goes on to show how 'the good-natured

[1] She died in 1919, the year following the death of her father, at the age of fourteen, during an epidemic of diphtheria. Some moving letters from the child, written shortly after Debussy's death, were published in the Belgian magazine *Terres latines* (March 1936).

[2] *Au cœur de Claude Debussy,* Paris, 1947.

animal consents to hobble through a clumsy dance on the knees of the astonished child. Soon they are seen sharing a glimpse of their imaginary world, and as child and elephant fall off to sleep, blissfully rejoining the fantasies they have just evoked, two magical notes mark with inexpressible wonder the transition from reality to illusion.' The seemingly innocent *Serenade*, superficially reminiscent of Massenet or Gounod, has subtle psychological undertones suggesting the fiction of a child's authority over her inanimate doll with its set smile:

The exquisitely delicate vignette, *The Snow is dancing*, hints at signs of sadness and solitude in a child's heart as it watches for the first time from its nursery window the ceaseless fall of snow-flakes enveloping the familiar landscape. The toy shepherd, dispatched into the depths of nature, appears to awaken a childish wonder in unseen visions of nymphs and naiads as he listens to the remote and mysterious echoes of his pipes. And finally, the *Golliwog's Cake Walk,* with its impertinent hint at the Prelude of *Tristan,* presents an hilariously comic caricature (note the guffaws of the *sforzandi*) in which, as M. Oleginni suggests with so much perspicacity, Debussy intends to convey that the child has glimpsed some of the artificiality and preten-tiousness of real life. Indeed, the authenticity of each of the little pieces of *Children's Corner* resides precisely in the fact that they so wonderfully confront the minds of the child and the artist, discovering and tracing in the one and the other the thin, almost imperceptible border-line between reality and fantasy.

It is at this point that I think one may discern the several planes on which Debussy's mind was working in attempt to integrate his many psychological, artistic and technical dis-coveries. The innocence of *Children's Corner* conceals, as we have seen, an intimate communion with the child mind, the source, as modern psychology teaches, of all artistic experience, which he was to explore in much more elaborate fashion in the ballet, originally written for piano, *La Boîte à joujoux.* I do not wish to overrate the importance of Debussy's children's music, but one can hardly doubt that the discipline of perception which its creation imposed upon the composer authorized the more richly introspective poetry of the twenty-four Preludes with their quest of visions as yet unrecorded in music and their endless musing on so many imaginative and symbolical associations. At the same time the unrivalled accuracy and intelligence of the craftsman compelled a severely practical approach to the keyboard, in which we see the composer analysing and defining the vast complexity of the instrument's purely physical properties, all of which, ultimately, are to be obtained by the action of ten human fingers upon the piano's unchanged, material mechanism. If the piano was to be transformed into an instrument of illusion—Debussy insisted that performers of his music should imagine the piano as an instrument without hammers—the transformation could only be effected by the closest analysis of touch and vibration, of keyboard harmony and figuration, of the immeasurable scale of contrasts in tone and register—in short by an analysis of all the technical resources of an instrument whose very limitations and defects were to be turned by Debussy into newly discovered virtues. We have, accordingly, the last and perhaps the greatest of the piano works, the twelve Studies, appropriately dedicated to the memory of Chopin, and representing a summary of the composer's entire pianistic creation.

In the two books of Preludes we are escorted on many novel journeys, the focus of Debussy's musical telescope—surely the nearest approximation to the piano of these extraordinary pieces—continuously changing as exotic images are revealed of the Orient, Spain, Italy and (not less exotic for the French) Scotland; as harsh, magnified caricatures are presented of the Victorian music-hall; as legend, prose and poetry are delineated in music; as the mysteries of nature are yet again evoked—the howling hurricane or the swift race of wind over plain; as, finally, the spy-glass having been put away, the artist peers into the primary symbols of notes on paper and keyboard in order to produce abstractions of thirds, whole-tone music and polytonality. The novelty of these musical explorations may have become familiar as other composers have set out on similar journeys, yet the impact on the listener of the Debussyan vision has lost none of its qualities of freshness and surprise, so amazingly does Debussy cut across all the accumulated rhetoric of piano writing in order to probe music's sharply defined realistic associations. Let us make bold to say that the description of the Preludes as realistic is used here advisedly; and, indeed, the term 'Impressionism,' so long associated with Debussy's piano music and not without significance in regard to the obvious aesthetic parallels between this music and the work of the French Impressionist painters, is ultimately misleading, since it is likely to convey none of the minute accuracy of expression which, for both the interpreter and the listener, must after all be the paramount consideration.[1]

On another plane it has been said that Debussy shows himself in the Preludes to be as much a clairaudient as a clairvoyant. His mysterious conception of the tactile properties of music is equally remarkable, and there are pages which might almost bring music to the borders of an odoriferous or even— so completely are we regaled by this music of the senses—a saporific art. 'Les sons et les parfums tournent dans l'air du soir,' the line of Baudelaire from *Harmonie du soir,* set in the earlier song of this title and serving again as a title of one of the Preludes, might in fact have been chosen as a generic description of the entire series. So intimate is the sensuous aspect of this music that the impression is created that Debussy did not write the pieces for public display, but imagined the beguiled listener creeping into his confidences and his visions almost unobserved. Here is the mechanical limp and grimace of General Lavine— who was this general whose effigy, so the story goes, was made to perform such quaint antics on the stage of the Folies-Bergère? Here is the mercurial Puck, swiftly vanishing into the depths of the Shakespearean forest, and Pickwick, a caricature of himself, as he appears to the French, knowingly whistling some snatch of a ditty and pathetically sketched out against the background of a comic reference to *God save the King.* Here is an extraordinary Hebridean vision, one of Leconte de Lisle's four Scottish beauties, *The Girl with the Flaxen Hair,* companion to

[1] Incidentally the term 'Impressionism' was sharply criticized by Debussy in its application to his own technical procedures. (See the letter to Durand referring to the orchestral *Images* on page 199.)

Jane [1] and to the well-known *Nell,* set to music by Fauré; and the picture in *Minstrels* of a black-faced pair of acrobats, incorporating a suggestion (according to Thompson) of an old-time Broadway song. The Mediterranean is revisited, and here is the musical imagery of Spain—*La Puerta del vino,* the famous gate of the Alhambra, with its imaginative reference to the Andalusian *cante jondo,* and *La Sérénade interrompue* with its strumming guitar effects and its reminiscence, so strangely transformed, of *Ibéria* (or was it a preliminary sketch?); or a glimpse, from the hills of Anacapri, of the Gulf of Naples, with snatches of a tarantella, a suggestion of cowbells and the steady trot of donkeys picking their way through the mountain slopes. India—an altogether imaginary India, though how original and authentic—is evoked in *La Terrasse des audiences au clair de lune,* the title derived from a contemporary French description of the 1912 Indian Durbar; and in *La Cathédrale engloutie,* the tolling bells of the legendary cathedral of Ys, said to rise from the sea off the coast of the ancient Breton province of Armorique. And beyond, in the realm of mythology, what else does this gallery of musical mirages still not embrace? The mother-of-pearl *Ondine* (to borrow Oscar Thompson's apt metaphor) is brought to life, and so are the Debussyan fairies who, as we are certainly prepared to believe, are at least the exquisite dancers of the prosaic title. Two ancient funereal urns from Canopus inspire a meditative reverie, and the sculptured bacchantes surmounting a Greek pillar, the noble *Danseuses de Delphes.* Delicate sketches of mists, heathland and snowscape are among the

[1] An early song by Debussy, sung by Claire Croiza in England before the war. There was also an early setting for voice and piano of *La Fille aux cheveux de lin*:

> Sur la luzerne en fleurs assise
> Qui chante dès le frais matin?
> C'est la fille aux cheveux de lin,
> La belle aux lèvres de cerises . . .

nature studies, and the ambiguous *Voiles* (sails or veils, we cannot be quite sure) would seem almost deliberately to leave the listener pondering upon an associative imagery of his own. As a conclusion to the two books something more than a prelude is presented in the virtuoso, Lisztian rhapsody of *Feux d'artifice,* a brilliant portrayal of the fireworks of a 14th July celebration with, at the close, a fleeting reference to the *Marseillaise* as the wonder-struck revellers finally disperse and disappear like the good-natured bumpkins who are somehow fatalistically compelled to depart from the fair-scene of *Chevaux de bois.* But where do these revellers disappear? Those solitary footsteps marked out in the desolate snowscape of *Des pas sur la neige,* where do they lead? And the fleeting wind, vanishing into thin air in *Le Vent dans la plaine,* into which mysterious world of the beyond has it entered? Or the mercurial Puck, or the fragile *Fille aux cheveux de lin,* or even the shadowy Mélisande —where, as the last sounds float to the top of the mind, do these lingering illusions vanish? Debussy takes music to the borders of mystery, and discovers there—well, what does he discover? Not the future of an illusion, but the illusion of an illusion, the dream of a dream, the phantom-like, almost unheard notes of the music of silence. And the miraculous circle is closed 'and nothing has ever been heard, and nothing has ever been seen:

> Tout fuit,
> Tout passe,
> L'espace
> Efface
> Le bruit.' [1]

The parodies, bugle calls and miniature battle scene of the children's ballet, *La Boîte à joujoux,* bring us back to the material world, or rather to those fanciful marionettes of the

[1] See Vladimir Jankélévitch, *Debussy et le mystère,* Neuchâtel, 1949.

material world whom we had seen in *Children's Corner*. The scenario, by André Hellé, presents a triangular love story among marionettes who, somewhat in the manner of the scenario of *La Boutique fantasque,* inhabit not the Derain shop of the Diaghilev ballet, but the large, old-fashioned toy-box of the composer's daughter. 'Toy boxes,' Hellé explains in the published preface to the score, 'are really towns in which toys live like real people. Or perhaps towns are nothing else but boxes in which people live like toys.' It is in this paradoxical spirit that Debussy's pointed and provocative score is conceived. His aim, he explained, was to achieve effects of striking and natural simplicity, to endow the puppets with an appropriately burlesque character and at the same time to display, as he amusingly writes in a letter to Durand, 'that the soul of a doll does not readily tolerate the kind of clap-trap so many human souls put up with.' The *Leitmotiv* technique, the Wagnerian associations of which were considered by Debussy to be so needlessly naïve, is used with much delicacy and humour to underline the parody of the three principal characters; musical-box effects, folk tunes—even a Hindu chant and themes from *Carmen* and *Faust*—are good-humouredly guyed; and both scenic and psychological evocation is conveyed with a sensitiveness showing how far Debussy was prepared to travel in the world of child-fantasy since the companion work of *Children's Corner*. The music accompanying the entrance of a toy English soldier is reminiscent of the *Golliwog's Cake Walk* and, appropriately, is a satire on the band music, heard by the composer in London, of the Grenadier Guards. Other memorable pages illustrate the riotous battle between soldiers and punchinellos, their ammunition, as we clearly hear in the score, consisting of nothing more dangerous than dried peas; or reveal the tender love-music of the soldier and the doll and, in the final tableau, the doll's ironic pathos. Twenty years later she is now comfortably settled with her soldier husband (turned park-keeper) and the mother of a large family, though understandably enough she can no longer go through the steps of her attractive little dance. Shrewdly commenting on human vanity, Debussy makes her sing the tune of her dance in a halting, cracked voice.

The last piano works, the extraordinary two books of studies, were written in 1915 in the short space of a few months or even weeks (we cannot be quite sure). Debussy was by this time extremely ill. His life was menaced by the advancing inroads of cancer and he had been, moreover, both morally and materially severely stricken by the upheavals of the war. The composition of these wonderful pieces under such conditions was a triumph of idealism, all the more remarkable since, as we have seen, so many long years of patience and waiting had been lived through before (in *Pour le piano*) even the first glimpses of the Debussyan piano style could be made apparent. But the reward for so much travail was not to be withheld, and perhaps Debussy was more conscious of this final triumph of idealism and independence represented by the studies than might be imagined. So much, at any rate, may be inferred from the published preface in which, under the guise of giving advice to his interpreters on matters of fingering—any indication of fingering is purposely omitted—he concludes with an enthusiastic endorsement of the saying: 'If you want a thing well done, do it yourself.'

The Studies do, in fact, present a synthesis of the manifold aspects of Debussy's original and independent conception of the piano. The first study, *Pour les cinq doigts,* opens with something of a burlesque on Czerny, the amusing evocation of the simple five-finger exercise soon to be made the subject, however, of a highly organized and elaborate fantasy. Seen in its relation to earlier experiments, this first study is the logical development and extension of *Doctor Gradus ad Parnassum*. The study in thirds similarly develops the technique of the Prelude *Les Tierces alternées.* The study in fourths with its fluid sense of tonality suggests the harmonic experiments of Bartók, and the one in sixths recalls something of the spirit of Chopin (though how transformed!). The tremendously difficult fifth study, in octaves, is a Debussyan vision of the style of the *Valse caprice,* and the final study of the first book, *Pour les huit doigts,* is an extraordinary virtuoso piece of vivacity of which the predecessors seem to be both *Mouvement* (from the *Images*) and *Le Vent dans la plaine.*

In the first three studies of the second book the keyboard resources of chromaticism, of ornamentation and of repeated notes are in turn explored, suggesting earlier explorations in certain of the preludes (*La Sérénade interrompue* and *Les Fées sont d'exquises danseuses*) and more especially the *Six Épigraphes antiques* for piano duet of 1914. The study in contrasted sonorities (*Pour les sonorités opposées*) presents the widest range of effects to be obtained both from the contrast of registers and variety of tone; while the eleventh study, strangely entitled *Pour les arpèges composés,* shows the composer experimenting with illusions of chords completely disintegrated, as it were, and reformed in lacy arpeggios. In the final study, *Pour les accords,* these chords are displayed in the stark outlines of concrete reality, or, let us say, they are rather chords of iron brutality hammered out of the keyboard to form one of the most powerful examples of modern piano music, reaching far beyond the Debussyan art of illusion to something approaching the hard clarity of the later neo-classical style of Stravinsky. The limits of Debussy's art are wrenched apart in this study, and the conception is established of the piano as a percussive instrument, the instrument of the piano works not only of Stravinsky, but of Bartók and of Hindemith.

Eventually, as the end is reached of this gallery of poetic musings, with its myriad associations and memories so miraculously wrought out of the unpliable mechanism of hammers and strings, with its bold visions too, as we may see in the Studies, of the pianistic art of a future generation — eventually the creation of the Debussyan piano stands out, like the creation of the Chopin piano, as a unique artistic phenomenon in the history of music, radically changing the musician's whole conception of what the instrument can be made to convey. The instrument Debussy created is unique technically, and it is unique imaginatively. More than that, the quality of uniqueness extends, after the early uncertain essays, to almost each individual work. And even beyond the Studies, in the *Six Épigraphes antiques* for piano duet, a worthy pendant to the earlier *Chansons de Bilitis,* or the dramatic portrayals of the first world war in the suite for two pianos, *En blanc et noir,* the quest goes on of still unexplored provinces of the imagination, in a manner comparable only to the explorations of Beethoven's late works. For like Beethoven, Debussy knew that the burden of the explorer is that the promised land is never reached, and that each discovery, miraculous as it may be, is yet another of music's imperishable illusions.

CHAPTER XIV

THE CHAMBER WORKS

THE songs show Debussy to be the poet's musician, and many of the piano works the painter's musician. He is seldom the musician's musician, at any rate not in the sense that he wrote works deriving inspiration from the technical resources of music alone. With his abhorrence of professionalism, his great service was to bring music out of its own isolated world into a wider world where painting, literature and music interact on each other freely.[1] In the realm of absolute music, therefore, we see the composer confronted with something like the skeleton of his imaginative soul—the bare bones of his art, so to speak, which we have already seen uncovered in such works as

[1] The well-known letter from Mussorgsky to Stassov would express Debussy's feelings exactly. 'Tell me,' Mussorgsky asks, 'why, when I listen to the conversation of young artists, painters or sculptors, I can follow their thoughts and understand their opinions and aims, and I seldom hear them mention technique, save in certain cases of absolute necessity? On the other hand, when I find myself among musicians I rarely hear them utter a living idea; one would think they are still at school; they know nothing of anything but technique and shop-talk. Is the art of music so young that it has to be studied in this puerile way?' (Translation by Gerald Abraham, *Studies in Russian Music*.)

the *Fantaisie* and the Studies.   In these works, as in the Quartet and the three Sonatas of his last years, an abstract conception of form was the original source of inspiration, and it is instructive to see how Debussy is attracted first to the cyclic form and later, during the years of his maturity, to a revival of the form of the eighteenth-century French suite.

The use of the cyclic form in both the *Fantaisie* and the Quartet may have been prompted in the first place by the examples of César Franck, but one can hardly ignore that, any influence of Franck apart, there was also in Debussy's musical nature a predisposition to a form in which more significance should be attached to the recurrence and transformation of motives than to their contrast and logical development.   Risking a generaliza- tion, one may say that, on the one hand the cyclic form, adapted as it is to Debussy's needs, provides for the expression of an obsessional, imaginative art; while on the other hand, the sonata forms as they have been used chiefly by the German romantic composers, allow for an expression of music's more intellectual aspects.   When Debussy exhausts the possibilities of the cyclic form he turns, in the late sonatas, not to the traditional forms which Saint-Saëns, d'Indy and Fauré had still been able to use in an original manner, but to a new conception of the forms of the seventeenth- and eighteenth- century masters—Couperin, Leclair and Rameau.   Only once, in the piano and violin Sonata, the last of the chamber works, does he toy with the orthodox sonata form, and then in an experimental manner which must ultimately rank this work as an illuminating failure.

The G minor string Quartet—published as 'Premier Quatuor, Op. 10' (this is the only work of Debussy to bear an opus number)—was several times recast before its final version and presents what amounts to a fusion of the variation form and the cyclic form.   Subtle transformations of a single motive predominate throughout the four movements.   The first movement opens with this motive in the Phrygian mode:

In the exposition there are two episodes (not counter-themes) which come and go with the minimum of effect on the general structure since, in fact, they are not to be reintroduced. The main motive appears with prismatic changes of harmony though melodically it remains almost unchanged. Here is an example of one such harmonic transformation:

Only at the very end of the exposition is a second subject introduced:

Replacing the development section is a series of minute
variations, mainly derived from the second subject, pieced
together into a mosaic. Examples of this procedure may be

seen in these two short extracts showing the theme on the first violin:

One arrives at the final section of this movement, not as in Beethoven, to see a deeper significance in the subject-matter, but to be enthralled a little longer by still further variations, designs and shifting harmonies. The movement ends with a short codetta based on the first half of the main germinal motive.

The second movement, a scherzo in the ternary form of the *Lied,* is one of the most arresting and animated pieces of string writing in the whole range of chamber music. The oriental influences suggested by the Javanese *gamelang,* so readily seized upon at its first performance by the Ysaÿe Quartet in 1893, are still immediately striking to modern ears. The generating theme of the first movement, recast in rhythm and mode, is

l:eard on the dark tones of the viola amidst a wonderfully
delicate pattern of flying *pizzicati*:

The opening section of an intermediary passage is built on an augmented version of the same theme heard on the first violin against a throbbing semiquaver accompaniment on the second violin and viola, while the cello maintains a *pizzicato* bass. This motto theme is subsequently subjected to a series of swiftly changing melodic transformations, the rhythmic animation is intensified into a whirlwind of broken *pizzicato* chords, and the movement ends leaving the listener with an unsuspected variety of macabre and ethereal effects.

Also in the *Lied* form, at any rate in its broad outlines, for the elements still consist of mosaic-like variations, is the beautiful slow movement, suggesting the contemporary score of *L'Après-midi d'un faune*. The technique of transformation is used here with much more freedom. There are moving soliloquies on the viola and cello, and Debussy experiments with the contrapuntal device of imitation. Characteristic of the more static nature of this move-ment with its trance-like mood of contemplation is this passage which is sometimes held to mark the climax of the entire work:

Debussy

170

The finale attempts to convey a synthesis of the preceding movements with the now familiar guises of the generating motto theme re-presented in much the same manner as are the snatches of themes from preceding movements in the finale of the ninth Symphony. Debussy may have been making a concession here to the current conventions of his audience at the Société Nationale where, as Vallas points out, Bach, Beethoven and the German Romantic composers were erroneously held to be the source of inspiration for the new French musical renascence. However this may be, the movement is unmistakably Debussyan in its constantly agile inventiveness. The scherzo version of the motto theme is reintroduced in the form of a fugato (a rarity indeed in a Debussy score) and we are even offered an amusing glimpse of the great instinctive composer toying with the scholastic device of the inversion. But the battle between freedom and convention is won in the end, and, as the movement impetuously drives its way through the too restrained cyclical form, some memorable passages explore still other novel transformations of the original theme. These two examples from the concluding pages must suffice to show the

wide range of invention of this quartet conceived, after all, out of
material amounting to little more than a single theme:

When the work is over, and so many prismatic sensations recede into memory, one is aware of the accuracy of Franck's appraisement of Debussy—'C'est de la musique sur les pointes d'aiguilles' (idiomatically, the split hairs of music or, shall we say, the nerves of music)—an appraisement made doubly apparent, though not in the derogatory sense Franck had in mind, by a comparison of the Debussy quartet with the more broadly sensuous quartet in the cyclic form by Franck himself.

Like Franck, Ravel and Fauré, Debussy left but a single example of the quartet. In an earlier chapter we have seen that, shortly after its performance in 1893, he had contemplated a second example in which, acting on Chausson's criticism of the work, he was going to 'bring more dignity to the form.' According to Vallas, a Belgian newspaper announced that the third movement of this second quartet had actually been finished. Whatever was committed to paper seems to have disappeared, and the same is true of a projected piano and violin sonata on which some work was done in the summer of 1894. In explanation of a reluctance either to complete these works or to attempt any further such essays, Vallas argues that the developments which French chamber music were following under the influence of Franck, d'Indy and Fauré were far from the ideals of the composer who had just completed *L'Après-midi d'un faune*. And indeed, before the individual contribution to chamber music of the late sonatas, we have to consider only a few smallish works in this sphere, written as a result of commissions.

The first of these is a *Rapsodie* for saxophone commissioned about 1895 from Debussy by Mrs. Richard J. Hall, an American patron of the Boston Orchestral Society. Variously entitled, during the several stages of its composition, *Fantaisie, Rapsodie orientale* and *Rapsodie mauresque,* it was finally entitled *Rapsodie* and the score for saxophone and piano was dispatched to Mrs. Hall in 1911. This score, however, was still incomplete. The final version of the saxophone *Rapsodie* was made after the composer's death, in 1919, by Roger-Ducasse, who also orchestrated the accompaniment. Vallas tells the amusing story of its composition:

For the sake of her health this lady [Mrs. Hall] had devoted herself to an instrument which had not yet achieved the popularity it has since acquired, thanks to the triumph of jazz. Wishing, regardless of cost, to build up a special repertoire for herself, she had given various French composers orders for important compositions. Debussy was very dilatory in the matter; he was almost incapable of composing to order, and, besides, he knew very little about the technique of this solo instrument. On 8th June [1903] he wrote to Messager: 'The Americans are proverbially tenacious. The saxophone lady landed in Paris at 58 Rue Cardinet, eight or ten days ago, and is inquiring

174

about her piece. Of course I assured her that, with the exception of Rameses II, it is the only subject that occupies my thoughts. All the same, I have had to set to work on it. So here I am, searching desperately for novel combinations to show off this aquatic instrument. . . . I have been working as hard as in the good old days of *Pelléas.* . . .'[1]

The following year, 1904, Mrs. Hall gave a public performance in Paris of another work she had commissioned, the *Choral varié* by d'Indy. Debussy 'thought it ridiculous to see a lady in a pink frock playing on such an ungainly instrument; and he was not at all anxious that his work should provide a similar spectacle.' The *Rapsodie,* which in its incomplete state was finally presented to the courageous lady unorchestrated (hence its consideration here) is a work of more obvious Spanish or Moorish associations and of only minor significance in a general survey.

Of the year 1910 there are two works for clarinet, the piano accompaniments of which were subsequently orchestrated. The first is another *Rapsodie,* intended as a competition piece for students at the Paris Conservatoire, where Debussy adjudicated at the wind instrument examinations; the other, *Petite Pièce,* was conceived as a sight-reading test. They are both exquisitely written for the instrument and were first performed by P. Mimart, the French clarinettist who appears to have inspired their composition. On the occasion of the performance of the small-scale *Rapsodie* Debussy spontaneously declared that it was 'one of the most pleasing pieces I have ever written.' The tiny piece, *Syrinx,* for unaccompanied flute (originally entitled *Flûte de Pan* and intended as a piece of incidental music to Gabriel Mourey's drama, *Psyché*) is the last of these occasional works. It is a most delicate and expressive conception of Pan's death song.

[1] Translation by Maire and Grace O'Brien.

The three sonatas written between 1915 and 1917 were
originally planned as part of a series of six sonatas for various
combinations of instruments. The first is for cello and piano,
the second for flute, viola and harp (the viola part was originally
conceived for oboe) and the third for violin and piano. A note
on the manuscript of the last sonata informs us that the fourth,
had it been written, would have been for oboe, horn and harpsichord. A much leaner sense of both melody and harmony
marks these three works. This greater economy may create at
first an erroneous impression of impotence; but, as is so often
characteristic of the later, more spiritualized works of the great
hedonistic artists (Verlaine and Stravinsky are other examples)
it is presently seen to represent a purification of the hedonistic
aesthetic, an art not so much to be indulged in as displaying
a new wisdom and a more serene acceptance of an ultimate
disillusionment. On this aspect of the sonatas Wilfrid Mellers
has written with much perspicacity.[1] Commenting upon
Debussy's preoccupation with the symbolic figure of Harlequin,
as exemplified in so many of the works inspired by Watteau, and
noting in particular that the ethereally pathetic cello sonata was
to have been entitled *Pierrot fâché avec la lune*, Mr. Mellers has
been the first, to my knowledge, to discover the fascinating link
between these sonatas and such later illustrations of what may be
called the aesthetic of disillusionment as one may find not only
in Stravinsky, but in Busoni and also in Picasso. 'It is not
surprising,' he contends,

that the more isolated modern artist should see in Harlequin the
divine Fool, a symbolization of his own difficulties and nostalgia; one
thinks immediately of Picasso, while among musicians Busoni wrote
one of his most personal operas around this legendary creature. In
his early work Debussy accepts the mythological pierrot world, the

---

[1] See the chapter 'The Later Work of Claude Debussy' in *Studies
in Contemporary Music*.

world of the Mask, as something intrinsically good, positively valuable; at the end of his life, worn out by disease and the attrition of
war, he begins to see through himself, to see that the Mask and the
Phantoms are not enough, that they cannot be permanently satisfying. . . . He looks back on his life and sees in it the likeness of
a puppet-show, himself, moon-eyed, desiring but perpetually dissatisfied in the mask of Harlequin. . . . This newly won honesty and
self-knowledge finds its manifestation in the consummate felicity of
the technique of the last works, in the consistency of their conventional
stylization. Debussy's Mask and Phantom have failed him; and the
failure is a new start. And so, disillusioned though it may be in
the strict sense, this music conveys an impression not of spiritual
sickness, but of freshness and health.

The declamatory Prologue with which the cello sonata opens
is in the form of a noble soliloquy. The Debussyan intimacy,
so often conveyed in harmonic refinement of detail, is here more
articulate. The score of this first movement occupies no more
than four pages, yet within the tiny framework the cello part
exhibits a constant renovation of melodic ideas, some no more
than a bar or two in length, made to follow each other in the
manner of a narrative. What is this sorrowful tale so eloquently
declaimed? It is impossible not to be aware of reminiscences of
earlier works—*Le Tombeau des naïades* and, even, in the recurrent
triplet figure, of the elementary and long-forgotten second piano
Arabesque. These reminiscences are recalled, however, not in a
spirit of sentimental nostalgia, but rather in the other-worldly
spirit of *Le Colloque sentimental*. A ghostly rumbling, in the
short passage marked *agitato,* provides a dramatic interruption,
and the cello, accompanied only by a few hollow chords, calmly
restates its moving message, lingering finally upon the eerie
harmony of an open fifth.

The second movement is a bitter, almost tragic Serenade in
which the cello is called upon to imitate a guitar, a mandoline,
a flute and even the tambourine. The original *pizzicato* and
portando effects are extremely expressive and leave one amazed

at the vivacious character Debussy was able to impart to this normally slow-moving instrument of the string family. In the last movement, of folksong character, there is a pathetic Harlequinesque semblance of high spirits, interrupted in the course of its hurried pace by this heart-rending passage marked *con morbidezza*. Harlequin is at last unmasked and the artist is faced with the desolation of his solitude.

The longer and more elaborate second Sonata is usually considered the work especially evocative of Couperin, though its classical grace and elegance—those overworked epithets which too easily mark the limitations of French music—are not in themselves the most enduring qualities of the work. In none of the later works of Debussy is the significance more apparent of the beautiful dictum of Vauvenargues, 'C'est la clarté qui nous révèle les profondeurs.' Indeed the clarity and the merciless precision of detail in both the solo and the ensemble writing is so poignantly expressive that the composer was himself forced to declare (in a letter to Godet) that the music he had written is 'so terribly melancholy that I can't say whether one should laugh or cry. Perhaps both?' And he adds: 'The further I go, the more I am horrified by a deliberate disorder, which is nothing but aural bluff, and also by those eccentric

179

harmonies which amount to nothing but flirting with fashion [qui ne sont que jeux de société]. How much has to be explored, and discarded, before reaching the naked flesh of emotion!'

Each of the three movements, *Pastorale, Interlude* and *Final,* presents, in place of thematic development, a series of subtly contrasted arabesques. Themes from the first movement are recalled in the second movement, in the form of a highly developed minuet, and in the finale, in the form of a fantasia. But there is no juxtaposition of so-called masculine and feminine themes, nor, in fact, is there any decided contrast between the movements themselves. Sometimes passages are repeated, but not in the form of a recapitulation. The sequence of ideas is maintained by the similarity of mood. It is a sonata of a single piece, a triptych of a single conception.[1] The harmony is extremely varied. Noting the affinity with Couperin, Vallas draws attention, too, to elements suggesting the monodic style of the trouvères and troubadours, and, in the solo writing for the viola, the *melisma* of Gregorian chant. On the other hand, there are passages of colliding tonalities suggesting the polytonal writing of the ballet *Jeux.*

Though the piano and violin Sonata was written, as we learn from a letter to Godet of 7th June 1917 'only to get rid of the thing, spurred on as I was by my dear publisher,' it nevertheless contains some beautiful pages. The first movement, the weakest of the three, is cast in a more or less orthodox form with subject and counter-subject developed, it must be admitted, without much imaginative resource.[2] Echoes of the Stravinsky

[1] In a letter to Godet of 4th September 1916 an allusion is made which confirms this impression: '[This sonata] recalls a very old Claude Debussy, the composer of the *Nocturnes,* I should say.'

[2] Wilfrid Mellers observes in this movement a fragmentary construction which, in my opinion, is much more ingeniously illustrated in the two earlier sonatas.

of *Le Sacre du printemps* can be heard in some of the bridge passages. The second movement is again one of those Harlequinesque interludes, the last of Debussy's serenades, less mordant than the slow movement of the cello sonata, but with many touches of a tender, benign melancholy. The finale opens with a reminiscence of the first movement and proceeds with an exuberant rondo on a theme recalling *Ibéria*. This theme, the composer explains in a letter to Godet of 7th May 1917 'is subjected to the most curious deformations and ultimately leaves the impression of an idea turning back upon itself, like a snake biting its own tail.' The finale is undoubtedly the most alive and inventive of the three movements. On the whole, however, though the inspiration of this Sonata is clearly on a lower plane than that of the two preceding examples, its place among the later works cannot be contested: it does not mark a return to an earlier style.

CHAPTER XV

THE ORCHESTRAL WORKS

I⊤ is hardly necessary, at this stage, to dwell at any length on Debussy's juvenilia in the orchestral sphere. Several early choral and instrumental works written as examination pieces and preserved in manuscript at the Paris Conservatoire library have been commented upon by Vallas and others, and the general opinion seems to be that apart from an obvious historical interest, they foreshadow little or nothing of the orchestral genius of the composer as it was quite suddenly to manifest itself in *L'Après-midi d'un faune*. These student works include the cantata *Le Gladiateur* with which, at the age of twenty-one, Achille, as he was still called, won the second prize at the Prix de Rome competition; a short orchestral work inspired by Heine's *Intermezzo*; fugues on subjects provided by Gounod and Massenet; and two choral pieces, both entitled *Printemps*, on poems by the Comte de Ségur and Jules Barbier. In 1887, during the sojourn in Italy a third work bearing the title *Printemps*, for chorus and orchestra and inspired by Botticelli's *Primavera*, was completed as the last of the so-called *envois de Rome* which holders of the Prix de Rome are required periodically to send to the French Academy. The original score appears to have been lost in a fire, and the version of *Printemps* known to-day, usually listed as Debussy's first published orchestral work, is actually a reconstruction of the work, for orchestra without chorus, made by Henri Büsser in 1913.

The two movements of *Printemps* are somewhat misleadingly described as a symphonic suite. Especially remarkable is the modal harmony and also a preoccupation with harmony in thirds and ninths which Vallas is inclined to attribute to the influence of *Götterdämmerung*. Wagner, rather than an evoca-tion of Botticelli, seems to have provided the underlying inspiration of the work which, as we have seen in an earlier chapter,[1] aims at conveying a pantheistic conception of spring. There are also passages of a broad, Massenet-like lyricism and sometimes a lingering, unaffected sentimentality recalling the mood of the early Paul Bourget songs. Occasionally a bar or two seems to hint, however remotely, at *L'Après-midi* or even *La Mer*, but in truth the Debussyan character of this charming score is recognizable only with the knowledge of his later works. The form of the two movements consists of several adroitly combined sections and the work concludes with a bacchanalian dance foreshadowing the ecstatic rhythmic vigour of *L'Isle joyeuse*. A curious feature of Büsser's orchestration is the inclusion of a part for piano duet which often doubles wood-wind and string parts and which was probably transcribed from the version made by Debussy himself and published in 1904 for piano duet and voices.

The work of the early Rome years it would have been especially interesting to see is the setting of the comedy by Théodore de Banville, *Diane au bois*. This was begun about 1883, the vocal score having long been in the possession of Alfred Cortot. But we have it on record from Paul Vidal that the music for *Diane au bois* was similar to if not identical with sections of the later *L'Après-midi d'un faune*. A significant fact in this connection is that it was Banville who urged Mallarmé to write *L'Après-midi*, going so far as to supply the younger poet with the theme of his famous poem based on this very play by Banville. All of which would seem to justify ascribing, if not the composition, at any rate the origin of *L'Après-midi* to an earlier period than the years to which it is usually ascribed, namely 1892–4. Moreover, it was of *Diane au bois* that, as far back as 1884, the wise and perspicacious Guiraud had said: 'All this is very interesting, but you must keep it for later. You will never get the Prix de Rome with that.'

The historical work must surely have passed through several stages before reaching its definitive form bearing the title *Prélude à l'Après-midi d'un faune*. As we have seen in an earlier chapter, the work was planned and actually announced for performance under the exceedingly cumbersome title of *Prélude, interludes et paraphrase finale pour l'Après-midi d'un faune*; and since we know that Mallarmé's poem was originally written as a monologue to be declaimed on a stage by the actor Coquelin *aîné*, it might reasonably seem that Debussy conceived his score as incidental music to accompany such a presentation. The publication, however, of a letter (dated 10th October 1896) from Debussy to the critic Henri Gauthier-Villars alludes, however tantalizingly, to the associations of the work as 'the remains of dreams in the recesses of the faun's flute.' 'More precisely,' he goes on, 'the work conveys the general impression of the poem . . . it follows the ascendant movement of the poem and illustrates the scene marvellously described in the text. The close is a prolongation of the last line:

Couple adieu! Je vais voir l'ombre que tu deviens.'

Elsewhere he states that 'This Prelude is a very free interpretation of Mallarmé's poem. It has no pretensions of presenting a synthesis of the poem. It is rather a series of scenes against which the desires and dreams of the Faun are seen to stir in the afternoon heat.'[1] Clearly, then, the wonderful *Prélude* is not, as it had earlier been supposed, the opening movement of a triptych. Though the title may be misleading —*Postlude à l'Après-midi d'un faune* might have been a more

[1] See *Achille-Claude Debussy* by Léon Vallas (Paris, 1949).

appropriate choice—the work may be considered as a musical counterpart of the entire poem. The opinion of Mallarmé expressed in a letter sent to the composer after the 1894 performance was that the score is an 'illustration . . . which would present no dissonance with my text. Rather does it go much farther into the nostalgia and light with subtlety, malaise and richness.'

The clotted imagery and complexity of associations which Mallarmé uses to trace out his apotheosis of sensualism form the inevitable technique of this recondite poet. Emotion is not spiritualized by successions of single images or symbols as in lyrical poetry; Mallarmé adopts almost a psycho-analytic approach in which complexity would seem to be cultivated for its own sake. The obscure poem of *L'Après-midi* reminds one, in fact, of nothing so much as that process which Freud himself describes whereby the pursuit of truth is traced as one might continuously uncover the layers of an onion, ultimately to discover—well, what may we discover? The answer in the case of Mallarmé's eclogue is music—the music which such poetry purports in fact to be, the music not fertilized by poetry, but perceived on the further less conscious side of poetry where, to adapt Walter Pater's famous dictum, 'all art recedes to the state of music.' In this respect Debussy's score stands not, as it seemed to earlier generations, as a challenge to Wagner but as the logical development of the Wagnerian theories—or, let us say, as a supreme example of their humanization. Poetry and music in this score are indissolubly one.

It was once said by Busoni of *L'Après-midi* that 'it is like a beautiful sunset; it fades as one looks at it.' It would have been truer to say that since the work reproduces the essentially fleeting qualities of memory, the myriad sensations of forgotten dreams pass through the score, and that what remain are the inexhaustible treasures of memory's indefiniteness. Predominant in this score, therefore, are the twin elements of Silence and the Unexpected to assist in what amounts to a new musical definition of the unconscious. No sooner has the piece begun than the remote and tenuous flute solo, with its finely calculated contrasts of inertia and improvisation, symbolizes the ravishment of long buried sensations made to live anew. A harp *glissando* colours a delicate background of horns and woodwind, and as the mosaic of sensations is being slowly pieced together in these five introductory bars a masterly silence mysteriously renews all these tiny sensations with an unexpected brightness. The strings have in the mean time made discreet entries and so has the second harp on low *pianissimo* chords. In the first ten bars of the work, then, the main elements of the orchestra have been glimpsed, but no instrument has, so to speak, committed itself. Veils are drawn apart to disclose, not yet the poem's voluptuousness, but a hint only of what may still come. Ten bars later, when repeated *crescendi* of the full orchestra seem to announce the faun's truer intentions, Debussy provides an even subtler example of artistic deception by deliberately letting these full-blooded effects languish in the empty, hollow notes of a solo clarinet.

The surprising and for ever novel effects of Debussy's orchestra may thus be followed bar by bar, almost note by note throughout the ten-minute apparition until, in the final bars, two notes on the tiny antique cymbals gleam in the fading dream, and from so many fantastic associations and visions an ordered lucidity is at last established. The miracle of the Debussyan orchestra is precisely this: that the most intricate complexity, the most refined and sophisticated instrumental combinations, are ultimately resolved into music of unassailable simplicity. And this impression is created, I suggest, because Debussy's orchestra is disintegrated in the first place and is then built up anew—timbre by timbre, the composition of the orthodox symphony orchestra consisting not of the so-called families of wood-wind, brass and strings, regimented in solid formation, but as far as possible of individual players called upon for their particular contributions. One may follow the evolution of this Debussyan orchestra clearly enough through its main stages— *La Damoiselle élue, L'Après-midi, La Mer* and *Jeux*. Each time the timbre and character of the contributing instruments are infused with a new spirit; a new agility is released, new tone-colours are brought into prominence, or instruments are made to develop an expressiveness in deep or shrill registers hitherto considered beneath the dignity of musical consideration. The flute, the mythological echoes of which are never far away from any Debussyan score, is made to flash and glitter, or alternatively, to linger on a melancholy phrase as if some unheard music was still to be described. The sharp, pointed, acid tones of the oboe are often apportioned to indicate undertones of irony or sarcasm. The clarinet with its great compass and variety of colour is made to twitter and gurgle in all manner of trills and shapely arabesques. The brass instruments, too, are transformed and regenerated. And how longingly does Debussy dwell on the infinite gradations of the lush horn timbres and how mercilessly accurate in effect is his writing for the strident trumpets! But these are still not more than the outer appurtenances of the orchestra. For Debussy, as for all great orchestrators, the flesh and bones of the orchestra are the strings, and to these he imparts so much suppleness and grace and strength, such a variety of colour in his manner of dividing the constituent groups or in his extraordinary combinations of bowed and plucked effects, that the string department of his orchestra is like some larger-than-life chamber-music *ensemble*, each player alive with a personal message of his own.

In all this Debussy teaches that the instruments of music are in themselves nothing: they are the dead pipes and keys, strings and hammers, handed on to us in their several curious forms which can only be made to live if the spirit of music passes through them, endowing them with gestures and a personality (and ultimately a technique), each time born afresh as the rare spirit descends among us. And so it is that the instruments of Berlioz are hardly the instruments of Wagner, and the instruments of Wagner are hardly the instruments of Strauss. The instruments of Debussy are surely the most magical of all media of music—as a discoverer of instrumental character Debussy is challenged by Ravel alone—and as such, let us admit, the progenitors of most of our mid-twentieth-century instrumental creations.

As the last bars of *L'Après-midi* fade away to rejoin, as the composer informs us, the nymphs' shadows, one is left with something like the amazed questioning of Shelley:

> And what is that most brief and bright delight
> Which rushes through the touch and through the sight,
> And stands before the spirit's inmost throne
> A naked Seraph?

An answer, or at any rate a partial answer, is provided by the score which Debussy completed in the last year of the nineteenth century. Here we leave the imagery of poetic emotional association to discover the orchestral equivalent of visual perception. For if *L'Après-midi* is the blossom of Mallarmé's poem, the orchestral triptych *Nocturnes* is a collateral illustration of the aesthetic of the Impressionist painters. The Impressionist Nocturnes of Whistler are said to have suggested the title, though none of the three pieces recalls to us to-day the canvases of this talented painter so much as those of his French contemporaries. Nor, in fact, can any aspect of this music be properly described as nocturnal. On the contrary, each of the three pieces is remarkable for the manner in which a sense of luminosity is evoked. To my mind, it is music which is able to convey the precise equivalent of the play of light in Impressionist painting—the soft, whitish-grey light of the Île de France, as in *Nuages,* and in Monet; the dappled, southern light with its fierce contrasts and blinding freshness, as in *Fêtes,* and in Renoir; and the whole universe of light, as in the seascape *Sirènes,* and in Turner. The composer has himself provided an often-quoted description of the triptych, which, though it was obviously hastily written and purports only to touch upon some of the more superficial aspects of the score, nevertheless indicates the music's essentially pictorial basis.

The title *Nocturnes* [he writes] is to be interpreted here in a general and, more particularly, in a decorative sense. Therefore it is not meant to designate the usual form of the nocturne, but rather all the various impressions and the special effects of light that the word suggests. *Nuages* renders the immutable aspect of the sky and the slow, solemn motion of the clouds, fading away in grey tones lightly tinged with white. *Fêtes* gives us the vibrating atmosphere with sudden flashes of light. There is also the episode of the procession (a dazzling fantastic vision) which passes through the festive scene and becomes merged in it. But the background remains persistently the same: the festival, with its blending of music and luminous dust, participating in the cosmic rhythm. *Sirènes* depicts the sea and its countless rhythms and presently, amongst the waves silvered by the moonlight, is heard the mysterious song of the Sirens as they laugh and pass on.[1]

Some further details illuminating the origins of the *Nocturnes* are contained in an account of a conversation between the composer and his friend Paul Poujaud:[2]

One day, in stormy weather, as Debussy was crossing the Pont de la Concorde in Paris with Poujaud he declared that on a similar day the idea had occurred to him of his symphonic work *Nuages*: he had seen those very thunder-clouds swept along by a stormy wind; a boat passed, its hooter bellowing. These two impressions are recalled in the dragging succession of chords and by the short chromatic theme on the cor anglais. Debussy also recounted that *Fêtes* had been inspired by a recollection of old-time public rejoicings in the Bois de

[1] Translation by Maire and Grace O'Brien.
[2] See Vallas, *Achille-Claude Debussy* (Paris, 1949).

189

Boulogne attended by happy, thronging crowds; the trio with its fanfare of muted trumpets suggests the former drum and bugle band of the Garde Nationale, beating the tattoo as it approached from afar and passed out of sight.

The shadows of those storm-laden clouds are mirrored clearly enough in *Nuages* as the long, monotonous theme—it is in fact hardly a theme at all, but rather a series of chords spaced out into infinity—passes from wood-wind to strings, subdivided into ten, twelve and sometimes fourteen parts. Clearly Debussy was imposing upon himself here the discipline of sobriety in the choice of orchestral timbres: ' A study in grey,' as the piece in its original form (for violin and orchestra) was described, is still the most accurate metaphor. And if the solo violin has completely disappeared from the score—for there is nothing to suggest that a solo part has either been incorporated or omitted— well then, let us imagine that Debussy came to realize in the end that a soloist would have been too articulate for such shadowy visions and that, in music as in human experience, the accompanying associations of a theme or idea are those that are richest in poetry, sufficing ultimately in themselves. How otherwise can one interpret that amazing passage where, after a deliberately colourless stretch of wood-wind unisons, the string section seems suddenly to disintegrate into a spray of minute *pizzicato* particles? The sharp timbre of the cor anglais is alone retained among these string soloists to recall the mournful but futile sound of the navigator's siren, for futile any such earthly contrivance must inevitably seem amidst this vast, mysterious cloudscape. The details of the scene, at once sombre and luminous, may be followed in unhurried succession as flutes and horns, violin and viola solos, discreetly enter and pass through the score like wisps of clouds; as the 'immutable aspect of the sky' is portrayed by a fragment of the opening theme on one half of the cellos, while the other has a slow chromatic figure, *tremolando*; and as, finally, the flute makes its last graceful appearance, the horns cast a faint glow of warmth, and the piece ends with the softest *pizzicato* against a drum roll.

'One commentator,' Oscar Thompson informs us in an attempt to bring us near the spirit of *Nuages*, 'thinks of Baudelaire's prose poem, *L'Étranger,* and of the Enigmatical Man's reply, when asked what it was he really loved in this world, since he had neither father, mother, sister, brother, friends nor country. "I love the clouds, the clouds that pass yonder, the marvellous clouds."' Debussy was the solitary poet of the clouds, but *Fêtes* shows that he was the solitary poet, too, of humanity—of the bustling, thronging crowds of humanity, of humanity in aspects of irrepressible excitement and profusion. I will not apologize here for quoting the remarkable description of this piece given by Oscar Thompson, who not only seizes upon the instrumental genius of the scoring, but also vividly suggests the work's pictorial connotations, albeit these must be the figment of any poetic listener's imagination.

In *Fêtes* [he writes] is a luminosity of vibration that even with Debussy was to stand alone. Muted brass assumed a new importance in scoring. The harp became something aerial and atmospheric rather than an accompaniment or a decoration. The play of rhythm is no less dazzling than that of instrumental colour. Wisps of melody jostle one another in a tonal *Mardi gras*. The spirit is that of high revelry until there comes upon the auditory carnival a miracle as from another sphere, the visionary procession which the composer likened to 'luminous dust.' There is a sudden hush in the gay swirl of the celebrants; from the harps, drums and *pizzicato* basses comes a marchlike accompaniment above which are sounded faint fanfares, approaching nearer and mounting to a scintillant but still disembodied climax, a *divertissement* in a world of pure fantasy. Muted trumpets and cymbals tingle in the air. As the vision passes, echoing from afar, the dancelike swirl of the opening is resumed, there is an amorous interlacing of woodwinds in the sultry evening air and the music dies away, leaving, like *Pelléas et Mélisande*, the afterglow of 'a dream within a dream.'

191

A disembodied, phantom *divertissement*—here is indeed the clue to this wonderfully illuminated music whose nervous and vivid realism is after all seen to have been one of the most power⁄ ful of Debussyan illusions. This all too human revelry, this joyousness on earth, could ever poet glimpse such mundane content unless to carry it to his more habitable world of unreality? In *Sirènes* a small female chorus is introduced to simulate the altogether fantastic vision of mermaids heard amidst 'the countless rhythms of the waves silvered by the moonlight.' But the wordless song of these mermaids appears to be less the human chant of choristers assembled with the orchestra than an evocation of the very instruments which are called upon to suggest their mystery—clarinets and horns, violins, violas and cellos. The symbolical descriptiveness of this piece is at once so complex and so accurate that pictorial interpretations are almost infinite of one phrase or another, as they gleam and shimmer in the spacious, airy texture. And in a manner of a *tour de force* this mirage of a remote, moonlit sea⁄ scape is built out of the simplest melodic material: for the most part two notes, a tone apart, rise and fall in duple and triple time to portray the monotonous motion of the waves, while the vast expanse and mysterious undercurrents of the sea are built up in all manner of delicate arabesques and changing harmonies.

In Burgundy in 1902, directly after the production of *Pelléas*, work was begun on *La Mer*. It was completed three years later, the rough draft of the orchestral score bearing the precise indication, as if of an historic moment, 'Sunday, 5th March 1905, at six o'clock in the evening.' We have seen that these years had been a critical period in the composer's personal life. At the same time Debussy was facing a major artistic crisis. The flight from Lily Texier, the divorce and the second marriage were external events coinciding with the storm over *Pelléas* and the imperative need to begin once again the penetrating, introspective search. The correspondence with Messager [1] shows clearly that during the summer spent with Lily and her parents at Bichain the composer's childhood impressions were still alive of the Mediterranean at Cannes and of the career, once planned for him by his father, of a sailor. 'I have endless memories which are worth more than reality.' During the subsequent eventful years spent in Paris, but with summers at Pourville on the Normandy coast and in the Channel Islands at Jersey, these memories were pursued and, with the experience of maturity, magnificently reconstructed into a work of quite unforeseen strength and power.

With his characteristic inclination to understatement Debussy describes La Mer, in the form of a sub-title, as 'Three Symphonic Sketches.' The three movements of this great work are not sketches. In a careful study of the composer's styles, Ladislas Fábián maintains that La Mer foreshadows the formal sonatas written during the war. And indeed, from the technical viewpoint of construction a new stage among the orchestral works is marked by La Mer. It shows the adoption of a classical mould earlier rejected. The amorphous form of L'Après-midi or the Nocturnes is replaced here by a structural sequence of ideas resembling the sonata form. Vallas goes so far as to say that these 'symphonic sketches' might very well be entitled Allegro, Scherzo and Finale, and assume the appelation of a symphony. The harmony, for all its extraordinary embellishments, is basically simple. The first movement is built out of three clearly recognizable themes, the first and third in D flat major, the second in B flat major. The Scherzo, opening in C sharp minor and concluding in the relative E major, is actually in the form of a free rondo where the importance of the principal theme is often subjugated to the thematic development of the episodes. The fantasia-like form of the Finale is admittedly more difficult to define, but it is nevertheless remarkable for

[1] See page 87.

long passages of thematic development, and also for the incorporation, according to the canons of the cyclic form, of two themes from the first movement. As opposed to so many tenuous motives in the earlier works, the full-blooded themes of *La Mer* are more sharply delineated and more strikingly contrasted. Sometimes they are set against a piece of intricate orchestral filigree work, or they may be enunciated without adornment as this counter-theme of the first movement, of bold, determined contours, given to the cellos in four parts:

In the last movement the long passage of arpeggios on the upper strings against which the bassoons and basses mark out a dramatic theme punctuated by sharp interjections from the horns, is one of the most remarkable effects in modern orchestration. A climax of overpowering intensity is created when this arabesque-like theme:

persisting throughout the movement in a variety of decorative guises, finally breaks into this tremendous utterance from the brass:

Strength and a new-found vitality are the impressive features of this score. A latent force that for years had been lying dormant is brought to a head. But the suppleness and nostalgia

of the earlier manner are still not far beneath the surface. They
are given a more concrete line and shape. They have emerged
from the nineteenth century into the twentieth. The dreamy
stuff of the orchestra of *L'Après-midi* is now brightly illuminated,
and in those mirages of gleaming spray, of the crash of waves or
of the gurgling backwash are pages as beautiful and as pregnant
with meaning as anything ever conceived by a composer of
music. In recollection, the mind lingers on such pages as a
permanent enrichment of musical experience. That passage,
for instance, in the second movement where the nasal cor anglais
picks its way through a maze of chattering trills, lightened by
the sparkling glockenspiel and triangle: *Jeux de vagues* is the
title given by the composer, though such a teasing, nervous
portrayal can only be symbolical of all that human emotion
knows of agility, malice and vivacity. Most unexpected of all,
and amazing in its grandeur, is the passage at the end of the
first movement, surely the greatest evocation of nature in a work
for orchestra, where the rocking barcarolle rhythm of the strings
leads to those foreboding block-chords on the horns accompanied by eerie harp patterns. Here is not merely a great
pantheistic drama of the sea; it is also the musical equivalent of
a Proustian drama of mankind.

Indeed, we have seen *La Mer* acquire the appeal and significance for our generation of a work such as the Beethoven
fifth Symphony at, let us say, the beginning of the century.
And from all accounts it seems that, like the Beethoven
symphonies, it was more than a generation after its first performance that *La Mer* received anything approaching an
adequate interpretation. Even the performances that Debussy
himself conducted in Paris and London seemed not yet to have
provided the full impact of the work's enduring and prophetic
qualities. The true revelation of *La Mer*, or at any rate one of
its true revelations, came with the unforgettable performances
conducted in the thirties by Toscanini. As Vallas rightly

points out, the work up till then had simply not been under-stood. In more recent years we have seen it used as one of the favourite war-horses of the virtuoso conductor. There is not one *La Mer,* but many versions of the work. So that whatever its authentic quality might have been—and it would be wrong to assume that that quality was specifically French—it has entered, now, a wider, universal world to become, like the work of those few chosen luminaries, greater than it was.

Before considering the orchestral works of the last decade of the composer's life, mention should be made of two unfinished works. Of the incidental music for Antoine's production of *King Lear,* two short pieces of little significance were discovered after the composer's death and published in 1926 under the title *Musiques pour le roi Lear.* One is a Fanfare for trumpets, horns, drums and two harps edited from the manuscript sketch by Roger-Ducasse; the other is entitled *Le Sommeil de Lear* for two flutes, four horns, harp, drums and strings. The 'Egyptian ballet' *Khamma* commissioned by Maud Allan for performance in London was merely sketched out by Debussy and completed and orchestrated by Charles Koechlin. First performed at a concert in Paris in 1924, it has not yet been produced as a ballet. The spectacular scenario by W. L. Courtney and Maud Allan apparently provided little inspiration and the work is essentially of a more immediately picturesque appeal. In a letter to Durand, Debussy expressed his too condemnatory opinion of *Khamma* as 'that queer ballet with its trumpet calls, which suggest a riot or an outbreak of fire and give one the shivers.'

There was much controversy over the early performances of *Images,* the orchestral triptych for orchestra written between 1906 and 1912, and forty years later some controversy still persists. This work consists of *Gigues,* begun in 1909 and completed and orchestrated in 1912 under the composer's direction by his amanuensis André Caplet; *Ibéria,* a three-panelled movement within the larger triptych, completed in 1908; and

Rondes de Printemps of 1909. The second and third movements were originally conceived as compositions for two pianos.
Each of the movements is designed to represent the character
of a country—England, Spain and France—and to this end
they embody folk or traditional songs in a highly original
manner. The *Images* for orchestra, therefore, represent a
development not of the contemporary works of the same title for
piano, as is often stated, but of the earlier piano triptych *Estampes,*
which similarly purports to evoke in music aspects of the soul
and character of countries. In both works, moreover, folkmusic of Spain and France inspire respectively the second and
third movements.

I find it hard, in a revised appraisement of Debussy's work,
to follow Vallas in his opinion that the *Images* were written,
or at any rate completed, albeit with the aid of Caplet, under
pressure from the composer's publisher Durand. 'By formal
contract with his publishers,' Vallas states, 'he had relinquished
his cherished freedom as a composer; the bohemian of former
days, who followed only his own inspiration, had reluctantly
become a bourgeois, a purveyor to the firm of Durand, a kind of
galleyslave of music.' However disconcerting the style of the
Images, at once more acrid and more ethereal, may have seemed
and seems still to those who would have wished to linger in the
more indulgent sensuousness of the Debussyan orchestra, here
are surely no signs either of a work hastily written or of the
large personality of genius constrained in development. That
opinion may reasonably have been expressed at the time of the
appearance of the *Images,* but it can hardly be maintained at this
distance of time. As for the accusation from the same shrewd
critic in his most recent study,[1] that in approaching the age of
fifty Debussy was foreseeing the end of his creative life and may
have therefore drawn on folkmusic from a lack of inspiration,

[1] *AchilleClaude Debussy* (Paris, 1949).

here is manifestly an unfortunate appraisement of one of the monuments of the composer's later years which I feel bound to challenge.

'What I am trying to do,' the composer explains in a letter to Durand written during the composition of *Images,* 'is something "different"—an effect of reality, but what some fools call Impressionism, a term that is utterly misapplied especially by the critics who don't hesitate to apply it to Turner, the greatest creator of mysterious effects in the whole world of art.' The expression 'an effect of reality' surely gives a clue to the paradoxical nature of the work in which well-known tunes are alluded to, usually in a fragmentary form, but are so strangely harmonized or so artfully concealed in the polyphonic writing that only their spirit, so to speak, is in the score, appearing and disappearing in many ironic and gruesome transformations. *Gigues,* originally entitled *Gigues tristes,* itself a contradiction in terms, has a long, plaintive melody in 6–8 time played by the oboe d'amore with which are mingled fragments of another theme, said to derive from a song by Charles Bordes entitled *Dansons la gigue.* I have unfortunately not been able to trace this supposed reference, but there can be little doubt that this second theme, which had been hinted at in the opening bars, is none other than the well-known Northumberland traditional song, *The Keel Row.* The fact that the use of this song in *Gigues* should so far have escaped the notice of any of Debussy's historians is perhaps not surprising, for it is presented in such a deceptive manner and distorted by so many unexpected modulations. Its component elements are so cunningly split up— the song is never heard in its entirety—that *Gigues* might at first seem to be a parody of *The Keel Row.* But once the tragic, Harlequin-like spirit in which Debussy approaches this popular song is realized, the whole piece takes on an extraordinarily weird and grotesque character, foreshadowing works of the first world war years such as the fantastic serenade of the cello

Sonata. Let us admit that this musical portrayal of England is less authentic than Debussyan.

Ibéria, on the other hand, is so completely and authentically Spanish that Manuel de Falla hailed it, with *Soirée dans Grenade,* as an example of all that Debussy was able to teach the composers of Spain about a more civilized use of their own folk-music. The extent to which its composition was prompted or influenced by the piano cycle *Iberia* by Albéniz has been discussed by Vallas and others, and it seems that although the first book of the Albéniz work was known to Debussy when writing *Ibéria,* an instinctive affinity with Spanish folk-music had so often been declared that Debussy would hardly need to seek inspiration from this source. The work consists of three sections romantically entitled *Par les rues et par les chemins, Les Parfums de la nuit* and *Le Matin d'un jour de fête.* The orchestration, with its many arresting percussive effects, is both vivid and suggestive, and the themes used are so unmistakably Spanish in character—Falla refers to the opening theme of the first movement as 'a kind of *Sevillana'*—that they may well pass for the authentic article. In point of fact none of the themes in *Ibéria* is borrowed from Spanish folklore. Yet the illusion is complete. As for the element of buffoonery or parody, which is never far removed in Debussy from expressions of intimacy—and there are many in *Ibéria*—it is inherent in the very nature of Spanish popular music. That pathetic violin solo in the last section so rudely interrupted by the jingling tambourine—how imaginatively a vision is created of some solitary guitarist elbowed out of the way of the thronging crowds! Or the ironic twist given to the pert little theme heard on the wood-wind at the beginning of this section, deliberately guying the soulful music of the slow movement! Or the evocation of 'the intoxicating spell of Andalusian nights,' to use Falla's description of the slow movement—what a vast and varied panorama of the animated Spanish scene is presented in these three tableaux!

Most memorable is the use of three pealing bells heard very softly at the close of the slow movement and gradually increasing in resonance to mark the transition from the atmosphere of a hot, perfumed night to the blinding sunshine of a southern dawn. Inescapable in this score are these stark suggestions of light, colour and animation, as well as of pathos and of caricature, combined to immortalize in music the romantic soul of Spain.

Rondes de Printemps bears an inscription taken from an old Tuscan song called *La Maggiolata*, which Debussy found in a book on Dante by Pierre Gauthier. The inscription runs: 'Vive le mai! Bienvenu soit le mai avec son gonfalon sauvage.' For the third and last time the children's song *Nous n'irons plus au bois* is utilized, and there is also a reference to *Do, do, l'enfant do*. France is the country to be illustrated in this movement, the springtime of France, which is suggested in a delicate, murmurous fashion with many tremolos, trills and glissandos and only wisps of melody vanishing through the airy score. Like *The Keel Row* in *Gigues*, the well-known French round is not heard in its entirety: it is subjected to augmentations and diminutions, it is given alarming harmonizations, so that in the end the whole character of the spontaneous song has been transformed. Or, let us say, that it has really not been heard at all. *Rondes de Printemps* is an essay, not so much in the art of illusion as in the art of laconic understatement. Its rhythmic structure is extremely complex. The rare performances of this movement have unfortunately seldom succeeded in conveying much of its intangible character: if it is to produce an impression comparable to that recorded by the young composers who heard it at its first performance, among them Ravel and Stravinsky, it remains still to be discovered.

The ballet *Jeux*, commissioned by Diaghilev, similarly remains little known. Nizhinsky's scenario aims rather pretentiously at presenting 'a plastic vindication of the man of 1913,' though the story of the three tennis players who, having lost their ball, turn their search into a flirtation scene, is in itself not more than attractively naïve. As a ballet, however, the work achieved little success, either in the form produced by Diaghilev two weeks before the first performance of Stravinsky's *Le Sacre du Printemps* or in the subsequent productions by the Swedish Ballet in the early twenties. Present-day audiences have therefore had no opportunity of seeing this ballet, nor, for that matter, are musicians able to judge the manner in which the score follows closely the precise indications of Nizhinsky. A commentary on each of the episodes of this short but extremely compact score, quoted by Vallas and taken from a programme of a Paris performance in 1914 in concert form, may therefore be a useful guide:

Following a prelude of a few dream-like bars in which a chord composed of all the notes of the whole-tone scale is heard against a high B minor tonic on the violins, the first theme marked *scherzando* and in 3-8 time is introduced, soon to be interrupted by the return of the prelude accentuated by figures in the lower strings. The *scherzando* now proceeds with a second theme. The action has begun by a tennis ball falling on to the stage. A young man in tennis clothes holding his racket high in the air leaps across the stage and disappears. Two girls appear, shy and inquisitive. They have something to confide to each other and are seeking a suitable corner. They begin their dance, first one, then the other, but suddenly stop, put off by the sound of rustling leaves. The young man has been watching them through the branches. They wish to run away, but he gently leads them back, and persuades one of them to dance with him. He even manages to steal a kiss from her, whereupon the jealousy of the other is immediately aroused which she expresses in a mocking dance (in 2-4 time). By this means she wins some attention from the young man who tries to teach her the steps of a waltz (in 3-8 time). The girl at first mimics him but is eventually won over. Her abandoned friend now wishes to make off, but the other, in a slower passage in 3-4 time, retains her, and the three now join in a dance (in 3-8 time) which is built up with much verve until at the climax (return of the 3-4 section) they are interrupted by another lost tennis ball falling on the stage and causing them to flee. The chords of the opening prelude are reintroduced; a few rapid notes slyly steal through the score, and the work is over.

It was this close that gave the composer much difficulty since, as he explained, 'the music has to convey a rather *risqué* situation.' 'But of course,' he banteringly goes on, 'in a ballet any hint of immorality escapes through the feet of the *danseuse* and ends in a pirouette.' In truth, the extremely delicate score which Debussy wrote to illustrate this simple story is a model of diaphonous clarity. The rhythmic variety and the many *rubato* effects surpass even the complexity of *Rondes de Printemps*. As if written in obedience to a dictum of Ravel, the work is complex but not complicated. Very different from its predecessors, it suggests, in one aspect, a Debussyan counterpart of the dawn scene and final dance from Ravel's ballet *Daphnis et Chloé*. Polytonal writing, in which a theme is heard simultaneously at intervals of a minor second and a minor third, contributes to the work's harmonic originality. Some critics see in the audacious harmony of *Jeux* the origin of the polytonal passages in *Le Sacre*. But what is especially remarkable is the pointedness and delight of the orchestration with its ingenious writing for the strings and its lightning effects for quadruple wood-wind. The relative simplicity of the action on the stage allowed Debussy in this final work for orchestra, to produce a *tour de force* of nimble-footed agility and at the same time discoveries of prophetic technical significance.

CHAPTER XVI

THE CHORAL AND DRAMATIC WORKS

DEBUSSY'S earliest stage work—the lyrical scene *L'Enfant prodigue,* written in twenty-five days at the age of twenty-one, and the work with which he won the Prix de Rome in 1884—is usually declared to be predominantly Massenet-like in character, graceful and melodious with many picturesque effects and charmingly and acceptably sentimental. The early months of 1884 saw the first production in Paris of two major operas by Massenet, *Manon* and *Hérodiade*; and Delibes's opera *Lakmé* had been produced the previous year. These character-istic French theatrical works of the 1880s must surely have impressed the Conservatoire student. Moreoever, as we have seen, Guiraud, to whom *L'Enfant prodigue* is dedicated, had been imploring his talented pupil to abjure such originality as might have prevented him from winning the Rome prize. It would seem reasonable, therefore, that this hastily written work was designed not to incur censure from the judges of the Academy, among whom was the far-sighted Gounod. On the other hand, it is worth observing that behind its apparently conventional façade, Gounod was able to discern qualities in the slender work which he did not hesitate to ascribe to genius. And although when Debussy came to revise the instrumentation twenty-five years later he high-mindedly dismissed his student effort as 'theatrical, amateurish and boring,' it nevertheless shows a personal use of the Massenet style, and, as we hear the work to-day, at least as much evidence of originality as of imitation.

After the composer's death *L'Enfant prodigue* was produced as a one-act dramatic work in Paris and London. In this form it appears to have met with little success; and understandably enough, for this 'scène-lyrique,' for three solo voices (Azaël, the Prodigal Son, and his parents, Lia and Siméon), orchestra and optional chorus, doubling the solo parts in the final trio, is actually a small-scale cantata. The libretto by Édouard Guinand provides for a scheme of orchestral interludes, recitatives, arias and concerted pieces, illustrating in uncomplicated verse Lia's distress at the loss of her son, his destitution, his return, the father's pardon and the final rejoicing. The well-known *Air de Lia* displays not only a charmingly lyrical flow of melody but the ability peculiar to Debussy to express dramatic tension by reticence: the more intense the sentiment, the more sparse and laconic the texture, the fewer notes, for either soloists or orchestra. The expression of love, for instance, is heart-rendingly conveyed in the broad opening bars of the aria ('Azaël! Azaël! Pourquoi m'as tu quittée?'), but even more moving is the barren, almost motionless recitative suffusing the lines, 'Douleur involontaire! Efforts superflus! Lia pleure toujours l'enfant qu'elle n'a plus,' with a genuine sense of grief. Here is not merely a reflection of Massenet; a hint, though as yet only a very vague hint, of the tragic element in Debussy's dramatic music is apparent. The two arias of Azaël and Siméon, though much less well known, similarly contain some surprising contrasts of lyricism and dramatic intensity, the former particularly with its notable effects of repeated notes to suggest a mood of hopelessness; while both the recognition and the pardon episodes convey an arresting conception of humility. The short prelude and the instrumental interlude entitled *Cortège et air de danse* are picturesquely sketched out in a style resembling the future *Suite bergamasque* and also the *Petite Suite*. There are, indeed, many conventionalities in *L'Enfant prodigue*— the suggestion of a class-room chorale in the final chorus, the bland arpeggios and unisons in the duo of Lia and Azaël—and one is ready to concede that the work as a whole was primarily designed for academic acceptance. Yet, however unadventurous the mould and idiom, the underlying psychology is not meretricious: the simple fervour of the parable is illustrated in a manner that comes from the heart, and although this short cantata is demonstrably a student work its melodic charm is already more pointed and less superficially seductive than many a page by the irresistible Massenet.

Elements of Franck rather than Massenet and also of *Parsifal,* which the composer had recently journeyed to hear at Bayreuth, are ingrained in the tenuous and sweet setting of sections of Dante Gabriel Rossetti's well-known Pre-Raphaelite poem *The Blessed Damozel.* A host of period associations surround this beautiful cantata of the late 1880s, laid out for contralto narrator, soprano (taking the part of the Blessed Damozel), a small choir of female voices and orchestra. Franck, Chausson and especially d'Indy (who referred to it in 'terms that would bring a blush to the lilies that lie asleep between the fingers of the Blessed Damozel') hailed it as a creation not far from their own ideals: echoes of the Rosicrucian music of Satie, with its obvious parallel in the Pre-Raphaelite poetry and painting of Rossetti, may be heard in the fourths and fifths of the opening bars of the Prelude; while the second of the themes heard in the Prelude, which are woven into the score in the manner of *Leitmotive,* has been shown by Vallas to have been prompted by the *a cappella* chorus in *Parsifal,* 'Durch Mitleid wissend.' Yet *La Damoiselle élue* was, at the time of its composition, and is still to-day, an entirely personal creation, proving that Debussy, inevitably a product of his period, was nevertheless able to transcend it and to discover a style, certainly very different from that of either *L'Enfant prodigue* or *L'Après-midi,* that was to be recaptured and developed only very much later, in *Le Martyre de saint Sébastien.* The bluntly sentimental narrative of Rossetti, describing the transformation of earthly to spiritual love as the angelic Damozel imagines the arrival in heaven of her terrestrial lover' is so sensitively blurred in Debussy's setting, so tastefully and so musically etherealized, that most of the Pre-Raphaelite garishness of the poem is at once dispelled, and we are made aware in its place of that mystical, almost medieval, candour that had in fact originally inspired the aesthetic of the Pre-Raphaelite Brotherhood.

From the manner in which the three themes of the short Prelude are subsequently used they would appear respectively to symbolize conceptions common to *The Blessed Damozel* and to *Parsifal* of redemption, suffering and regret.   As typical of Satie as they are of Debussy, the opening chords:

suggest a child-like vision of Paradise delineated in much the same manner when the Damozel in her solo song describes the aureole around the head of her guileless lover.   The entrance of the female choir is a little marvel of naïvety and innocence: the voices are treated homophonically and create the effect of nothing more than a whisper as they gently evoke the lily-bearing damsel seen from beyond 'the gold bar of Heaven.' Narrator and chorus now proceed to alternate in the form of duet.   The lines are chosen from the first ten stanzas of the poem, but nowhere is one disturbed by the unfortunate mawkishness of Rossetti's lily-bearing and etiolated angels. The translation by Gabriel Sarrazin is commendably free,[1] and

---

[1] The English text published in the Durand edition attempts to adhere to the original, but the composer's intentions are falsified where

in any case Debussy was concerned to find the equivalent less of the pictorial than of the spiritual art of Rossetti. (The same, incidentally, may be said of Vaughan Williams's song cycle on poems by Rossetti, *The House of Life*). The long aria of the Damozel which follows constitutes approximately half of the entire cantata. This is actually a magnificent scena celebrating the joy and peace of sublimation. Recitative and flowing melody are combined, not yet in the highly cultivated manner of *Pelléas,* but with an abundance of lyrical invention sustained by ornate developments of the germinal themes in the orchestral accompaniment. One must go to the Baudelaire songs, particularly to *Le Balcon,* to find, among the earlier works, an example of vocal writing of such intensity. Sublimation and redemption are the themes illustrated, but the hedonist in Debussy is revealed in the beautiful close of the song where the 'regret' motive soars above the setting of the lines

> There will I ask of Christ the Lord
>> Thus much for him and me.
> Only to live as once on earth
>> At peace—only to be
> As then awhile, for ever now
>> Together, I and he.

---

lines of Rossetti's not set by Debussy are printed below the French version of other lines. The lines, for instance,

> Et voilà qu'elle parla à travers l'air calme.
> Sa voix était pareille à celle des étoiles
> Lorsqu'elles chantent en chœur,

are printed below lines, adapted from Rossetti's previous stanza:

> From the fixed lull of Heav'n, she saw
> Time like a pulse shake fierce
> Through all the worlds,
> Shake fierce through all the worlds.

Chorus and Narrator resume their innocent duet, and the work
ends with a short orchestral postscript surely inspired by the
touching pathos of the final words of Rossetti's poem—'I
heard her tears.'

In approaching the hushed and exalted *Pelléas et Mélisande,*
it is a matter of prime historical importance to observe that over
a period of twenty years Maeterlinck's play was prompting a
new aesthetic in the minds of composers all over Europe. An
opera on *Pelléas et Mélisande* had been contemplated by Puccini;
the incidental music by Fauré was written for the production of
the play in London; in England Cyril Scott wrote an overture
bearing the play's title; and the orchestral works inspired by
Pelléas by composers so dissimilar as Sibelius and Schoenberg
suggest that there must have been elements in Maeterlinck
calculated to arouse a new and universal musical consciousness.[1]
The drama of *Pelléas* preaches the fatalistic philosophy that
man's incapacity to escape from the hidden unconscious forces
which determine the course of his life is the tragedy of his
existence. In Maeterlinck's pessimistic view there is only one
certain reality—death. Death hovers over all his plays,
liberating his creatures from their world of dreams. Character,
then, in its stoical sense, as it is displayed in, let us say, the plays
of Somerset Maugham, has no place in the tenuous, shadowy
world of Maeterlinck. On the contrary, the vogue of this
playwright at the beginning of the century was based precisely
on a denial of free-will and leads, ultimately, to the despairing
predicament of humanity illustrated by such writers of our time
as James Joyce, Virginia Woolf or Franz Kafka. The musical

---

[1] Maeterlinck's earlier play, *La Princesse Maleine* (1889), had made a
similar appeal to forward-looking composers, among them Satie,
d'Indy, and Debussy himself, though one conjectures that it was too
early for their projects to materialize. Vallas reveals that in 1891
Debussy went so far as to seek Maeterlinck's authorization to set
La Princesse Maleine.

counterparts of these later explorations of the unconscious mind are Alban Berg's operas *Wozzeck* and *Lulu*; and it is therefore entirely comprehensible that *Pelléas* has been considered, on the one hand as a logical extension of *Tristan* and, on the other, as a musical and psychological forerunner of *Wozzeck*. The wonderful work stands astride the nineteenth and twentieth centuries as the symphonies of Beethoven bridge the classical and romantic eras.

The action of *Pelléas et Mélisande* passes in the imaginary kingdom of Allemonde in a remote and undetermined past. Mélisande is weeping by a well in the forest. Golaud, grandson of Arkel, the king, has lost his way and approaches her. He is a giant compared to her frail young self and she forbids him to touch her. All have done her a wrong; she has fled from far. She will not, cannot tell him any more. Golaud discovers her name and, on condition that he does not touch her, persuades her to come with him. 'But where will you go?' she asks. 'How can I tell, for I too am astray.'[1] Those words, as the two go out, set the mysterious tone of the play.

In the following scene Arkel is informed of their marriage. He does not view it with much approval, but consents to it as a manifestation of fate. Fate, too, compels Pelléas, Golaud's half-brother, to postpone his departure to a friend's deathbed. Some days later, when Mélisande is in the dark gardens that surround Arkel's castle, in which she has come to live with Golaud, Geneviève, her mother-in-law, shows her the light from the sea. Pelléas enters. Then the boat which brought Mélisande leaves the port, and together Pelléas and Mélisande return to the castle.

The second act presents a string of symbolic events. With Pelléas, by a well in the park, Mélisande is playing with her wedding-ring and drops it into the water. 'I threw it up too

[1] This and the following extracts are taken from the excellent translation of the libretto by Henry G. Chapman.

high in the rays of the sun,' she says. In the next scene we learn that, at the moment it fell, Golaud was thrown from his horse, which suddenly, at the stroke of twelve, 'ran like a blind fool straight into a tree trunk.' 'No doubt I fell,' he tells his young wife, 'the horse, I take it, fell upon me; but it seemed as though the woods themselves lay on my body. I felt sure that my heart had been torn in two.' Mélisande tends him and for no apparent reason bursts into tears. What has happened to you?' Golaud inquires. 'Has someone done you wrong? . . . Is it the king? Is it my mother? Is it Pelléas?' 'No, no, it is not Pelléas. It is no one. Oh! I know you can't understand me.' Golaud takes hold of her hands and sees that she has not her ring. She must go and find it at once. 'Ask Pelléas if he will not go with you.' She has not told Golaud that the ring had dropped into the well—the clear and deep well that 'could heal the eyes of the sightless.' She goes with Pelléas to find it in a grotto 'full of very dark blue shadows,' knowing perfectly well that it is not there. Frightened by the sight of three paupers revealed by a flood of light from the moon, she runs away, dragging Pelléas after her.

In the first scene of Act III Mélisande is combing her long hair at a window of one of the castle towers. Pelléas passes and greets her cheerfully. As she leans out to let him have her hand, her hair suddenly falls down by the side of the tower, enveloping Pelléas down to his knees. There follows a sensuously poetic passage rather like *La Chevelure* from Pierre Louÿs's *Chansons de Bilitis*. 'They are here in my hands,' Pelléas sings, 'in my mouth too I hold them. . . . Can you not hear my kisses all along your hair?' Doves come out of the tower and fly about them in the darkness. But Golaud enters, perturbed. 'Stop playing like this out here in the dark. You're children, both of you'; and he dismisses them with a nervous laugh.

In the castle vaults of the following scene Golaud symbolically shows Pelléas the stagnating water from which there rises a stench of death and a chasm of which he sees the 'very bottom.' When they come out on to the terrance Golaud warns his brother that this childish play with Mélisande must stop. He has become fiercely jealous and his anxiety drives him, in the next scene, to question his little son (by his first wife), Yniold. One evening in the woods they seat themselves under Mélisande's window and Yniold says that his mother and Pelléas quarrel 'about the door' and 'about the light,' and that once they kissed when it rained. Golaud can get little out of the child beyond these frightening replies, but when suddenly the window is lighted he hoists him up to spy. Pelléas is there, but still he learns only that they are close to each other and looking at the lamplight.

Arkel is a character of patriarchal nobility. 'An old man feels the need now and then just to touch with his lips the brow of a maid or the cheek of a child, to keep on trusting in the freshness of life and drive away for a moment the menaces of death.' But it is Mélisande who is threatened by death. 'Thou hast the strange mien and errant look,' he tells her, 'of a creature ever waiting for some dreadful doom, in the sun, in a garden. . . .' Golaud breaks into this touching scene to announce that Pelléas is leaving that night. Mélisande had already been told of the decision and had arranged to meet Pelléas for the last time. As she approaches Golaud to wipe some blood off his forehead, he angrily casts her aside. 'Do you see those great eyes?' he says to Arkel. 'I know them well, those eyes, I have seen them at work. Keep them shut! Keep them shut! or I'll close them for many a day.' He catches hold of her feverish hands and becomes hysterical: 'Get you away! 'Tis your flesh that disgusts me!' Then seizing her by the hair he drags her on her knees, calling on Absalom and laughing like an old man. Arkel runs up,

Golaud affects a sudden calm, and the scene ends with Arkel's fine line:

If I were God I should have pity on the hearts of men.

The next scene is again one of those interpolations which rather too naïvely symbolize the fatality of the drama. By the well in the park Yniold tries in vain to lift a rock to regain his golden ball. Then he hears the bleating of sheep, crowding now to the right, now to the left. Suddenly they are quiet. 'Why don't they talk any more?' he asks the shepherd. 'Because they are not on their way to the fold.' The only excuse for this interpolation is that it separates the last dramatic scene from the next, in which Pelléas and Mélisande meet for the last time and confess their love. As the doors of the castle are bolted against them and their fate seems decided, Golaud appears 'at the end of their shadows.' As he draws his sword they embrace desperately, and he falls upon them. Pelléas is killed and Mélisande flees through the wood.

The last act is in one scene only. Mélisande, who has given birth to a child, is on her deathbed, surrounded by Arkel, Golaud and a physician. Golaud begs her forgiveness. 'Yes, yes, I have forgiven you. But what is there to be forgiven?' she asks in all innocence. Still Golaud is harassed by doubts and implores her to tell him the truth about her love for Pelléas. 'Did you love with a love that's forbid?' he stammers out. He will never know. Mélisande is shown her child, the serving women line the walls in silence and fall on their knees as she dies.

Such is the libretto of Debussy's opera. It is by no means the whole of Maeterlinck's play, nor does the text as it stands always conform to the original. Four whole scenes and a number of passages are cut and certain lines have been altered. Now the scenes that are cut (Act I, scene i; Act II, scene iv; Act III, scene i, and Act V, scene i of the play) are for the most part highly symbolical, like the scene of Yniold and the

213

sheep in Act IV of the opera which, too, is generally cut at performances, presumably at Debussy's wish. The general opinion to-day is that these scenes merely hold up the action of the play by their too obvious insistence on the fatalism of the work. It is easy to see now why Maeterlinck was so displeased with Debussy's adaptation which, he said, was 'strange and almost hostile' to him.[1] That was probably an exaggeration. But, unlike the play, the libretto may be read without being greatly disturbed by the obviousness of the symbolic scenes, the number of which, as we have seen, Debussy reduced to a minimum. In the opera their obviousness disappears entirely.

This is not to say that this fatalistic element is not apparent in the opera. I do not think that in composing the score it was uppermost in Debussy's mind, but it was always present. When Arkel says to Mélisande: 'At my age there has grown upon me the belief one can often rely on events themselves,' and follows this by: 'Thou wilt be the one to open us the door for such a new era as I foresee,' the theme typifying Mélisande is heard at the same time as a rising figure on the horns:

Et c'est toi, main - te - nant, qui vas ou-vrir la

p

cresc. molto

---

[1] See Maeterlinck's letter to *Le Figaro* on page 81.

porte   à   l'è-re nou-   vel - le que j'entre - vois

(Mélisande's theme)

Hns

a theme that recurs when Arkel approves Golaud's marriage with the words: 'It may be there never occurs any event that is useless':

Il n'ar-ri-ve peut- ê - tre   pas__ d'é-vè-ne-

ments i - nu - ti - les

and, among many other examples, when, at Mélisande's death,
Arkel, refusing to let Golaud speak to her alone, says to him:
'Ah! you do not know this being, the soul':

vous ne sa-vez pas - ce que c'est que l'â - me

It is the *Leitmotiv* of destiny.

Now let us turn to the great and special beauty of the score,
which lies in the extremely subtle way the music brings into
relief the meaning of the words. It has often been said that
aesthetically Debussy and Maeterlinck were perfectly matched.

Recitative in 'Pelléas'

But this is only half stating the case. The prose of Maeterlinck in *Pelléas* is poetic, but not intensely so. His lines are
never charged with the bottled-up passion of the lines of
Mallarmé. On the contrary, they are extremely simple, resort-
ing to imagery only for occasional high-lights. What Debussy
achieved in *Pelléas* is Maeterlinck intensified, as *L'Après-midi*
is Mallarmé clarified. The very simplicity of the lines allowed
him, almost compelled him, to create a richer and a greater drama.

Yet the music never stifles the lines. In his excellent
analysis [1] Maurice Emmanuel quotes a prophecy of Jean-
Jacques Rousseau that a French musician would one day
realize the 'recitative appropriate to the simplicity and clarity
of our language.' This recitative, Rousseau said, 'should
proceed by very small intervals. The voice should neither
rise nor descend very much. There should be few sustained
notes; no sudden bursts and still less any shrieking; nothing
that resembles song; and little inequality in the duration or
the value of the notes.' This would be an exact description
of the recitative in *Pelléas*; and it is poignantly expressive.
Here is an example from the letter that Geneviève reads to
Arkel announcing Golaud's marriage. The words are simply:
'I know neither her age, nor who she is, nor where she belongs
and I do not dare to ask her yet.' This is rendered:

Je ne sais ni son â-ge, ni qui elle est, ni d'où el-le

[1] *Pelléas et Mélisande : étude historique et critique.* (Paris, n.d.)

* H   217

vient et je n'o-se pas l'in-ter-ro-ger,

Very similar in feeling is a line of Yniold in the scene with his father:

Oui, oui, toujours, petit père ; quand vous n'êtes pas là.

and Mélisande's meeting with Golaud when, in the last act, he asks her forgiveness:

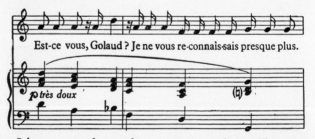

Est-ce vous, Golaud ? Je ne vous re-connais-sais presque plus.

p très doux

I have purposely put these passages together as illustrating the candour and innocence of this new-born music. Their beauty may not be immediately apparent, but gradually it creeps on one, as one might perceive the smile on some Gothic Virgin.

Was not d'Annunzio thinking of such passages when he wrote
in the preface to *Le Martyre de saint Sébastien*:

> Très douces gens, par lui, par lui,
> Vous entendrez chanter la Vierge,
> Qui est la douleur de l'aurore!

Pelléas provides the answer to those who complain of the arti-
ficialities of classical and romantic opera with its stylized recitatives
and high-flown arias overwhelming or obscuring the meaning of
the words. No composer, unless it be Mozart, has ever made
music accentuate speech more carefully, nor indeed more variedly.
In the first scene of the opera, when Golaud suggests recovering
Mélisande's crown which has fallen into the water, he has a line
in which one can recognize the inflections of the spoken voice:

219

Mélisande will not hear of it. 'Leave it alone! If you do take it out I shall throw myself down there.' And she has an impassioned phrase spread over a whole octave: she breaks into song:[1]

[1] For a detailed analysis of this fusion of dramatic recitative and song that is a special characteristic of the vocal writing in *Pelléas* see M. Emmanuel's study. It is most interesting to note that this was the ideal of Mozart who, in 1778, wrote to his father about Benda's duologues *Medea* and *Ariadne auf Naxos*: 'You probably know that there is no singing, but declamation; sometimes, indeed,

In the passage where Pelléas reassures Mélisande on the loss of her ring an expression of nascent love is conveyed, not directly, but by means of this laconic, reticent recitative with lingering repeated notes and unexpected drooping fifths. 'It is naught, perhaps the ring will be recovered. If not, no doubt we can find you another':

words are spoken while the music is playing, and then the effect is most magnificent.' And he gives his opinion that 'most recitative should be treated in opera in this way; and only occasionally when the words are suitable for musical expression, should there be singing in the recitative.'

Debussy

en re-trou-ve-rons une au - tre

And as Mélisande refuses, there is no mistaking her assent to
Pelléas's advances—her lines are, of course, symbolical of this:

Non, non, nous ne la re-trou-ve-rons

plus, nous n'en trou-ve-rons pas d'au-tres non plus.

Golaud's love for Mélisande is from the first shot through with apprehension and fear. 'You're very young, I fancy. How old may you be?' In the first scene this is about all he manages to say to her:

The fear is apparent and it is also infectious. To this over-abrupt approach Mélisande elusively answers, 'I begin to feel so cold.' And how gracefully she recoils in the downward phrase (see page 224)!

One could quote such subtly suggestive touches from almost every page. Golaud's doubts, superstitions, fury, repentance, Mélisande's whimsical moods, Pelléas's sudden streaks of passion, Arkel's 'pity for the hearts of men,' all this is treated simply and beautifully and in a way that makes one feel, as with the music of Mozart, that it could not possibly have been

done in any other way. That is the test of the greatest art; one has to make no excuses. It is something to love—entirely. And above all it is simple. 'Take hold of Eloquence and wring her neck,' wrote Verlaine. Compare, then, with the passion of Isolde, fiercely triumphant in her defiance of death, this simple confession of love from these creatures of fate :

224

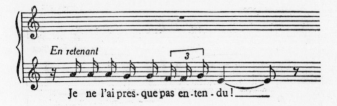

The nudity of such music, so replete with unconscious fantasy, would seem to represent the antithesis of the art of Wagner. The writing for the voices brings out the finest shades of the words, but the drama is developed in the orchestra. This was the principle of Wagner, and there is no denying that *Pelléas* would never have been possible without *Tristan*. I like to think of Mélisande as the illegitimate daughter of Tristan and Isolde. Like them, she has a *Leitmotiv,* and so have each of the other characters. There is also a theme for destiny (already noted), the lost ring, death and pardon. Maurice Emmanuel, apologizing for such an 'outrage against Debussy's tastes,' gives a list of thirteen. It would be an outrage if one ticketed each theme off—'visiting cards' Debussy called the *Leitmotive* in the *Ring*—and said nothing more. But actually Debussy's *Leitmotive* are distinguishable as such only after careful searching and only by painfully extracting them from their flimsy context. See how discreetly, after Golaud's 'I cannot permit it, Méli‑sande, so come, come, give me your hand' (Act I, scene i), Melisande's theme enters on the double bass (see page 226). And then, as he warns her that 'the night will be so dark and so chilly,' the theme that opens the opera is heard on the violins (in minims) (see page 226). This theme, says M. Emmanuel, 'represents nothing, and nobody. It evokes only a far‑off past.'

Throughout, the orchestration is a model of delicacy, transparency and discretion, and it is such that if the singers

Debussy

226

enunciate clearly not a word is missed. Like a mirage of the drama, it rises behind their lines, giving perspective to the words of the moment. From a purely technical point of view this was a wonderful feat. Romain Rolland has put it well:

Rien de trop: that is the artist's motto. Instead of amalgamating the instruments for mass effects, he throws into relief their individuality or delicately grafts one timbre on to another, without anything of their true nature being spoilt. Like the Impressionist painters of those times, he paints with pure colours, with that delicate sobriety that spurns all harshness and ugliness.

Standing back and looking at the main lines of the composition, one is struck by the dramatic inevitability in the sequence of scenes. Consider the various scenes between Pelléas and Mélisande. There are in all six, so constructed that there is not the slightest drag in the way the drama proceeds to its goal—which, given the dreamy nature of the subject, there might well have been. Of these six scenes, the three love scenes stand in the middle of the canvas, making a progression towards Golaud's mad killing of Pelléas, while the three shorter ones—the meeting of Pelléas and Mélisande by the sea, their frightened visit to the grotto, and their hurried exchange of a few words in the castle before Golaud appears to drag Mélisande by her hair—offset the development of the love scenes like counter-themes in a movement of a symphony. The balance of the composition is supplied by the scenes between Golaud and Mélisande, growing in intensity in the opposite direction, as it were. The framework, it is true, is Maeterlinck's, but this does not detract from Debussy's achievement. In Yniold's spying scene and the scene in the vaults there is something Mussorgskian; in Golaud's fury and despair, contrasted with the magnificent serenity of Mélisande's death, there is something Shakespearian. It is a musical drama of overpowering candour and acuteness of psychological perception, irradiating the whole of Debussy's work and indeed the whole course of romantic and modern opera from Wagner to Alban Berg.

If the present generation can hardly have had the opportunity of judging *Pelléas* by anything approaching an ideal per-formance, the incidental music to Gabriele d'Annunzio's mystery play *Le Martyre de saint Sébastien,* has fortunately, in recent years, had a more favourable fate. Following the failure, recounted in an earlier chapter, of the 1911 production of *Le Martyre* in Paris and subsequent unsuccessful attempts in France, Italy and America to present the work as a hybrid form of either a play, a ballet or an opera, the extraordinary score was boldly rescued from these associations and performed in the concert-hall as an oratorio. It is in this entirely acceptable form that the work is usually performed to-day. Appropriate ex-tracts from d'Annunzio's play, chosen by Roland-Manuel and spoken by a narrator (the part has often been taken by Jean-Louis Barrault) introduce the various musical interludes. Another version of the work, in the form of a suite in five movements for orchestra alone and made by André Caplet, who was responsible for the original orchestration, is not more than a pale reflection of the composer's intentions and is seldom performed.

It was d'Annunzio who conferred on Debussy the imaginary title of 'Claude de France'—as Monteverdi was to be 'Claudio d'Italia'—a sign of pretentiousness noticeable also in this poet's use of language and his sense of the theatre. The fact that the libretto was written in French by an Italian has naturally prejudiced critics appreciative of Debussy's prosody. Yet if allowances are made for a style of writing seemingly less suited to French than Italian, d'Annunzio's *Martyre* has some fine poetry, often of great concentration and nobility.

In a statement signed by d'Annunzio and Debussy, and issued to the press in response to the censure on the work pronounced by the Archbishop of Paris, *Le Martyre* is described as 'the lyrical glorification not only of the splendid Christian athlete [i.e. Saint Sebastian] but of all Christian heroism.' The confusion of Christian and pagan virtues arising from the identification in the course of the play of Christ and Adonis provoked an enraged onslaught from many contemporary writers led by the profoundly devout Charles Péguy. It may reasonably be argued, however, that Debussy had an equally profound conception of divinity exemplified in *Le Martyre* itself and aptly described as 'the work of a pagan musician who sees God in all things.'

The confusion of the libretto derives from the deliberate intermingling of Christian and pre-Christian virtues. And here Louis Laloy traces the origin of d'Annunzio's treatment of Sebastian's martyrdom to Anatole France's *Thaïs* and to Flaubert's *La Tentation de saint Antoine*. At the opening Sebastian, captain of a body of Asiatic archers in imperial Rome, offers encouragement to the Christian twins, Marcus and Marcellus. In the course of their interrogation by the Romans he takes their unenviable place and, as an act of faith, performs a wild dance on the burning coals. In the next act an occult element is introduced. Sebastian enters the magic chamber of the Chaldean fortune-tellers who are seen gazing at the planets. The voice of Erigone, virgin daughter of Icarus, is heard and presently a sick woman appears, her aching wound caused by a fragment of the winding-sheet of Christ kept close to her breast. Sebastian snatches it from her and perceives on it the face of the Saviour. Erigone is converted to Christianity and now the movements of heavenly bodies in the firmament are seen to be ordered not by any occult force but by the Virgin Mary and the Infant Jesus.

In the next act Sebastian has been summoned to the emperor's palace to give an account of his actions to an assembly of pagan divinities. His answer to their summons is a recitation of the Passion. The pagan women of Byblos assume Sebastian to be

Adonis and mourn his death. Fastened to a laurel tree, Sebastian is alone in perceiving the Good Shepherd just as his body is about to be pierced by the archers' arrows; and the play ends with a scene in Paradise where the Saint is greeted by a chorus of angels.

Sebastian's part is entirely spoken. In the last act his soul is impersonated by a soprano, and other solo soprano parts are for a celestial voice and the virgin Erigone. To the five acts, representing the *mansions* of French medieval drama, orchestral preludes are provided, setting an appropriate mood. The prelude to the first act, 'The Court of Lilies,' opens with an *organum* effect in the manner of *La Cathédrale engloutie* leading to a chaste recitative passage ('Frère, que serait-il le monde') mostly unaccompanied and sung by two contraltos impersonating the twin brothers Marcus and Marcellus. There follows a tier-like contrapuntal section in eight parts introducing the Saint, his ecstatic dance on the burning coals and a magnificent poly-phonic chorus, reminiscent of *La Damoiselle élue* and con-cluding with the glorious proclamation 'Tout le ciel chante!'

The prelude to the second act, 'The Magic Chamber,' is a glittering piece of orchestral writing with an undercurrent of terror suggesting the uncertainties of the future as divined by fortune-tellers. The virgin Erigone, converted by the Saint and about to be tortured to death, sings a most graceful aria derived, according to Caplet, from a medieval Italian song. As the Saint challenges the forces of evil the spirit of Christianity is symbolized by a celestial chorus developed over a succession of common chords and concluding with an ethereal impersonation of an angel in heaven.

In 'The Council of False Gods,' the prelude with its cruel fanfares depicts the court of Caesar Augustus. There is a modal hymn to Apollo which leads to an extended scene illustrating the apprehension of the women of Byblos at the imminent death of their Adonis. This is the central musical episode of the play.   The orchestration is rich and varied.   The taut chromatic writing for chorus and soloists is not merely picturesque; it is tragic and devout.   One would have to go to Bach, to the St. John Passion, to find something comparable to this symbolical expression in music of tears.   As the chorus of women pour out their anguish, their bitter command 'Pleurez, pleurez!' is repeated with intolerable insistence and intensity. At the close of the act the grief of the worshipping women is finally released and flows into a mood of reassuring serenity.

The eerie tremolos and the plaintive cor anglais solo in the prelude to the fourth act foreshadow the martyrdom.   The appearance of the Good Shepherd is suggested by a contemplative symphonic interlude, but the chorus re-enter to reaffirm their grief at the death of the Saint who is now bound to the laurel tree and made the target of archers.   The gates of Paradise are opened and in the final act Debussy provides a series of majestic polyphonic choruses, recalling the style of the Villon and the Charles d'Orléans songs and designed to celebrate the arrival in heaven of the Saint greeted in turn by the martyrs, the virgins, the apostles and the angels.   The voice of Sebastian's soul soars above chorus and orchestra and the work concludes with a tremendously impressive hymn, *Louez le Seigneur*, the words of which are the French version of Psalm CL.   The last dramatic work of the great hedonist composer, *Le Martyre* is his *Parsifal* or his *L'Enfance du Christ*.   The pretentiousness and confusion of the libretto are largely eliminated in a performance of the work as an oratorio; and what remains is a potent and underlying faith, hedonistic or pantheistic as it may be, but ultimately expressed in terms of the universal Christian qualities of sacrifice and redemption.

CHAPTER XVII

THE LITERARY WORKS

THE literary works of Debussy it would be especially interesting to talk about are still in manuscript, and I have unfortunately not been able to consult them. These are the opera librettos adapted from the tales of Poe, a study of which should illuminate the composer's conception of the stage during the latter part of his life. This study was at one time to have been undertaken by Gabriel Mourey, Debussy's associate in the project for an opera on Tristan, and still waits to be written. In the mean time one can only point again to a lifelong hankering after the musical stage as one of Debussy's important characteristics as a composer. Apparently he considered himself a competent literary dramatist, for, over a period of eighteen months, about the year 1900, he gave lessons in writing for the stage to his young friend René Peter. Together they contemplated a fairy play entitled *Les Mille et une Nuits de n'importe où et d'ailleurs* and began a dramatic satire called *F.E.A.* (*Les Frères en art*). This, René Peter writes, 'is the story of an evil-minded painter who, at the height of his fame, managed, by the aid of a mutual assistance league (*Les F.E.A.*), in which he had complete authority, to stifle budding talents and to imperil the honour of his favourite pupil.' This play was accepted by a Paris theatre manager, but at the last moment Debussy seems to have thought it unworthy. 'I am just an old romantic,' he wrote to a friend of Peter's, 'who has chucked all desire for success out of the window.' Three acts of the play are still in manuscript. There is one other stage-work to be mentioned, a scenario for a ballet, *Masques et Bergamasques*, written at the request of Diaghilev. It is a

232

conventional love-story from the Italian comedy which passes in eighteenth-century Venice. The music was never composed.

The main concern of this chapter, then, are Debussy's critical writings and his essays in musical journalism which are to be found in a number of Paris journals between the years 1901 and 1914. The bulk of these writings is in three series of articles: *La Revue blanche,* April to December 1901; *Gil Blas,* January to June 1903; and *La Revue S.I.M.* (the publication of the French section of the International Society of Music), November 1912 to March 1914. The complete critical writings have been listed and commented upon by Léon Vallas in his book, *Les Idées et les théories de Claude Debussy, musicien français,* to which the reader who wishes to investigate the subject more thoroughly may be referred.[1]

The title of this book was perhaps not very apt, for strictly speaking Debussy had no theories. In his first article in *La Revue blanche* of 1st April 1901 he makes this clear:

Having been asked to speak about music in this review, may I be allowed to explain what I intend to do? On these pages will be found sincere and honestly felt impressions rather than criticism; for this too often takes the form of brilliant variations on the theme of: 'You're wrong because you didn't do as I did': or 'You're talented and I'm not; that can't go on.' I will try to discover the forces that have brought works of art into being, which I think is more worth while than taking them to pieces like an old watch.

People hardly remember that as children they were never allowed to open the insides of their dolls. That would be a crime of *lèse*-mystery. Yet they still insist on sticking their aesthetic noses where they have no business. They no longer break their dolls; but they take them to pieces and kill the mystery in cold blood. Then they have something to talk about. Oh, yes—some may be excused

---

[1] The translations of Debussy's articles in this chapter are partly taken from the English translation of this book by Maire O'Brien, partly from *M. Croche the Dilettante-hater,* and are partly my own.

on the ground of ignorance, but others, more harmful, premeditate the crime. Well, mediocrity must be defended and those who undertake its defence may be sure of support.

I shall speak very little of works established by success or tradition. Once for all, Meyerbeer, Thalberg, Reyer are men of genius, and nothing more need be said.

On Sundays, when God is kind, I shall hear no music. Please accept my apologies. Lastly, remember the word 'impressions,' for I insist on keeping my emotion free from all parasitic aesthetics.

This harsh, wry sarcasm which grins in so much that Debussy wrote is curious, particularly as it is hardly noticeable in his music, at least not until the later works. The musician and the writer in Debussy were certainly very different people. It seems that he flung all his animosity, of which he had a great deal, into his prose, his conversation or his letters, which often show the same harsh tone, so that he could preserve that inner glow of warmth for his music. One has to remember in reading his criticisms that, as Vallas notes, he was 'detested by reactionary artists who condemned, anathematized and excommunicated him'; and that he 'took little interest in these notes, which he never wrote except from sheer necessity in order to earn a little money.' A barbed tongue is evident in his article on Nikisch:

On Sunday the overpowering glare of the sun seemed to make it unthinkable to listen to music. The Berlin Philharmonic Orchestra, conducted by Nikisch, took the opportunity of giving its first concert. I hope that God will forgive my having gone back on my resolutions and that others more fortunate paid homage to the grass generously spread by Him for the reception of sausage skins and the logical **development** of idylls.

To people to-day his style seems strained and self-conscious. It is precious. Preciosity was a characteristic of the Symbolist writers when they did not attain the stature of Mallarmé or Verlaine, or of Jules Laforgue, a young writer of genius who

died at the age of twenty-eight and with whose style Debussy's
biting manner has often been compared, though it is difficult
for me to see any resemblance. In his prose Debussy seemed
to have little regard for the principle of 'economy of means.'
A style more replete with adjectives and images it would be
difficult to imagine. It reminds one that *La Revue blanche,*
for which the first articles were written, was almost contemporary with those *fin-de-siècle* reviews in London, the *Yellow
Book* and the *Savoy,* in which extravagance was the keynote.
In some ways Debussy's prose is like the drawings of Aubrey
Beardsley: it has that same baroque excess of energy that runs
into wild curlicues. What it certainly never reminds one of
is Debussy's music. Here is an example from a criticism of
some songs of Delius performed at the Société Nationale:

> They are very sweet and innocent songs, music to rock the con-
> valescents of the rich neighbourhoods. There is always a note
> hanging over a chord like a water-lily in a lake, tired of being
> watched by the moon, or like a little balloon blocked by the clouds.

Apparently Debussy thought this passage so good that two
years later he reproduced it exactly as it stands in a notice of
some songs of Grieg. He added then that another piece of
Grieg's music was like a 'pink sweet filled with snow.'

This brings us to an episode in Debussy's journalistic career
that left some unpleasantness. About 1900 Grieg protested
against the condemnation of Dreyfus by refusing to come to
France. Some years later, however, in 1903, he accepted an
engagement to play at the Concerts Colonne and Debussy, who
had instinctively taken sides with the nationalists, seized the
opportunity to pour abuse of a purely personal kind on Grieg
which, in a concert criticism, would certainly be out of place
to-day.

> To begin with [he wrote] the number of Norwegians who usually
> haunt the Concerts Colonne was tripled; we had never before been

privileged to see so much red hair or such extravagant hats—for the fashions in Christiania seem to me rather behind the times. Then the concert opened with a double turn: the performance of an overture called *Autumn* and the ejection of a crowd of Grieg's admirers, who, at the bidding of a police-constable, a slave to duty rather than to music, were sent to cool their enthusiasm on the banks of the Seine. . . .

At last I saw Grieg. From in front he looks like a genial photographer; from behind his way of doing his hair makes him look like the plants called sunflowers, dear to parrots and the gardens that decorate small country stations.

He then went on to say that Grieg was an exquisite musician when he interpreted the folk-music of his country, but 'apart from this he is no more than a clever musician, more concerned with effects than with genuine art.' Grieg was naturally very much offended, and in a letter to M. D. Calvocoressi made it clear how much he deplored Debussy's 'utter lack of comprehension of my art' and especially 'his venomous and contemptuous tone . . . A genuine artist,' he added, 'ought to strive to maintain a high level in all things of the mind, and to respect the point of view of other artists' [1]—a feat of which such a subjective artist as Debussy was not always capable.

His quips, which sometimes suggest Erik Satie, were not everywhere appreciated. In an article entitled 'Open-air Music,' written for *La Renaissance latine,* he proposes, among other things, that 'M. Gavioli, the famous maker of street organs, . . . should be induced to make his instruments worthy of playing the *Ring*. Did not Wagner declare again and again that he could be understood only in France? . . . The Opéra does not shrink from playing *Pagliacci*; shrink then no longer from making street organs worthy to perform the *Ring*.' M. D. Calvocoressi explained why this article never appeared

[1] This letter is quoted in M. D. Calvocoressi's *Musicians' Gallery.*

in the journal for which it was written: 'The article was duly set in type, and lay waiting, when suddenly *La Renaissance latine* changed hands. The new proprietor and editor, coming across it, gave it a glance, exclaimed: "Mais c'est idiot!" and decreed, despite my expostulations, that it was not to be published.' It appeared in *La Revue blanche* of 1st June 1901.

And now, I think, we may turn to the more gratifying aspects of Debussy's journalism—of which there are many. He loved to watch as much as to listen at a concert. Often he would devote the whole of his notice to the performer's appearance ('le côté décoratif' so dear to the sensualist). In an account of the *Ballade* for piano and orchestra by Gabriel Fauré he says:

> The *Ballade* is almost as lovely as Mme Hasselmans, the pianist. With a charming gesture she readjusted a shoulder-strap which slipped down at every lively passage. Somehow an association of ideas was established in my mind between the charm of the afore-mentioned gesture and the music of Fauré. It is a fact, however, that the play of the graceful, fleeting lines described by Fauré's music may be compared to the gesture of a beautiful woman without either suffering from the comparison.

Very charming. Debussy could be harsh and petulant in his notices; but beyond this exterior he also showed a child-like simplicity and had a loving, ingenuous manner of seizing upon the humour of the irrelevant. He tells that during a performance of the unfinished Symphony a flock of sparrows came to sit on the window-sill and that 'Nikisch had the grace not to demand their expulsion.' Such touches are those of a man who had a fine contempt for officialdom, grandiloquence and bombast. Virtuosity was anathema to him: 'The attraction of the virtuoso for the public is very much like that of the circus for the crowd. There is always a hope that something dangerous may happen; M. Ysaÿe may play the violin with M. Colonne on his shoulders; or M. Pugno may conclude his piece by lifting the piano with his teeth.' Not only virtuosity, but the whole machinery of the concert world, seemed to him suspect:

Music, nowadays, tends to become more and more an accompani-ment for sentimental or tragic incidents, and plays the part of the showman at the door of a booth behind which is displayed the sinister form of 'Mr. Nobody.' True lovers of music seldom frequent fairs; they merely have a piano and feverishly play a few pages over and over again; as sure a means of intoxication as 'just, subtle and mighty opium,' and the least enervating way of spending happy hours.

In the decade before the first world war it was feared that the growing popularization of music would threaten the remaining ivory-tower strongholds. The following passage, written in *La Revue S.I.M.* of 15th May 1913, must be one of the first forebodings of an evil with which we have since come to terms:

At a time like ours, in which mechanical skill has attained un-suspected perfection, the most famous works may be heard as easily as one may drink a glass of beer, and it only costs ten centimes, like the automatic weighing machines. Should we not fear this domestication of sound, this magic that any one can bring from a disk at his will? Will it not bring to waste the mysterious force of an art which one might have thought indestructible? Why don't they understand that there is really no reason to have so many centuries of music behind us, to have thus profited by this magnificent intellectual heritage and to seek childishly to re-write history? Is not our duty, on the contrary, to find the symphonic music appro-priate to our age, that which is demanded by progress, bravery and modern victories? The century of aeroplanes has a right to a music of its own.

In his numerous opinions of composers there is no attempt at objective criticism. He said what he liked or did not like, for any one who wanted to know, but his innermost feelings about music were not to be put into words. He was often exceedingly scathing. And the impression is left that he was always more interested in the music that he had not yet written than in the finished product of someone else.   A composer is, after all, not a wine-taster.

The great value of these criticisms is that they taught, in an age when reverence was apt to be blind, that what counted most were 'honestly felt impressions.' He disliked the 'Pastoral' Symphony, and said so.   Some songs of Schubert were like 'dried flowers . . . photographs that are dead indeed! The effect is repeated through endless verses and by the time the third is reached one begins to wonder if the time has not come to produce our own Paul Delmet.' The expression of such opinions was deliberately intended to be provocative and reveals an affinity with writers whose waspish aim was to 'épater le bourgeois.'

His preferences went to the very old and to the very new. Bach, he wrote, was 'a benevolent god, to whom musicians should offer a prayer before setting to work so that they may be preserved from mediocrity.' He admires in him 'that musical arabesque, or rather that principle of ornament, which is the basis of all forms of art' and which he sees too in Palestrina, Victoria and Orlandus Lassus.   He appreciated Beethoven's orchestra (curiously enough), the ninth Symphony, but not *Adelaide,* which 'the old master must have forgotten to burn,' nor the concertos.   In later years he contemptuously referred to Beethoven as 'le vieux sourd.'   He was very critical of Gluck, to whose shade he wrote an open letter (published in *Gil Blas* on 23rd February 1903) on the occasion of the revival of *Iphigénie en Aulide.*   In this curious letter he says: 'Between ourselves, your prosody was very bad; at least, you turn the French language into an accentuated language when it is, on the contrary, a language of fine shades.'   That is interesting, but he objected to Gluck on other grounds.   Elsewhere he says: 'Queen Marie Antoinette, who always remained an Austrian—a sentiment for which she was made to pay once and for all—imposed Gluck on French taste. Thus our beautiful traditions became warped, our desire for clarity stifled, and, via Meyerbeer, we arrived quite logically at Richard Wagner.' The composer he opposed to Gluck was Rameau, who, he maintains, 'was infinitely more Greek.'

Of the romantic composers he placed Weber highest. Berlioz 'is an exception—a monster. He is not a musician at all. He creates the illusion of music by means borrowed from literature and painting. Besides, there is, as far as I can see, little that is French in him.' And further: 'His passion is satisfied with leaves which literature has dried between the pages of its books. . . . His genius found a bitter pleasure in airing its longings in an artificial-flower shop.' He admired *L'Enfance du Christ,* the *Symphonie fantastique* and *Roméo et Juliette,* but not *Les Troyens.*

Of the more modern composers, Mussorgsky receives special praise. Speaking of the set of songs called *The Nursery,* he says that 'no one has given utterance to the best within us in tones more gentle or profound: he is unique and will remains so because his art is spontaneous and free from arid formulas.' But the contemporary vogue for Russian folk-music was condemned. 'The fashion for popular airs has spread quickly throughout the musical world. From east to west the tiniest villages have been ransacked, and simple tunes, plucked from the mouths of hoary peasants, find themselves, to their consternation, trimmed with harmonic frills.' Of Rimsky-Korsakov he admired *Antar,* but not *Schéhérazade,* which reminded him less of the Orient than of a bazaar.[1] In his criticisms Borodin is not mentioned. His later opinion of Tchaikovsky I have not come across, but Vallas notes that he disapproves of him, 'like all Frenchmen.'

The music of Massenet is 'vibrant with thrills, transports

[1] See the letter to Raoul Bardac on page 284 (Appendix E).

240

and would-be embraces. The harmonies are like enlacing arms, the melodies are the necks we kiss . . .' and so on. He 'amply succeeded in what he set out to do, a fact which caused some to believe that they were taking their revenge by calling him—*sotto voce*—Paul Delmet's best pupil. That is merely a joke in the worst possible taste.'[1] It is curious to see his admiration for Richard Strauss, whose 'irresistible domination it is not possible to withstand.' He is 'very nearly a genius.' Debussy was, of course, not blind to Strauss's vulgarity and begins a notice on *Tod und Verklärung*: 'In the cookery book, under "Jugged Hare," will be seen this wise recommendation: "Take a hare." Richard Strauss proceeds otherwise. To write a symphonic poem he takes anything.' Still he admits that 'he is one of the most assertive geniuses of our time.'

On Wagner there is little to be added that would further eluci-date both the love and the fear of the great dominating figure of his life. He speaks of the *Leitmotive* in the *Ring,* which suggest 'a harmless lunatic who, on presenting his visiting-card, would declaim his name in song.' Yet this work 'is irresistible as the sea. . . . One does not criticize a work of such magnitude as the *Ring*. . . . Its too sumptuous greatness renders futile the legitimate desire to grasp its proportions.' And he grandilo-quently concludes: 'He can never quite die. He will eventually feel the cruel hand with which time destroys the most beautiful things. Some splendid ruins will, however, remain, in whose shade our grandchildren will dream of the past greatness of a man who, had he been but a little more human, would have been great for all time.' He heard this performance of the *Ring* at Covent Garden, and 'as a reward for good behaviour' spent an evening at the Empire music-hall.

During the first world war Debussy made a selection of his

[1] It was, however, a joke made by Debussy himself. See the letter to Pierre Louÿs on page 73.

articles for publication in book form. Some were developed, others cut, and the first proofs of the twenty-five articles thus adapted were sent to G. Jean-Aubry in 1917. But the printing-presses were then in invaded territory and it was not possible to publish the book before 1921. Its title, *M. Croche antidilettante,* is the name of an imaginary interlocutor, an *alter ego* who is sketched in the first two essays.

M. Croche, whose 'features are best pictured by recalling those of Tom Lane, the jockey, and M. Thiers,' had an 'intolerable smile . . . especially evident when he talked of music.' Here is the explanation of the epithet following his name:

I suddenly decided to ask him what his profession might be. He replied, in a voice which checked any attempt at comment: 'Dilet-tante-hater. Have you noticed the hostility of a concert-room audience? Have you studied their almost drugged expression of boredom, indifference and even stupidity? . . . I try to forget music because it obscures my perception of what I do not know or shall only know to-morrow.'

Those last words, the most striking in the book, are the kernel of Debussy's philosophy. 'Music is a sum total of scattered forces,' M. Croche goes on. 'You make an abstract ballad of them! I prefer the simple notes of an Egyptian shepherd's pipe. . . . To see the sun rise is more profitable than to hear the "Pastoral" Symphony. What is the use of your almost incomprehensible art?' This superb challenge to the accumu-lated burdens of habit was the double-edged weapon with which he defended himself against the mummification of music's idols and which at the same time enabled him to glimpse the wondrous candour of a new-born art. As a matter of fact, Debussy sketched the character of M. Croche after reading Paul Valéry's *Soirées avec M. Teste,* where a similarly wrinkled old man symbolizes a quest for the instinctive art. 'I haven't had any books for twenty years,' M. Teste says. 'I've burnt my papers too. . . . I can remember what I want. But the difficult thing is not that, but to *remember what I shall want to-morrow.*' These thoughts are almost identical with those of M. Croche; but M. Teste goes further. 'Je rature le vif,' he says (literally 'I cross out the living'), by which he means to renounce the instinctive life in search of a sublimated spiritual ideal. This forms part of the philosophy of Valéry, as it does of the later Stravinsky, T. S. Eliot and *Parsifal.* And if the hedonist in Debussy would have shunned such a bleak call to sacrifice at the time of his association with the Mallarmé of *L'Après-midi,* the experience of *Pelléas, Le Martyre* and above all the late sonatas led him to seek a reflection in the lonely conscience of Valéry and to reveal himself as a stoic of music, an exile from himself who may show us still the promised land.

APPENDICES

APPENDICES

APPENDIX A

CALENDAR

(Figures in brackets denote the age reached by the person mentioned during the year in question.)

Year	Age	Life	Contemporary Musicians
1862		Achille Claude Debussy born August 22, at Saint-Germain-en-Laye, near Paris, son of Manuel Achille Debussy (26), then a keeper of a china shop.	Delius born, Jan. 29; Halévy (63) dies, March 17. Albéniz aged 2; Alkan 49; Arensky 1; Auber 80; Balakirev 25; Balfe 54; Berlioz 59; Bizet 24; Boito 20; Borodin 29; Bossi 1; Brahms 29; Bréville 1; Bruckner 38; Bruneau 5; Chabrier 21; Charpentier 2; Chausson 7; Cornelius 38; Cui 27; Dargomizhsky 49; Delibes 26; Duparc 14; Dvořák 21; Elgar 5; Fauré 17; Franck 40; Gade 45; Goldmark 32; Gounod 44; Grieg 19; Heller 47; Humperdinck 8; d'Indy 11; Lalo 39; Leoncavallo 4; Liadov 7; Liszt 51; Loeffler 1; MacDowell 1; Mahler 2; Martucci 6;

Year	Age	Life	Contemporary Musicians
			Massenet 20; Mercadante 67; Meyerbeer 71; Mussorgsky 23; Offenbach 43; Parry 14; Pedrell 21; Ponchielli 28; Puccini 4; Raff 40; Rimsky-Korsakov 18; Rossini 70; Rubinstein 32; Saint-Saëns 27; Serov 42; Sgambati 19; Smetana 38; Stanford 10; Strauss (J. ii) 37; Sullivan 20; Taneiev 6; Tchaikovsky 22; Thomas (A.) 51; Verdi 49; Wagner 49; Wolf 2.
1863	1		Bordes born, May 12; Mascagni born, Dec. 7; Pierné born, Aug. 16.
1864	2		d'Albert born, April 10; Meyerbeer (73) dies, May 2; Ropartz born, June 15; Strauss (R.) born, June 11.
1865	3		Dukas born, Oct. 1; Glazunov born, Aug. 10; Sibelius born, Dec. 8.
1866	4		Busoni born, April 1; Satie born, May 17.
1867	5		Granados born, July 29.
1868	6		Bantock born, Aug. 7; Rossini (76) dies, Nov. 13; Sinigaglia born, Aug. 14.
1869	7	Visit to Cannes, where he has his first piano lessons from an old Italian teacher, Cerutti.	Berlioz (66) dies, March 8; Dargomizhsky (56) dies, Jan. 17; Pfitzner born, May 5; Roussel born, April 5.

Year	Age	Life	Contemporary Musicians
1870	8		Balfe (62) dies, Oct. 20; Mercadante (75) dies, Dec. 17; Novák born, Dec. 5; Schmitt (Florent) born, Sept. 28.
1871	9	Meets Mme Mauté de Fleurville, a pupil of Chopin and Verlaine's mother-in-law.	Auber (89) dies, May 12; Serov (51) dies, Feb. 1.
1872	10	Enters the Paris Conservatoire, October. Studies solfège under Lavignac (27) and piano under Marmontel (57).	Scriabin born, Jan. 4; Vaughan Williams born, Oct. 12.
1873	11		Rachmaninov born, April 1; Reger born, March 19; Séverac born, July 20.
1874	12		Cornelius (50) dies, Oct. 26; Holst born, Sept. 21; Schoenberg born, Sept. 13; Suk born, Jan. 4.
1875	13		Bizet (37) dies, June 3; Coleridge - Taylor born, Aug. 15; Montemezzi born, Aug. 4; Ravel born, March 7; Roger-Ducasse born, April 18.
1876	14	Enters the harmony class of Émile Durand. Sets to music poems of Théodore de Banville (53).	Falla born, Nov. 23; Wolf-Ferrari born, Jan. 12.
1877	15	Wins 2nd prize for piano playing and 1st for solfège.	Dohnányi born, July 27.
1878	16	Songs written on poems of Paul Bourget and André Girod.	Caplet born, Nov. 23; Palmgren born, Feb. 16; Schreker born, March 23.

Year	Age	*Life*	*Contemporary Musicians*
1879	17	Fails to win the first prize at either of the annual piano examination and his parents abandon their hopes of his becoming a virtuoso.	Bridge (Frank) born, Feb. 26; Delage born, Nov. 13; Grovlez born, April 4; Ireland born, Aug. 13; Respighi born, July 9; Scott (Cyril) born Sept. 27.
1880	18	First prize in score-reading enables him to enter a composition class. At the very time that his career is decided he meets Tchaikovsky's (40) patroness, Nadezhda von Meck (50) and journeys with her, as a domestic musician and tutor to her children, to Switzerland and Italy. Tchaikovsky gives his opinion of D.'s early compositions. On his return to Paris he enters the composition class of Ernest Guiraud (43).	Bloch born, July 24; Inghelbrecht born, Sept. 17; Medtner born, Jan. 5; Offenbach (61) dies, Oct. 5; Pizzetti born, Sept. 20.
1881	19	Preparation for the Grand Prix de Rome. Meets Mme Vasnier, the young wife of a civil servant, who is said to have been his mistress. Visit to Mme von Meck in Moscow in the summer.	Bartók born, March 25; Miaskovsky born, April 20; Mussorgsky (42) dies, March 28.
1882	20	Becomes acquainted with the poetry of Verlaine (38)	Kodály born, Dec. 16; Malipiero born, March 18;

Year	Age	Life	Contemporary Musicians
		and Mallarmé (40) and dedicates the first of the *Fêtes galantes* (on poems of Verlaine) to Mme Vasnier. Visits Plechtchevo, Moscow and Vienna.	Raff (60) dies, June 24–5; Stravinsky born, June 17; Turina born, Dec. 9; Vycpálek born, Feb. 23.
1883	21	Gains second Prix de Rome with the cantata, *Le Gladiateur.* Begins a stage setting of Théodore de Banville's *Diane au bois.*	Bax born, Nov. 8; Casella born, July 25; Szymanowski born, Sept. 21; Wagner (70) dies, Feb. 13; Webern born, Dec. 3; Zandonai born, May 28.
1884	22	Gains the first Prix de Rome with the lyric scene, *L'Enfant prodigue.*	van Dieren born, Dec. 27; Griffes born, Sept. 17; Smetana (60) dies, May 12.
1885	23	Leaves for the Villa Medici in Rome much against his will. Begins a choral work on Heine's drama, *Almanzor,* and continues to work on *Diane au bois,* but eventually abandons them both. He finds life at the Villa Medici distasteful but meets Liszt (74), and is also said to have met Verdi (72), Leoncavallo (27) and Boito (43).	Berg born, Feb. 9; Wellesz born, Oct. 21.
1886	24	Flees to Paris. Returns after a few weeks and writes *Printemps,* his only 'envoi de Rome.'	Kaminski born, July 4; Liszt (75) dies, July 31; Ponchielli (52) dies, Jan. 17.
1887	25	Flees again from Rome, this time for good. Begins	Borodin (54) dies, Feb. 28; Toch born, Dec. 7.

Year	*Age*	*Life*	*Contemporary Musicians*
		La Damoiselle élue. Meets poets of Mallarmé's (45) circle and is said to have met Brahms (54) in Vienna and to have visited London.	
1888	26	Visits Bayreuth to hear *Parsifal* and *Meistersinger.* Finishes *La Damoiselle élue* in Paris. Lives with Gabrielle Dupont known as Gaby Lhéry.	Alkan (75) dies, March 29; Durey born, May 27; Heller (74) dies, Jan. 14.
1889	27	Second visit to Bayreuth to hear *Tristan.* On his return he becomes acquainted with the score of Mussorgsky's *Boris Godunov,* which he admires, but not uncritically. He is impressed by the Javanese and Annamite music heard at the Exposition Universelle. Finishes the *Cinq Poèmes de Baudelaire.*	Shaporin born, Nov. 8.
1890	28	Begins to write *Rodrigue et Chimène,* the libretto, by Catulle Mendès (49), based on Guillem de Castro's *Las Mocedades del Cid.*	Franck (68) dies, Nov. 8; Gade (73) dies, Dec. 21.
1891		Meets Erik Satie (25), who is a pianist in a Montmartre café, and forms a lifelong friendship with him.	Bliss born, Aug. 2; Delibes (55) dies, Jan. 16; Migot born, Feb. 27; Prokofiev born, April 23; Roland-Manuel born, March 22.

Year	Age	Life	Contemporary Musicians
1892	30	Reads Maeterlinck's (30) drama, *Pelléas et Mélisande,* and immediately sets to writing some incidental music for it. Begins to write a *Prélude, Interludes et Paraphrase finale* for Mallarmé's (50) eclogue, *L'Après - midi d'un faune. Rodrigue et Chimène,* carried as far as the third act, abandoned.	Honegger born, March 10; Jarnach born, July 26; Kilpinen born, Feb. 4; Lalo (69) dies, April 22; Milhaud born, Sept. 4; Tailleferre (Germaine) born, April 19.
1893	31	*La Damoiselle élue* and the Quartet performed at the Société Nationale, the first large works of D. to be heard. They meet with little success. He decides to write an opera on *Pelléas* and visits Maeterlinck (31) at Ghent. Enters into intimate friendship with Pierre Louÿs (23) and Ernest Chausson (38).	Goossens born, May 26; Gounod (75) dies, Oct. 18; Tchaikovsky (53) dies, Nov. 6.
1894	32	The *Prélude à l'Après-midi d'un faune* performed at the Société Nationale, where it passes almost unnoticed. First version of the *Nocturnes* (for violin and orchestra, intended for performance by Ysaÿe (36)) begun.	Chabrier (53) dies, Sept. 13; Pijper born, Sept. 8; Rubinstein (64) dies, Nov. 20.
1895	33	First version of *Pelléas* finished.	Castelnuovo-Tedesco born, April 3; Hindemith born, Nov. 16; Sowerby born, May 1.

Year	Age	Life	Contemporary Musicians
1896	34	Begins *Pour le Piano* and a setting of Pierre Louÿs's (26) translation of Rossetti's *Willowwood*.	Bruckner (72) dies, Oct. 11; Sessions born, Dec. 28; Thomas (A.) (85) dies, Feb. 12.
1897	35	Orchestrates Satie's (31) *Deux Gymnopédies* and sets three of Pierre Louÿs's (27) *Chansons de Bilitis*.	Brahms (64) dies, April 3; Korngold born, May 29.
1898	36	End of relationship with Gabrielle Dupont.	Rieti born, Jan. 28.
1899	37	Marries Rosalie (Lily) Texier, a dressmaker, Oct. 19. Second version of the *Nocturnes* (for orchestra) finished.	Auric born, Feb. 15; Chausson (44) dies, June 10; Poulenc born, Jan. 7; Strauss (J. ii) (74) dies, June 3.
1900	38	The *Nocturnes* conducted by Camille Chevillard (41) with great success.	Křenek born, Aug. 23; Sullivan (58) dies, Nov. 22.
1901	39	D. acts as music critic to *La Revue blanche*.	Verdi (88) dies, Jan. 27.
1902	40	The performance of *Pelléas*, April 30, at the Opéra-Comique creates a scandal. D. accepts the Croix d'Honneur. Writes the libretto of *Le Diable dans le beffroi*, an opera based on Poe's *Devil in the Belfry*, and plans to write another opera on Shakespeare's *As You Like It*.	Walton born, March 29.
1903	41	Acts as music critic to *Gil Blas*. Makes further plans for *Comme il vous plaira* (*As You Like It*) and writes the *Estampes*.	Wolf (43) dies, Feb. 22.

Appendix A—Calendar

Year	Age	Life	Contemporary Musicians
1904	42	D. abandons his wife for Emma Bardac. Lily attempts suicide. *La Mer* begun.	Dvořák (63) dies, May 1.
1905	43	Birth of Claude ´ Emma (Chouchou). D. divorces his first wife and marries Mme Bardac. *La Mer* is finished and performed on Oct. 15.	Lambert born, Aug. 23.
1906	44	Begins *Ibéria* (of the *Images*) for orchestra.	Arensky (45) dies, March 11; Cartan born, Dec. 1; Shostakovitch born, Sept. 25.
1907	45	Finishes the *Images* for piano. Contemplates an opera on the legend of Tristan.	Grieg (64) dies, Sept. 4.
1908	46	Visits London and con´ ducts *L'Après´midi* and *La Mer* at Queen's Hall, Feb. 1. Writes *Trois Chansons de Charles d'Orléans* for mixed voices. Begins an opera on Poe's *The Fall of the House of Usher* and sells the rights to the Metropolitan Opera of New York.	MacDowell (47) dies, Jan. 23; Rimsky´Korsakov (64) dies, June 21.
1909	47	Conducts the *Nocturnes* in London. Becomes afflicted with cancer. *Pelléas* performed at Covent Garden.	Albéniz (49) dies, May 18; Bordes (46) dies, Nov. 8; Martucci (53) dies, June 1.
1910	48	Conducts in Vienna and Budapest. *Préludes* for piano begun.	Balakirev (73) dies, May 29.

Year	Age	Life	Contemporary Musicians
1911	49	Conducts in Turin, where he meets Elgar (54) and Strauss (47). Writes incidental music for d'Annunzio's (48) drama *Le Martyre de saint Sébastien* in a few weeks. It is performed at the Théâtre du Châtelet with little success.	Mahler (51) dies, May 18.
1912	50	Nizhinsky (22) produces for Diaghilev (40) a ballet on *L'Après - midi* which meets with no approval from D. He nevertheless consents to collaborate with Nizhinsky in *Jeux*. Begins the ballet *Khamma* for Maud Allan and entrusts its completion to Charles Koechlin.	Coleridge - Taylor (37) dies, Sept. 1; Massenet (70) dies, Aug. 13.
1913	51	*Jeux* produced with little success. Three songs to words by Mallarmé written. Second set of *Préludes* finished. Visit to Russia.	
1914	52	Composes the *Berceuse héroïque*, a war piece for King Albert's (39) Book.	Liadov (59) dies, Aug. 28; Sgambati (71) dies, Dec. 14.
1915	53	Composes numerous piano pieces—*En blanc et noir*, *Douze Études*, the song, *Noël des enfants qui n'ont plus de maison*, and two Sonatas published with the words 'musicien français' under the composer's	Goldmark (85) dies, Jan. 2; Scriabin (44) dies, April 27; Taneiev (59) dies, June 19.

Year	Age	Life	Contemporary Musicians
		name. His cancer develops and he undergoes an operation. From now on he is a sick man.	
1916	54	Composes no music for a year. Recasts the libretto for *La Chute de la maison Usher*.	Granados (49) dies, March 24; Reger (43) dies, May 11.
1917	55	Plans again to write music for *As You Like It*. His last work, the piano and violin Sonata, completed in the spring.	
1918	56	Debussy dies in Paris, March 25, while the city is being bombarded by German guns.	Boito (76) dies, June 10; Cui (83) dies, March 14; Parry (70) dies, Oct. 7.

d'Albert aged 54; Auric 19; Bantock 50; Bartók 37; Bax 35; Berg 33; Bliss 27; Bloch 38; Bossi 41; Bréville 57; Bridge (Frank) 39; Bruneau 61; Busoni 52; Cartan 12; Casella 35; Castelnuovo-Tedesco 23; Charpentier 58; Delius 56; van Dieren 34; Dohnányi 41; Dukas 53; Duparc 70; Durey 30; Falla 42; Fauré 73; Glazunov 53; Goossens 25; Griffes 34; Hindemith 23; Holst 44; Honegger 26; Humperdinck 64; d'Indy 67; Ireland 39; Jarnach 26; Kaminski 32; Kilpinen 26; Kodaly 36; Korngold

Year	*Age*	*Life*	*Contemporary Musicians*
			21; Křenek 18; Lambert 13; Leoncavallo 60; Loeffler 57; Malipiero 36; Mascagni 55; Medtner 38; Miaskovsky 37; Milhaud 26; Montemezzi 43; Novák 48; Palmgren 40; Pedrell 77; Pfitzner 49; Pierné 55; Pijper 24; Pizzetti 38; Poulenc 19; Prokofiev 27; Puccini 60; Rachmaninov 45; Ravel 43; Respighi 39; Rieti 20; Roger ‑ Ducasse 43; Roland ‑ Manuel 27; Ropartz 54; Roussel 49; Saint‑Saëns 83; Satie 52; Schmitt (Florent) 48; Schoenberg 44; Schreker 40; Scott (Cyril) 39; Sessions 22; Séverac 45; Shaporin 29; Shostako‑vitch 12; Sibelius 53; Sinigaglia 50; Sowerby 23; Stanford 66; Strauss (R.) 54; Stravinsky 36; Suk 44; Szymanowski 35; Toch 31; Turina 36; Vaughan Williams 46; Vycpálek 36; Walton 16; Webern 35; Wellesz 33; Wolf‑Ferrari 42; Zandonai 35.

APPENDIX B

CATALOGUE OF WORKS

THE dates of composition, except where works have been published in the last two or three years, or where I have discovered the existence of manuscripts, are based on those in the catalogue published in Léon Vallas's *Claude Debussy et son temps*. The names in brackets following the title are those of the authors of poems or librettos.

UNPUBLISHED WORKS

SONGS

Year	
1880	*Caprice.*
1880–4	*Chanson espagnole* for two voices.
	Rondel chinois.
	Romance (Paul Bourget).[1]
	Aimons-nous (Théodore de Banville).
	O floraison divine des lilas ⎫
	Souhait ⎬ Théodore de Banville.
	Sérénade ⎭
	La Fille aux cheveux de lin (Leconte de Lisle).[2]
	Jane (Leconte de Lisle).
	Eclogue (Leconte de Lisle) for soprano and tenor.
	Il dort encore from Banville's *Hymnis.*
	Flots, palmes, sables (Armand Renaud).
1908	*Berceuse* (René Peter) for the play, *La Tragédie de la mort.*

---

[1] Not to be mistaken for the published *Romance* (Paul Bourget) of 1891.

[2] Dedicated to Mme Vasnier with the inscription: 'All that is any good in my mind is here; judge for yourself.' This song has no connection with the *Prélude* of the same title.

Debussy

CHAMBER WORKS

Year
1880   Trio in G major for piano, violin and cello.
1900   *Chansons de Bilitis.* Incidental music for the poems of
       Pierre Louÿs for 2 flutes, 2 harps and celesta.

CHORAL, DRAMATIC AND LITERARY WORKS

1880–4 *Daniel* (Émile Cécile).   Cantata.
1883   *Le Gladiateur* (Émile Moreau).   Cantata.
1884   *Printemps* (Jules Barbier).   Chorus.
1891–2 *Rodrigue et Chimène* (Catulle Mendès).   Unfinished opera
        in three acts.
1900   *F.E.A.* (*Frères en art*).   Three scenes of a play, written with
        René Peter.
1903   *Le Diable dans le beffroi* (Poe–Debussy).   Sketch for scene i.
1908–18 *La Chute de la maison Usher* (Poe–Debussy).   Libretto
        (sketches and final version) and vocal score (incomplete).

PIANO AND ORCHESTRAL WORKS

1882   *Intermezzo* for orchestra based on a passage from Heine's
        Intermezzo.   Full score and piano duet arrangement.
1884 (?) Two short pieces for piano written at Moscow.

PUBLISHED WORKS
SONGS [1]

Dedicated to

1876 (?) *Nuit d'étoiles* (Théodore de Banville).
1878 (?) *Beau soir* (Paul Bourget).
         Fleur des blés (André Girod).   Mme E. Deguingand.

---

[1] The songs *Chanson d'un fou* (Alphonse Daudet) and *Ici-bas* (Sully
Prudhomme), published under Debussy's name and attributed to the
year 1882, are by Émile Pessard and the brothers Paul and Lucien
Hillemacher respectively.

Appendix B—Catalogue of Works

Year	SONGS—continued	Dedicated to
1880–3	*Mandoline* (Paul Verlaine). *La Belle au bois dormant* (Vincent Hypsa). *Voici que le printemps* (Paul Bourget). *Paysage sentimental* (Paul Bourget).	Mme Vasnier.
1881	*Zéphyr* (Théodore de Banville).	
1882 (1)	*Rondeau* (Alfred de Musset).	Alexander von Meck.
1882–4	*Pantomime* (Paul Verlaine). *Clair de lune* (Paul Verlaine).[1] *Pierrot* (Théodore de Banville). *Apparition* (Stéphane Mallarmé).	Mme Vasnier. Mme Vasnier. Mme Vasnier. Mme Vasnier.

1887–9	*Cinq Poèmes de Baudelaire.*
	    Le Balcon.
	    Harmonie du soir.
	    Le Jet d'eau.[2]
	    Recueillement.
	    La Mort des amants.
		Étienne Dupin.

1888	*Ariettes oubliées* (Paul Verlaine).
	    C'est l'extase . . .
	    Il pleure dans mon cœur . . .
	    L'ombre des arbres . . .
	    Chevaux de bois.
	    Green.
	    Spleen.
		Mary Garden.

1891	*Deux Romances* (Paul Bourget).
	    Romance.
	    Les Cloches.
	Les Angélus (G. le Roy).
	Dans le jardin (Paul Gravolet).
	Trois Mélodies (Paul Verlaine).
	    La mer est plus belle . . .
		
		Ernest Chausson.

[1] Not the *Clair de lune* (Paul Verlaine) of 1892.
[2] Piano accompaniment orchestrated by Debussy.

Debussy

Year	Songs—*continued*	Dedicated to
	Le son du cor s'afflige . . .	Robert Godet.
	L'Échelonnement des haies.	Robert Godet.
1892	*Fêtes galantes* (Paul Verlaine), first series.	
	En sourdine.	Mme Robert Godet.
	Fantoches.	Mme Lucien Fontaine.
	Clair de lune.	Mme Arthur Fontaine.
1892–3	*Proses lyriques* (Claude Debussy).	
	De rêve.	V. Hocquet.
	De grève.	Raymond Bonheur.
	De fleurs.	Mme E. Chausson.
	De soir.	Henry Lerolle.
1897	*Chansons de Bilitis* (Pierre Louÿs).	Mme M. V. Peter.
	La Flûte de Pan.	
	La Chevelure.	
	Le Tombeau des Naïades.	
1904	*Fêtes galantes* (Paul Verlaine), second series.	Mme S. Bardac.[1]
	Les Ingénus.	
	Le Faune.	
	Colloque sentimental.	
	Trois Chansons de France.	Mme S. Bardac.
	Rondel: Le temps a laissié son manteau . . . (Charles d'Orléans).	
	La Grotte (Tristan Lhermite).[2]	
	Rondel: Pour ce que plaisance est morte . . . (Charles d'Orléans).	

[1] The dedication runs: 'Pour remercier, le mois de juin, 1904. A.l.p.M.' The initials stand for 'A la petite Mie' (To my little darling).

[2] This is the same song as *Auprès de cette grotte sombre,* the first of the next group.

Appendix B—Catalogue of Works

Year	SONGS—continued	Dedicated to
1904–10	*Le Promenoir des deux amants* (Tristan Lhermite). *Auprès de cette grotte sombre* . . . *Crois mon conseil* . . . *Je tremble en voyant ton visage* . . .	Emma Claude- Debussy
1910	*Trois Ballades de François Villon.* *Ballade de Villon à s'amye.* *Ballade que feit Villon à la requeste de sa mère pour prier Nostre-Dame.* *Ballade des femmes de Paris.*	
1913	*Trois Poèmes de Stéphane Mallarmé.* *Soupir.* *Placet futile.* *Éventail.*	Dr. Bonniot and to the memory of Stéphane Mallarmé.
1915	*Noël des enfants qui n'ont plus de maison* (Claude Debussy).[1]	

PIANO WORKS [2]

(a) Piano Solo

1880	*Danse bohémienne.*	
1888	*Deux Arabesques*	
1890	*Rêverie.* *Ballade.* *Danse.* *Valse romantique.* *Nocturne.*	Mlle Rose Depecker.
1890– 1905	*Suite bergamasque.* *Prélude.*	

[1] There also exists a version of this song for children's chorus.

[2] See also under Chamber Works and Works for Solo Instrument and Orchestra.

Debussy

	Menuet.	
	Clair de lune.	
	Passepied.	
1891	Mazurka.	
1896–	Pour le piano.	
1901	Prélude.	Mlle M. W. de Romilly.
	Sarabande.	Mme E. Rouart.
	Toccata.	N. G. Coronio.
1903	Estampes.	Jacques-Émile Blanche.
	Pagodes.	
	Soirée dans Grenade.	
	Jardins sous la pluie.	
1903	D'un cahier d'esquisses.	
1904	Masques.	
	L'Isle joyeuse.	
1905	Images, first series.	
	Reflets dans l'eau.	
	Hommage à Rameau.	
	Mouvement.	
1907	Images, second series.	
	Cloches à travers les feuilles.	Alexandre Charpentier.
	Et la lune descend sur le temple qui fut.	Louis Laloy.
	Poissons d'or.	Ricardo Viñes.
1906–8	Children's Corner.	Claude-Emma Debussy (Chouchou).
	Doctor Gradus ad Parnassum.	
	Jimbo's Lullaby.	
	Serenade for the Doll.[1]	
	Snow is Dancing.	

[1] Should be, of course, *The Doll's Serenade.*

Appendix B—Catalogue of Works

The Little Shepherd.

Golliwog's Cake-walk.

1906 (?) *The Little Nigar (Le Petit Nègre).*

1909 *Hommage à Haydn.*

1910 *La plus que lente.*[1]

1910 *Douze Préludes,* first book.

Danseuses de Delphes.

Voiles.

Le Vent dans la plaine.

Les sons et les parfums tournent dans l'air du soir.

Les Collines d'Anacapri.

Des pas sur la neige.

Ce qu'a vu le vent d'ouest.

La Fille aux cheveux de lin.

La Sérénade interrompue.

La Cathédrale engloutie.

La Danse de Puck.

Minstrels.

1910–13 *Douze Préludes,* second book.

Brouillards.

Feuilles mortes.

La Puerta del Vino.

Les Fées sont d'exquises danseuses.

Bruyères.

General Lavine—eccentric.

La Terrasse des audiences au clair de lune.

Ondine.

Hommage à S. Pickwick, Esq., P.P.M.P.C.

Canope.

Les Tierces alternées.

Feux d'artifice.

---

[1] Orchestrated by Debussy.

Year	PIANO WORKS—*continued*	Dedicated to

1913   *La Boîte à joujoux.* Children's ballet. Scenario by André Hellé.

1914   *Berceuse héroïque pour rendre hommage à S.M. le Roi Albert Ier de Belgique et à ses soldats.*

1915   *Douze Études.*   The memory of Frédéric Chopin.

Book I:
Pour les cinq doigts.
Pour les tierces.
Pour les quartes.
Pour les sixtes.
Pour les octaves.
Pour les huit doigts.

Book II:
Pour les degrés chromatiques.
Pour les agréments.
Pour les notes répétées.
Pour les sonorités opposées.
Pour les arpèges.
Pour les accords.

(b) Piano Duet

1880   *Symphonie en si.* (One movement.)[1]   Mme von Meck.

1882 (?)   *Triomphe de Bacchus.* Orchestral interlude.

1889   *Petite Suite.*
En bateau.
Cortège.
Menuet.
Ballet.

---

[1] This and the next work were intended to be orchestral works. The piano duet arrangements by Debussy are all that is known.

266

Year	PIANO WORKS—*continued*	Dedicated to
1891	*Marche écossaise sur un thème populaire. (The Earl of Ross March.)*[1]	
1914	*Six Épigraphes antiques.*[2]	
	Pour invoquer Pan, dieu du vent d'été.	
	Pour un tombeau sans nom.	
	Pour que la nuit soit propice.	
	Pour la danseuse aux crotales.	
	Pour l'Égyptienne.	
	Pour remercier la pluie au matin.	

(c) Two Pianos

Year		Dedicated to
1901	*Lindaraja.*	
1915	*En blanc et noir.* (Three pieces.)	A.[3] Koussevitsky, Lieutenant Jacques Charlot and Igor Stravinsky.

CHAMBER WORKS

Year		Dedicated to
1893	String Quartet.	Ysaÿe Quartet (Ysaÿe, Crickboom, van Hout, Jacob).
1903-5	*Rapsodie* for saxophone and piano.[4]	Mrs. Elisa Hall.
1909-10	*Première Rapsodie* for clarinet and piano.[1]	P. Mimart.
1910	*Petite pièce* for clarinet and piano.[1]	

---

[1] Orchestrated by Debussy.

[2] There is also an arrangement of these pieces for piano solo.

[3] No doubt a misprint for S. (Serge) Koussevitzky, with whom Debussy stayed in Moscow in 1913.

[4] The piano accompaniment has been orchestrated by Roger-Ducasse.

Debussy

Year	CHAMBER WORKS—*continued*	*Dedicated to*
1912	*Syrinx* for unaccompanied flute.	Louis Fleury.
1915	Sonata for cello and piano.	Emma Claude-Debussy.
	Sonata for flute, viola and harp.	Emma Claude-Debussy.
1916–17	Sonata for piano and violin.	Emma Claude-Debussy.

WORKS FOR SOLO INSTRUMENT AND ORCHESTRA

1889	*Fantaisie* for piano and orchestra.	René Chansarel.
1904	*Danse sacrée* and *Danse profane* for harp and strings.	Gustave Lyon.

ORCHESTRAL WORKS

1887	*Printemps.*[1]	The memory of Auguste Durand.
1892–4	*Prélude à l'Après-midi d'un faune.*	Raymond Bonheur.
1893–9	*Nocturnes.*	Georges Hartmann.
	Nuages.	
	Fêtes.	
	Sirènes (with female chorus).	
1903–5	*La Mer.* Three symphonic sketches.	Jacques Durand.
	De l'aube à midi sur la mer.	
	Jeux de vagues.	
	Dialogue du vent et de la mer.	
1904	Incidental music for *King Lear* (Shakespeare).	
	Fanfare.	
	Sommeil de Lear.[2]	

---

[1] Orchestration revised by Henri Büsser.
[2] There are a few rough notes in manuscript for six further pieces.

Appendix B—Catalogue of Works

Year	ORCHESTRAL WORKS—*continued*	*Dedicated to*

1906–12	*Images.*
	    Gigues.[1]
	    Ibéria.
	    Rondes de Printemps.
		Emma Claude Debussy.

UNACCOMPANIED CHORAL WORKS

1908   *Trois Chansons de Charles d'Orléans*
        for sopranos, contraltos, tenors
        and basses.
        Dieu! qu'il fait bon regarder!
        Quand j'ai ouy le tabourin . . .
        Yver, vous n'estes qu'un villain . . .

CHORAL AND DRAMATIC WORKS

Year	Work	Dedicated to
1882	*Printemps* (Comte de Ségur). Chorus for female voices.[2]	
1883	*Invocation* (Lamartine). Chorus for male voices. Piano and vocal score only.	
1884	*L'Enfant prodigue* (Édouard Guinand). Cantata.	Ernest Guiraud.
1887–8	*La Damoiselle élue* (D. G. Rossetti–G. Sarrazin). Cantata for solo voices, chorus and orchestra.	Paul Dukas.
1892–1902	*Pelléas et Mélisande* (Maurice Maeterlinck). Opera in five acts.	The memory of Georges Hartmann and to André Messager.

---

[1] The orchestration finished by André Caplet.

[2] The piano and vocal score, which is all that is available, has been made by Marius-François Gaillard.

269

Debussy

CHORAL AND DRAMATIC WORKS—*continued*

Year		Dedicated to
1911	*Le Martyre de saint Sébastien.* Incidental music to the mystery play by Gabriele d'Annunzio, for solo voices, chorus and orchestra.	
1912	*Jeux.* Ballet. Scenario and choreography by Nizhinsky.	Mme Jacques Durand.
1912	*Khamma.* Ballet. Orchestrated by Charles Koechlin. Scenario by W. L. Courtney and Maud Allan.	
1916–17	*Ode à la France* (Louis Laloy). Cantata for solo, chorus and orchestra. Completed from sketches by Marius-François Gaillard.	

ARRANGEMENTS AND ORCHESTRATIONS

Gluck, C. W.	*Caprice* for piano on airs from the ballet of *Alceste*.
Raff, J.	*Humoresque en forme de valse.* Arrangement for piano solo.
Saint-Saëns, C.	Arrangement for piano solo of extracts from the opera *Étienne Marcel*.
	Introduction et Rondo capriccioso. Arrangement for two pianos.
	Second Symphony. Arrangement for two pianos.
Satie, Erik	Orchestration of *Deux Gymnopédies*.
Schumann, R.	*Am Springbrunnen.* Arrangement for two pianos.
	Six Studies in canon form. Arrangement for two pianos.
Tchaikovsky, P.	*The Swan Lake.* Arrangement of three dances for piano solo.
Wagner, R.	Overture to *The Flying Dutchman*. Arrangement for two pianos.

Appendix B—Catalogue of Works

LITERARY WORKS

Articles in :

Comœdia	November 4, 1909.
	January 31, December 17, 1910.
	January 26, May 18, 1911.
	February 1, 1914.[1]
Excelsior	March 9, 1911.
Le Figaro	May 8, 1908.
	February 14, 1909.
Gil Blas	January 12 to June 28, 1903.
Mercure de France	January 1903.
Musica	October 1902.
	May 1903.
	July 1906.
	January 1908.
	March 1911.
La Revue blanche	April 1 to December 1, 1901.
La Revue bleue	March and April 1904.
La Revue S.I.M.	November 1912 to May 15, 1913.
	November 1913 to March 1914.

M. Croche antidilettante. A selection of the above articles made by Debussy in 1917, but published posthumously.
Masques et Bergamasques. Scenario for a ballet written in 1910.

---

[1] These are all interviews.

APPENDIX C

Annunzio, Gabriele d' (*Gaetano Rapagnetto*) (1863–1938), Italian poet, novelist, dramatist and patriot. His style derives partly from Carducci and partly from Nietzsche. In 1919 he organized the military occupation of Fiume and played in important part in politics. Zandonai, Mascagni, Pizzetti and Nadia Boulanger were among the composers inspired by his plays.

Bailly, Edmond (born 1878), French writer, owner of the Librarie de la Revue Indépendante, biographer of Maeterlinck (q.v.) and publisher of Debussy's *La Damoiselle élue*.

Banville, Théodore de (1823–91), French poet, follower of Victor Hugo, Alfred de Musset and Théophile Gautier, and at the same time a precursor of the Symbolists. Part of his comedy, *Diane au bois* (1864), and several of his poems were set to music by Debussy.

Bédier, Joseph (1864–1938), distinguished scholar of French medieval literature, of which he held the chair at the Collège de France. The author of the *Roman de Tristan et Yseult* (1900), which Debussy started to set to music and of which a fine English translation was made by Hilaire Belloc.

Bourget, Paul (1852–1935), poet and novelist who made his name as a writer on psychological, social and religious questions. Became a member of the Académie in 1894 and subsequently an ardent Royalist.

Bruneau, Alfred (1857–1934), French composer, pupil of Massenet and great friend of Zola, who wrote the librettos of his operas, *L'Ouragan* and *Messidor*. One of the most prolific of modern French composers for the stage, though his works are little known outside of France.

Appendix C—Personalia

Caplet, André (1878–1925), French conductor and composer whose works were much influenced by Debussy. He completed the orchestration of several of Debussy's works and conducted chiefly in America.

Carré, Albert (1852–1938), succeeded Carvalho as director of the Opéra-Comique, where he produced *Pelléas et Mélisande* in 1902. He subsequently became director of the Comédie-Française.

Chausson, Ernest (1855–99), pupil of César Franck, of whom he was a devout admirer. He wrote two operas, *La Légende de sainte Cécile* and *Le Roi Arthus,* and a number of symphonic and chamber works. He was killed in a bicycle accident.

Chevillard, Camille (1859–1923), conductor and composer, pupil of Chabrier and son-in-law of Charles Lamoureux (q.v.). He earned a reputation for conducting Russian music and became the conductor of the Concerts Lamoureux.

Colonne, Édouard (1838–1910), violinist and conductor, founder of the Concerts Colonne. He was the first to popularize Berlioz and was well known for his performances of Wagner, Tchaikovsky and Rimsky-Korsakov.

Doret, Gustave (1866–1943), Swiss composer, studied the violin in Germany with Joachim and composition in Paris with Massenet. Became conductor of the Société Nationale, where he gave the first performance of *L'Après-midi d'un faune.*

Dujardin, Édouard (born 1861), French writer. The founder of *La Revue wagnérienne, La Revue indépendante* and *La Revue des idées.* He introduced Mallarmé to the music of Wagner.

Ghil, René (1862–1925), French poet who propounded an original theory by the application of which poetry was to become indistinguishable from music. He had an important influence on Mallarmé.

Godet, Robert (1866–1950), Swiss journalist, composer, translator of Houston Stewart Chamberlain and the author of a study of *Boris Godunov.* Debussy's lifelong friend.

Guiraud, Ernest (1837–92), Debussy's teacher of composition at the

Conservatoire. His operas include *Le Kobold, Madame Turlupin, Piccolino* and *La Galante aventure.*

Hébert, Ernest (1817–1908), French painter, pupil of David, friend of Gounod and director of the Villa Medici during the second year of Debussy's residence.

Huysmans, Joris-Karl (1848–1907), French novelist who in his books, *A rebours* and *Là-bas,* was a keen observer of the artistic sensibility of his times. At the end of his life he became a Trappist.

Koechlin, Charles (1867–1950), French composer and critic, pupil of Massenet and Fauré. He wrote valuable books on Fauré (translated into English) and Debussy.

Laforgue, Jules (1860–87), French writer who was engaged as a reader to the German Empress Augusta in Berlin. His poetry is a strange mixture of sadness, irony and fantasy. He had an important influence on the Symbolist movement.

Laloy, Louis (1874–1944), Debussy's intimate friend and his first biographer. Editor of the *Mercure musical.* In 1914 he became Secretary-General of the Opéra and in 1930 music critic of the *Revue des deux mondes.* He wrote a valuable book on Chinese music.

Lamoureux, Charles (1834–99), French violinist and conductor. Founder of the Concerts Lamoureux, at which he made Wagner known to a wide public.

Lavignac, Albert (1846–1916), teacher of *solfège* and harmony and editor of the great *Encyclopédie de la musique et dictionnaire du Conservatoire.* Debussy's first master at the Conservatoire.

Leroux, Xavier (1863–1919), French composer, pupil of Massenet and Debussy's friend at Rome. Wrote numerous operas.

Louÿs, Pierre (1870–1925), French poet and novelist. One of Debussy's most intimate friends. Other composers inspired by his *Chansons de Bilitis* were Georges Dandelot, Albert Dupuis and Roman Maciejewski. His best-known novel is *Aphrodite.*

Marmontel, Antoine-François (1816–1898), French piano teacher, the author of several important works on piano playing and Debussy's master at the Conservatoire.

Mauté de Fleurville, Antoinette-Flore, née Chariat (died 1884), a pupil of Chopin and the mother of Mathilde, the young forsaken wife of Verlaine. She was Debussy's piano teacher before he entered the Conservatoire.

Meck, Nadezhda Filaretovna von, née Fralovskaya (1831–94), patroness of Tchaikovsky. The daughter of a landowner, she married at seventeen a poor government engineer, Karl von Meck, who subsequently made a huge fortune which he bequeathed to her at his death in 1876. The same year she started her intimate correspondence with Tchaikovsky which lasted for sixteen years.

Mendès, Catulle (1841–1909), French writer, married Judith, the daughter of Théophile Gautier, and wrote librettos for Pessard (q.v.), Chabrier, Massenet, Debussy (*Rodrigue et Chimène*) and others.

Messager, André (1853–1929), French composer and conductor, pupil of Saint-Saëns. Wrote a number of ballets for the Théâtre des Folies-Bergère, many light operas, conducted the *Ring* at the Paris Opéra and the first performance of *Pelléas* at the Opéra-Comique.

Monet, Claude (1840–1926), French Impressionist painter remarkable for his delicate monochromes.

Moréas, Jean, real name *Papadiamantopoulos* (1856–1910), French poet born at Athens. Editor of *Le Symboliste* and a prominent member of the so-called 'décadents.' In his later years he wrote some beautiful, lucid poetry.

Mourey, Gabriel (born 1865), French writer. Has written several volumes of verse and translated Poe and Swinburne. He adapted Joseph Bédier's (q.v.) *Tristan* for Debussy's projected opera.

Péladan, Joseph (1858–1918), French writer. An eccentric personality who assumed the title of *Sar* and grouped together certain French painters under the title 'Salon de la Rose-Croix.' He was the librettist of Erik Satie's *Le Fils des étoiles.*

Pessard, Émile (1843–1917), a composer of light operas whom Debussy particularly admired in his early youth. He was a teacher of Ravel.

Pierné, Gabriel (1863–1937), French composer and conductor. A pupil of Franck and Massenet, he became conductor of the Concerts Colonne, where in 1910 he conducted the first performance of Debussy's *Ibéria*. His many dramatic and orchestral works are little known outside France.

Sivry, Charles de (1848–1900), French composer of light songs and operettas and accompanist at the Cabaret du Chat Noir. He introduced Debussy to his mother, Mme Mauté de Fleurville (q.v.), who prepared him for the Conservatoire.

Tiersot, Julien (1857–1936), French writer on music. Pupil of Massenet and César Franck. Edited the correspondence of Berlioz and wrote extensively on folk-music.

Toulet, Paul-Jean (1857–1920), a subtle and fanciful poet who became addicted to opium. He wrote a libretto for Debussy adapted from Shakespeare's *As You Like It.*

Vidal, Paul (1863–1931), French composer of ballets and operas, conductor at the Opéra. He was an intimate friend of Debussy's at the Villa Medici.

Willy, pseudonym of *Henri Gauthier-Villars* (1859–1931), an amusing and caustic musical critic, who wrote in the *Écho de Paris* under the name of 'L'Ouvreuse du Cirque d'Été.' Married the charming writer Colette (the librettist of Ravel's *L'Enfant et les sortilèges*), in collaboration with whom he wrote several books.

Wyzewa, Téodor de (1862–1917), French writer of Polish origin who helped to found *La Revue wagnérienne*. With Georges de Saint-Foix he wrote the first two volumes of one of the most important studies on Mozart.

Ysaÿe, Eugène (1858–1931), Belgian violinist, one of the great virtuosos of his time. Debussy's *Nocturnes* were originally intended for him, and his string quartet gave the first performance of the Quartet of Debussy.

APPENDIX D

BIBLIOGRAPHY

SHORT LIST

Dietschy, Marcel, 'La Passion de Claude Debussy.' (Neuchâtel, 1962.)

Jankélévitch, Vladimir, 'Debussy et le mystère.' (Neuchâtel, 1949.)

Laloy, Louis, 'Debussy.' (Paris, 1944.)

Lockspeiser, Edward, 'Debussy: His Life and Mind.' Vol. I (London and New York, 1962.)

Schaeffner, André, 'Debussy et ses rapports avec la musique russe' in *Musique russe.* Vol. I edited by Pierre Souvtchinsky. (Paris, 1953.)

Strobel, Heinrich, 'Debussy.' (Berlin, 1940, in German; and Paris, 1943, in French.)

Thompson, Oscar, 'Debussy: Man and Artist.' (New York, 1937.)

Tiénot, Yvonne, and *d'Estrade-Guerra, Oswald,* 'Debussy.' (Paris, 1962.)

Vallas, Léon, 'Claude Debussy: His Life and Works.' (English translation by Maire and Grace O'Brien.) (London, 1933.)

—— 'Achille-Claude Debussy.' (Paris, 1949.)

—— 'Claude Debussy et son temps.' Second edition. (Paris, 1958.)

LETTERS

'Lettres de Claude Debussy à son éditeur' (i.e. Jacques Durand). (Paris, 1927.)

'Correspondance de Claude Debussy et Paul-Jean Toulet.' (Paris, 1929.)

'La Jeunesse de Pelléas: Lettres de Claude Debussy à André Messager.' (Paris, 1938.)

'Lettres de Claude Debussy à deux amis (Robert Godet and G. Jean-Aubry). (Paris, 1942.)

'Correspondance de Claude Debussy et Pierre Louÿs.' (Paris, 1945.)

'Debussy et d'Annunzio: Correspondance inédite.' (Paris, 1948.)

'Lettres inédites à André Caplet.' (Paris, 1957.)

'Lettres de Claude Debussy à sa femme Emma.' (Paris, 1957).

'Tel était Claude Debussy' (Letters to Pasteur Vallery-Rodot). (Paris, 1958.)

'Segalen et Debussy' by A. Joly-Segalen and André Schaeffner. (Paris, 1962.)

OTHER SOURCES

Ambrière, F., 'La Vie romaine de Claude Debussy.' (*La Revue musicale,* Paris, January 1934.)

Debussy

Antoine, A., 'Mes souvenirs sur le Théâtre Antoine et sur l'Odéon.' (Paris, 1928.)

Arconada, M., 'En torno a Debussy.' (Madrid, 1926.)

Aubry, G. Jean-, 'Claude Debussy et la musique française moderne en Angleterre. (*La Revue S.I.M.,* March 1909.)

—— 'Some Recollections of Debussy.' (*Musical Times,* London, May 1918.)

—— 'L'Œuvre critique de Debussy.' (*La Revue musicale,* December 1920.)

—— 'La Musique et les nations.' (Paris and London, 1922.)

Barre, A., 'Le Symbolisme.' (Paris, 1911.)

Bérys, J. de. See under Caillard, C. F.

Bonheur, R., 'Souvenirs et impressions d'un compagnon de jeunesse.' (*La Revue musicale,* May 1926; special number entitled 'La Jeunesse de Debussy.')

Boucher, M., 'Debussy.' (Paris, 1930.)

Bruneau, A., 'Musiques de Russie et musiciens de France.' (Paris, 1903.)

Brussel, R., 'Claude Debussy et Paul Dukas.' (*La Revue musicale,* May 1926.)

Caillard, C. F. and Bérys, J. de, 'Le Cas Debussy.' (Paris, 1910.)

Calvocoressi, M. D., 'Musicians' Gallery.' (London, 1933.)

Casella, A., 'Claude Debussy.' (*Monthly Musical Record,* London, January 1933.)

Chennevière, D., 'Claude Debussy et son œuvre.' (Paris, 1913.)

Cœuroy, A., 'Appels d'Orphée.' (Paris, 1928.)

Cortot, A., 'The Piano Music of Debussy.' English translation by Violet Edgell. (London, 1922.)

Daly, W. H., 'Debussy: a Study in Modern Music.' (Edinburgh, 1908.)

Danckert, Werner, 'Claude Debussy.' (Berlin, 1950.)

Debussy, C., 'Monsieur Croche antidilettante.' (Paris, 1921.)

—— 'Monsieur Croche the Dilettante-hater.' English translation (anonymous). (London, 1927.)

Decsey, Ernst, 'Debussy.' (Vienna, 1936.)

278

Appendix D—Bibliography

Dᵉcsey, Ernst, 'Claude Debussy: Biographie.' (Graz, 1936.)
Dumesnil, Maurice, 'Claude Debussy: Master of Dreams.' (New York, 1940.)
—— 'How to Play and Teach Debussy.' (New York, 1932.)
Durand, J., 'Quelques souvenirs d'un éditeur de musique.' (Paris, 1924.)

Emmanuel, M., 'Pelléas et Mélisande.' (Paris, 1926.)
—— 'Les Ambitions de Claude-Achille.' (*La Revue musicale,* May 1926.)

Fábián, L., 'Claude Debussy und sein Werk.' (Munich, 1923.)

Gatti-Cassazza, G., 'Debussy.' (*New York Times,* March 15, 1925.)
Gianturco, E., 'Claude Debussy.' (Naples, 1923.)
Godet, R. (see also under Prunières, H.), 'Claude Debussy.' (*La Semaine littéraire de Genève,* April 13, 20 and 27, 1918.)
—— 'Le Lyrisme intime de Debussy.' (*La Revue musicale,* December 1920 and January 1921.)
—— 'En marge de Boris Godunov.' Vol. II. (Paris and London, 1926.)
—— 'En marge de la marge.' (*La Revue musicale,* May 1926.)
—— 'Weber and Debussy.' (*The Chesterian,* London, June 1926.)
Gosse, Sir E. W., 'French Profiles.' (London, 1905.)
Gui, V., 'Debussy in Italia.' (*Musica d'oggi,* Milan, December 1932.)
Gysi, F., 'Claude Debussy.' (Zürich, 1926.)

Inghelbrecht, D. E., 'Souvenirs.' (*La Revue musicale,* December 1920.)
Indy, V. d', 'Richard Wagner et son influence sur l'art musical français.' (Paris, 1930.)

Jakobik, Albert, 'Die assoziative Harmonik in den Klavier-Werken Claude Debussys.' (Würzburg, 1940.)
Jardillier, R., 'Pelléas.' (Paris, 1927.)

Klingsor, T., 'Les Musiciens et les poètes contemporains.' (*Mercure de France,* November 1900.)

Debussy

Koechlin, C., 'Quelques anciennes mélodies inédites de Claude Debussy.' (*La Revue musicale,* May, 1926.)

—— 'La Leçon de Claude Debussy.' (*La Revue musicale,* January 1934.)

—— 'Souvenirs sur Debussy, la Schola et la S.M.I.' (*La Revue musicale,* November 1934.)

—— 'Sur l'évolution de la musique française avant et après Debussy.' (*La Revue musicale,* April 1935.)

Kölsch, Hans Friedrich, 'Der Impressionismus bei Debussy.' (Düsseldorf, 1937.)

Kurt, E., 'Romantische Harmonik and ihre Krise in Wagners Tristan.' (Berne and Leipzig, 1920.)

Laloy, L., 'Debussy.' (Paris, 1909.)

—— 'Le Théâtre de Claude Debussy.' (*La Revue musicale,* December 1920.)

—— 'La Musique retrouvée.' (Paris, 1928.)

—— 'Debussy.' (*La Revue des deux mondes,* Paris, July 15, 1932.)

Leblanc, G., 'Souvenirs.' (Paris, 1931.)

—— 'Maeterlinck and I.' English translation by Janet Flanner. (London, 1932.)

Lépine, J., 'La Vie de Debussy.' (Paris, 1930.)

Liebich, L. S., 'Claude A. Debussy.' (London, 1908.)

—— 'An Englishwoman's Memories of Debussy.' (*Musical Times,* June, 1918.)

Liess, Andreas, 'Claude Debussy. Das Werk im Zeitbild.' 2 vols. (Strasburg, 1936.)

—— 'Claude Debussy und das deutsche Musikschaffen.' (Würzburg, 1939.)

Lockspeiser, Edward, 'Debussy et Edgar Poe.' (Paris, 1962.)

Meck, N. F. von. See under Tchaikovsky.

Newman, E., 'The Development of Debussy.' (*Musical Times,* May and August 1918.)

Niemann, W., 'Die Musik seit Richard Wagner.' (Berlin and Leipzig, 1913.)

Appendix D—Bibliography

Oleginni, Léon, 'Au cœur de Claude Debussy.' (Paris, 1947.)

Oulmont, C., 'Deux Amis. Claude Debussy et Ernest Chausson. Documents inédits.' (*Mercure de France*, Paris, December 1, 1934.)

Perrachio, L., 'L'Opera pianistica di Claude Debussy.' (Milan, 1924.)

Peter, R., 'Debussy. Vues prises de son intimité.' Revised edition. (Paris, 1944.)

Pierné, G., 'Souvenirs d'Achille Debussy.' (*La Revue musicale*, May 1926.)

Prod'homme, J. G., 'Claude-Achille Debussy.' (*Musical Quarterly*, New York, October 1918.)

Prunières, H., 'A la Villa Médicis.' (*La Revue musicale*, May 1926.)
—— 'The Youth of Debussy.' (*The Sackbut*, London, October 1926.)
—— 'Autour de Debussy.' (*La Revue musicale*, May, June and September 1934.) A detailed criticism of Léon Vallas's Claude Debussy et son temps,' incorporating notes by Robert Godet. The June and September numbers contain a rejoinder from Léon Vallas.

Rebois, H., 'Les Grands Prix de Rome de musique.' (Paris, 1932.)

Régnier, H. de, 'Souvenirs sur Debussy.' (*La Revue musicale*, May 1926.)

La Revue musicale. Special number entitled 'Wagner et la France.' (October 1923.) Other numbers listed under names of contributors.

La Revue wagnérienne. (Paris, 1885–8.)

Rolland, R., 'Musicians of To-day.' Translation by M. Blaicklock. (London, 1915.)

Santoliquido, F., 'Il dopo-Wagner: Claude Debussy e Richard Strauss.' (Rome, 1909.)

Setaccioli, G., 'Debussy è un innovatore?' (Rome, 1910.)
—— 'Debussy. Eine kritische-ästhetische Studie.' Translated from the Italian by F. Spiro. (Leipzig, 1911.)

Shera, F. H., 'Debussy and Ravel.' (London, 1925.)

Symons, A., 'The Symbolist Movement in Literature.' (London, 1899.)

Debussy

Tchaikovsky, P. I., 'Peripiska s N. F. von Meck.' Vols II and III. (Moscow, 1935–6.)

Templier, P. D., 'Erik Satie.' (Paris, 1932.)

Ternant, A. de, 'Debussy and Brahms.' (*Musical Times,* July 1924.)

—— 'Debussy and some Italian Musicians.' (*Musical Times,* September, 1924.)

—— 'Debussy and some Others on Sullivan.' (*Musical Times,* December 1924.)

Tiersot, J., 'Promenades à l'exposition universelle.' (*Le Ménestrel,* Paris, May 26, June 30, July 14, 1889.)

—— 'Un Demi-siècle de musique française. Entre les deux guerres.' (Paris, 1918.)

Vallas, L. (see also under Prunières, H.), 'Debussy.' (Paris, 1926.)

—— 'Les Idées de Claude Debussy, musicien français.' (Paris, 1927.)

—— 'The Theories of Claude Debussy.' English translation by Maire O'Brien. (London, 1929.)

Valéry-Radot, P., 'Souvenirs de Claude Debussy.' (*La Revue des deux mondes,* Paris, May 15, 1938.)

Vasnier, M., 'Debussy à dix-huit ans.' (*La Revue musicale,* May 1926.)

Verlaine, Mathilde, 'Mémoires de ma vie.' (Paris, 1935.)

Vidal, P., 'Souvenirs d'Achille Debussy.' (*La Revue musicale,* May 1926.)

Vuillermoz, E., 'Autour du Martyre de saint Sébastien.' '*La Revue musicale,* December 1920.)

—— 'Claude Debussy.' (Paris, 1920.)

Walch, G., 'Anthologie des poètes français contemporains.' Vol. II. (Paris, 1927.)

Woolley, G., 'Wagner et la symbolisme français.' (Paris, 1934.)

Ysaÿe, E., 'Lettres inédites de Claude Debussy à Eugène Ysaÿe.' (*Les Annales politiques et littéraires,* Paris, August 25, 1933.)

To Raoul Bardac

BICHAIN, 31*st August* 1901.

DEAR FRIEND,

My delay in replying in no way means that I was untouched by the delicate attention of your letter. But here in Bichain, where I am sorry that we shall not see you, the minutes pass, one knows not exactly how.

I have the feeling of being at the other end of the world from Paris. The beastly fever that worries us all more or less, can't play havoc here, and there's no mistaking that the movement of the trees against the river-banks forms a counterpoint less poor than ours. . . . But the people are much less lovely than their setting. I needn't tell you that 'le geste auguste du semeur'[1] is quite forgotten and that when the angelus gently orders the fields to sleep you never see any one striking that solemn pose of the lithographs. [2]

What you tell me of X . . .[3] is most praiseworthy. One can never spend too much time constructing that special atmosphere in which a work of art should move. I believe that one should never hurry to write but leave everything to that many-sided play of thoughts—those mysterious workings of the mind which we too often disturb, prompted (though we may not like to admit it) by materialism and even cowardice.

Thank you for the Quartet.[4] I shall be much indebted to you and don't know how I can repay you. Anyhow you can always

---

[1] Line of Victor Hugo.

[2] Allusion to the well-known pictures of Millet, *L'Angélus* and *Les Glaneuses.*

[3] Work of Raoul Bardac.

[4] An arrangement of Debussy's Quartet made by Raoul Bardac.

Debussy

count on me—for whatever that is worth, for I don't ever expect to become a big pot. I am far too unconcerned about my fellow beings, which is incidentally the only way to choose between them.

I shall be in Paris about 10th September and am afraid of being worried by more people than usual. But if you will come and see me it will make me forget how tiring they are.

Affectionately,

C. D.

Sunday, 25th February 1906.

MY DEAR RARA,

Forgive my laziness! Well, 'regonflons des souvenirs d'hiver,'[1] as Willy would make Mallarmé's Faun say. And what a winter! Rain, the trees look like disconsolate widowers, and for a change they've put the flowers inside and the poultry outside. Vain-glorious people try to fill the void with symphonic descriptions. Well, we heard *Schéhérazade*[2] again. It doesn't improve with age. It reminds one more of a bazaar than of the Orient. And of course Chevillard[3] isn't a bit like the princess. . . . We heard too *Un Jour d'été à la montagne* by Vincent d'Indy. This kind of d'Indy is from beyond the Cévennes.[4] As I am not very well informed on this place, I can hardly speak of it. There seemed to be an immoderate use of the bassoon—and fancy having a piano. I thought they had pianos only in the mountains of Switzerland.

---

[1] Play on the word 'divers' in the line from *L'Après-midi d'un Faune*:

'O nymphes regonflons des souvenirs divers.'
('O nymphs, recall with me remembered bliss!')

[2] By Rimsky-Korsakov.

[3] Camille Chevillard, the conductor.

[4] The implication here is that this is the old, authentic d'Indy. Allusion to the expression: 'C'est de derrière les fagots'—something genuine, and to the *Symphonie cévenole,* a work that d'Indy composed twenty years earlier.

Appendix E—Letters

You didn't have any luck at the Société X . . .[1] But you have no reason to feel very resentful. First of all you weren't properly backed, and then you don't belong to any of the groups who are allowed to mess things up. You have time to prepare your play—so don't strike out on a bad line or one that might lead to nothing.

You are talented, but you can never be too aware of the long road ahead. You know how little respect I have for the parasite development which has too long bolstered up the glory of the Masters. With such a feeling there comes a keener sense of values and one may discover a melodic line more sensitive to design and timbre. Let your ideas breathe, for they can so easily succumb to the pretentiousness of form.

In a word, have patience! It is a major and even a domestic virtue which helps a great deal. But I don't want to spoil a fine day for you with this shower of moral and aesthetic considerations. What's the good? Aesthetics have really only a relative value and I'm afraid that morals have too.

The description of your days is delightful. You are right! It is better to let one's mind soak in the sun—like the flowers and the photographs—while one's nerves can still react.

Gather impressions. But don't hurry to note them down; for music has this over painting, that it can bring together all manner of variations of colour and light.[2] It is a point that is not often observed though it is quite obvious.

And then, from time to time forget music altogether. 'Practice makes perfect' is a schoolmaster's notion. And it is not in very good taste to badger those one loves the most [3] with constant requests.

You mother has a wonderful cold. You know how opposed she is to all medicine, and that doesn't help matters.

---

[1] Allusion to some songs of Raoul Bardac which were badly sung at a concert of this society.

[2] Debussy was no doubt thinking of paintings such as the series of Claude Monet (in the Musée de l'Orangerie in Paris) of a lily-pond at different times of the day. Music, he implies is not bound to any particular *tone* of impression.

[3] Meaning musical inspiration.

Little Chouchou is going to have yet another nurse. The one she has at present says that her husband has been unfaithful to her. So she is going to find out the trouble for herself, which is not very wise and certainly not very economical.

I shan't speak to you of what I am doing. Although I have been writing very little, music offends my ear. The reason for that, we will say, is the colour of the sky.

Au revoir . . .

C. D.

To the Royal Philharmonic Society in London

CHÂTEAU DE PUYS, *27th August* 1906.

DEAR SIR,

Having been away from Paris, I have only recently received your kind invitation to conduct the orchestra of the Philharmonic Society.

Before replying I had to be sure of the date when *Pelléas* will be given at the 'Monnaie' at Brussels, for I have to go there and superintend the rehearsals. I can now be free on the 16th or the 30th of May 1907, the dates suggested in your letter.

It remains for me to say that I don't speak English at all and fear that this may prove a hindrance at the rehearsals with your excellent orchestra. Apart from this fear I shall be very glad to be amongst you.

Yours cordially,

C. D.

In his reply, the secretary suggested that he should conduct *Pelléas,* apparently not realizing that it was an opera, and adds: 'As the Philharmonic Society is not in the habit of paying a fee to those distinguished composers who honour us with their presence, we hope you will allow us to offer you £15 to cover your expenses.' Debussy scornfully replies (on 24th September):

Pelléas et Mélisande is a musical drama in five acts which lasts $2\frac{1}{2}$ hours, so that it is not possible to give it at a concert. Furthermore, as it is likely to be given in London, this is an additional reason for avoiding any concert performance.

When you asked me to conduct the Philharmonic Society I naturally thought of some symphonic work. I am sorry there was this misunderstanding, but once again, not only is it impossible to give *Pelléas* at a concert, but the composition of the work is such as to make extracts utterly impossible.

The secretary's note appended reads: 'I wrote and said "quite so," and would he come and direct some symphonic work—no reply.' A final refusal was sent on 19th October.

APPENDIX F

ACHILLE-CLAUDE DEBUSSY

Manuscript memoir by Nicholas von Meck in the Tchaikovsky Museum at Klin (U.S.S.R.)

This adds a few details to the account of Debussy's association with the von Meck family in Chapter II. The reader will easily interpret for himself the opinions expressed and may make the necessary rectifications of dates and places by referring to the correspondence of Mme von Meck which I have quoted. Nicholas von Meck seems not to have had a great appreciation of Debussy's character. There is something disconcertingly patronizing about his remarks (especially in view of the fact that they were written in 1926), and indeed when Debussy went to Moscow in 1913 his boyhood friend was only able to say that he was 'a funny, fat, and empty little man.' On the other hand it is interesting to see that the song, *Ici-bas tous les lilas meurent,* by the brothers Paul and Lucien Hille-macher, is referred to as by Debussy, for this apparently means that Achille unscrupulously passed off this composition as his own. It was recently published under Debussy's name (see Appendix B). On the friendship with Alexander von Meck, M. Georges de Meck, his son, informs me that a collection of letters from Debussy to his father was lost at the time of the Russian Revolution.

The translation of this document from the Russian was kindly made for me by Countess Benningsen.

In the year 1879 my mother, Mme N. F. von Meck, addressed herself to the Paris Conservatoire, requesting them to recommend her a pupil from the piano class who could teach my sisters music during the summer, accompany their singing, play four-hands with my mother and play in her trios and quartets.

The Conservatoire sent A. Debussy, who was then nineteen.

The little Frenchman arrived, dark, thin, sarcastic, and gave every-body amusing nicknames. For instance, he called our plump teacher 'petit hippopotame en vacances,' and we in turn nicknamed him 'le bouillant Achille.' He joined us in Switzerland, and from there we went to Italy and stopped in Rome. Once we walked past the Villa Medici, where the best students of the Conservatoire and the Academy of Arts [L'École des Beaux-Arts] reside for a year at the cost of the French Government. One of us, pointing to the villa, said to Debussy: 'This is your future home.' It was interesting to see how longingly he looked back on the Villa Medici.

From Rome we went to Florence, where we lived at the Villa Oppenheim, and from here, in October, Debussy returned to his studies in Paris. On leaving us he was very sad, and my mother had to comfort him, promising that in the spring of 1880 he would again return to us. He did join us the next year, in Moscow, and he spent the whole summer with us visiting various places and towns in Europe.

My mother considered Debussy a gifted musician, not only as a pianist, but also as a composer. He was a pupil of Massenet, and at that time his professor exercised a strong influence on him.

My mother acquainted him with Russian music and with Wagner. Of the Russians he got to know Tchaikovsky and all the members of the 'Kutchka,' Rimsky-Korsakov, Cui, Mussorgsky and Borodin.[1] Both Wagner and the Russian composers produced an unfavourable impression on Debussy, which was quite natural,

---

[1] 'All the members of the "Kutchka,"' but Balakirev is omitted. And we know that, in Moscow, Debussy did become acquainted with this composer. 'Dear friend, do you know Balakirev's songs?' writes Mme von Meck to Tchaikovsky (21st August 1881). 'I came across them recently, and they please me immensely. There is a picturesque element in them which appeals to the imagination. Not only do you hear a melody in them, but you hear it against a certain background.' Those are words which might have been written by Debussy himself; and indeed, it would not be surprising if Mme von Meck, who was apt to take her opinions from other people, got this one from her 'little pianist Bussy.'

since French music at that time was too near the music of the classical composers, and Debussy, following this tradition, did not react to all innovations.

But as he became better acquainted with Russian music he appreciated it, though by his French nature he was inclined to inter-pret it in a superficial and elegant manner. No doubt his acquaint-ance not only with Russian music and Wagner, but also with his contemporaries in other countries, widened his outlook and influenced his development. Of his compositions at that time his song, *Ici-bas tous les lilas meurent*, was frequently sung and played in our house by my sister Julia Pachulska [*née* von Meck]. The manu-script of this song was in the possession of my brother Alexander von Meck, who was in correspondence with Debussy for a long time.

Our prophecy in 1879 about Debussy's residence at the Villa Medici was fulfilled, for he finished his studies at the Conservatoire by obtaining the Prix de Rome, and having been assisted by my mother, went to Rome. In conclusion I may add that as a com-panion Debussy was a very pleasant, lively and even-tempered man, and we were always sorry when he left us.

When he returned to Moscow during the musical season of 1913–14, only my sister Sophia Galitzin [*née* von Meck], his former pupil, saw him. Debussy always remembered his sojourn with us with gratitdue and pleasure.

N. K. MECK.

1926.

APPENDIX G

Translation of Mallarmé's poem by Alex. Cohen [1]

I WOULD eternalize those nymphs.
>   Their rosy
Bloom's so light, it floats on the air drowsy
With tufted sleep.
>   Loved I a dream?
>   The mound
Of my dark doubt by subtle boughs is crowned,
That, palpably remaining trees, alas,
Bear witness my imagined triumph was
Delusion that the roses feigned for me.
Now think . . .
>   Suppose those girls thou speak'st of be
Desires that from thy fabulous senses rise!
The figment, faun, wells from the chaste blue eyes
Of the first, cold as weeping springs: yet she,
The other one, all sighs, can she but be
The breeze in thy fleece—the breath of a sultry noon?
Ah no! amid the weary, hot, still swoon
Choking the cool of the barely struggling breeze
No water murmurs save what dews the trees
In a shower of fluted notes.   The only wind
Is the puff from my twin-pipes before the sound
Scatters in arid rain, except that on
The far unruffled skyline can be seen
The visible calm breath of artifice
—Of the inspiration that regains the skies.

---

1 First published in *Musical Opinion*, September 1935, this translation has been amended by Mr. Alex Cohen and is reprinted here with his kind permission.

Debussy

Calm lakeside pillaged by my vanity,
That moves Sicilian suns to envy me,
Shore silent now under flowering sparks, TELL HOW
I here was cutting hollow reeds t' endow
With genius; when, where distant vines enfold
The wreathéd fountains 'mid the green and gold,
A living whiteness, wave-like, idly stirred:
How, when the first slow notes I piped were heard,
The swans, no! naiads, dived or flew away. . . .

The still noon fiercely flames, and naught could say
How that great rout of Hymen fled from me,
Who seek the *A* to pitch my melody.
Let me then wake old ardours, and, upright
And lone, lilies, 'neath ancient floods of light,
Let me be one of you for artlessness.
Unlike that furtive sweet naught of a kiss
—That token traitor-love breathes, to assure—
Though proof I've none, mysteriously here
My bitten breast attests a kiss divine;
But stay! such secrets must be told by mine
Elected confidant, who, 'neath the Blue,
—Great double reed—turns care to song, and who
In lingering arabesques dreams of amusing
The beauty hereabout by falsely confusing
Its charm with the illusion song creates:
At just the height to which love modulates,
Pursuing them with veiled eyes, I'd expunge
The common dream of flank and back, to change
It to a monotone of sounding line.

Essay then, instrument of flight—malign
Syrinx—to bloom again beside our lake!
Proud of my fame, of goddesses I'll talk
And picture them profanely, letting fall
The girdle from their shadowy shapes withal;

Thus, when the radiance of the grape I drain,
To cheat regret I fill the globes again,
Laughingly puffing the empty grape-skins tight,
Then gazing through the glowing spheres till night,
Athirst for drunkenness and ecstasies.

O nymphs, recall with me remembered bliss!
—'*Piercing the reeds, mine eye speared each immortal*
Bosom slaking its burning in the waters,
Crying that wildness to the forest sky;
In a shimmer of rays, a shudder of jewelry,
The glittering glory of their hair has gone.
I run, when, at my feet I see enlaced
Two girls, each in the other's arms embraced,
Both wounded by the pain of not being one.
I seize but part them not, then haste away
To the rosebank that the playful shadows shun,
Where the sun drains perfume, where our joy too may
Be sun-drunk, like the rosy, dying day.'
I love thee, virgin wrath, O sacred bliss
Of the naked burdens shrinking from the kiss
Of my lips on fire that thrill like a lightning flash
As they drink the secret terror of the flesh!
From the cruel one's feet to the timid heart of the other
It flies, and both lose innocence together,
With wild tears wet or some less dolorous dew.
'*My crime is this, that, gay as I quelled their fears,*
The tangled skein of kisses I unwound
That gods about the guileless pair had bound.
By a finger I held the smaller of the twain
So that her sister's quickened sense might stain
Her swan's unblushing purity: but when
I bent to hide my burning laughter in
The happy bosom of the elder one,
Lo! 'twas as though some vague death had undone
The prison of my drunken arms.   My prey,
Ingrate, deaf to my sobbing, slipped away.'

293

Debussy

No matter! others will drag me to caresses,
Binding my horns with bonds of amorous tresses.
Desire, thou knowest that to slake the thirst
Of murmuring bees the pomegranates will burst
Their ripe and purple fruit; and that our blood,
In love with all that seeks it, is in flood
For all the everlasting swarms of passion.
At evening, when this wood grows gold and ashen,
The dying leafage blazes festively.
'Tis then, O Etna, Venus visits thee,
Come forth as is her wont from her retreat,
To tread thy lava with her artless feet
When thy flames die in slumbrous thunder, spent.
I hold the goddess!

            O sure chastisement! . . .

But, quelled at length by conquering, silent noon,
My wordless soul and heavy body swoon:
On thirsty sand be now my sin in sleep's
Oblivion stilled; I'd drink with ravished lips
Dream's starry wine.

            Farewell; I go to see,
O Nymphs, the shades that ye already be.

INDEX

Index

Index

Index

Index

Index

Index

Nerval, Gérard de, 38
Nikisch, Artur, 234, 237
Nizhinska, Romola, 100
Nizhinsky, Vaslav, 99, 100, 201, 202
Nocturne, piano, 143
Nocturne, violin and piano, 19
Nocturnes, orchestra, 61, 62, 65, 66, 77, 94, 145, 180, 188–193
Noël des enfants qui n'ont plus de maisons, 104, 141, 142
Novello & Co., 43, 74
Nuit d'étoiles, 13, 118

O'Brien, Grace, 83, 84, 89, 100, 175, 189
O'Brien, Maire, 83, 84, 89, 100, 175, 189, 233
Ode à la France, 105
Offenbach, 10, 31
Ojetti, Ugo, 69
Oleginni, Léon, 152, 154
Ombre des Arbres, L', (*Ariettes oubliées*), 127
Ondine (*Préludes II*), 157
Orléans, Charles, Duke of, 136–139, 231
Orphée-roi, 107, 108, 112

Pachulska, Julia. *See* Meck, Julia von
Pachulsky, pianist, 15
Pachulsky, violinist, 13, 14
Pagodes (*Estampes*), 147–8
Palestrina, 27, 239
Pantomime, 120, 121
Parry, Hubert, 43, 74
Pater, Walter, 185
Paysage sentimental, 16, 119, 120
Péguy, Charles, 229
Péladan, Joseph, 47, 275
Pelléas et Mélisande, (39), 41,

46, 50, 53–8, 61, 65, 67, 68, 73, 79–87, 89, 95, 97, 110, 113, 118, 131, 133, 143, 149, 175, 191, 192, 209–28, 243, 286, 287
Périer, Jean, 82
Pessard, Émile, 10, 11, 275
Peter, René, 72, 75–7, 92, 113, 232
Petite Pièce, clarinet, 175
Petite Suite, 144, 205
Philipp, Isidore, 60
Picasso, Pablo, 176
Piccinni, 92
Pierné, Gabriel, xii, 6, 20, 24, 29, 96, 106, 276
Pissarro, Lucien, 148
Placet futile (*Trois Poèmes de Stéphane Mallarmé*), 101, 141
Poe, Edgar Allan, 35, 107, 112, 113, 232
Poèmes de Baudelaire. See *Cinq Poèmes*
Poèmes de Stéphane Mallarmé. See *Trois Poèmes*
Poissons d'or (*Images* for piano II), 151, 152
Poujaud, Paul, 189
Poulenc, Francis, 46
Poulet, Gaston, 105
Pour ce que plaisance est morte, 136–7
Pour le piano, 146, 147, 160
Prélude (*Pour le piano*), 146
Prélude a l'Après-midi d'un faune. See *Après-midi*
Préludes, Set I, 96, 124, 155–8
Préludes, Set II, 155–8
Primoli, Joseph, Count, 27
Printemps, 2 choral works, 182
Printemps, for orchestra, 32, 51, 182, 183
Promenoir des deux amants, Le, 96
Proses lyriques, 131, **132**
Proust, Marcel, 42

301

Index

Prunières, Henry, xiii, 4, 19, 20, 30

Puccini, 209

Puerta del vino, La (Préludes II), 157

Pugno, Raoul, 56, 237

Quartet for strings, 41, 55, 59, 66, 145, 146, 164–74, 283

Rabbe, 32

Rabutin, Roger de, 3

Rameau, (106), 108, 146, 150, 164, 240

Rapsodie, clarinet, 175

Rapsodie, saxophone, 174, 175

Ravel, Maurice, 46, 92, 119, 122, 148, 151, 173, 188, 201, 203

Read, Meredith, General, 144

Recueillement (Cinq Poèmes de Baudelaire), 124, 125

Redon, Odilon, 37, 91

Reflets dans l'eau (Images for piano I), 149, 150

Régnier, Henri de, 42, 54, 131, 132

Renan, 35, 36, 72

Renoir, 189

Réty, Émile, 18

Rêverie, 41, 143

Reyer, Ernest, 234

Rimbaud, Arthur, 39, 102, 127, 128, 148

Rimsky-Korsakov, 16, 41, 143, 147, 240, 284, 289

Rodin, 100

Rodrigue et Chimène, 50, 75, 83

Roger-Ducasse, 174, 197

Roger, Thérèse, 75

Roi Lear, Le. See *King Lear*

Roland-Manuel, 228

Rolland, Romain, 83, 93, 102, 133, 227

Roman de Tristan, Le, 107, 108

Rondeau, song, 14, 120

Rondel chinois, 19

Rondes de printemps (Images for orchestra), 94, 96, 119, 198, 201, 203

Ronson, 82

Ropartz, Guy, 59, 60

Rossetti, Dante Gabriel, 51, 62, 206–9

Rostand, Edmond, 127

Rousseau, Jean-Jacques, 217

Roustan, Mme, 4, 5, 7

Rubinstein, Anton, 11, 13, 16

Rubinstein, Ida, 97

Rubinstein, Nicholas, 11

Saint-Saëns, Camille, 7, 10, 29, 49, 60, 61, 74, 144, 164

Samazeuilh, Gustave, 50

Sand, George, 38

Sarabande (Pour le piano), 146

Sarrazin, Gabriel, 51, 207

Satie, Erik, 46–9, 63, 64, 76, 102, 146, 206, 207, 209, 236

Saulaie, La (Willowwood), 62

Savard, Augustin, 26

Scherzo, violin and piano, 19

Schoenberg, Arnold, 100, 139, 209

Schott, publisher, 13

Schubert, 45, 131, 148, (237), 239

Schumann, 9, 10, 124, 148, 234

Scott, Cyril, 69, 209

Segalen, Victor, 108

Ségard, Achille, 64

Ségur, Comte de, 182

Serenade for the Doll. See *Doll's Serenade*

Sérénade interrompue, La (Préludes II), 157, 161

Sévigné, Mme de, 3

Sgambati, Giovanni, 28, 29

Shakespeare, 29, 32, (90), 107–110, 227

Shelley, 32, 188

302

Index

303